GEOGRAPHY WIZARDRY for KIDS

Margaret Kenda and Phyllis S. Williams

BARRON'S

For Bill Kenda
and the Other Favorite World Travelers,
Explorers, and Geography Wizards
Who Came to Our Aid,
With Love and Thanks

● ● ● ● ● ● ● ● ● ●

All inquiries should be addressed to:
Barron's Educational Series, Inc.
250 Wireless Boulevard
Hauppauge, New York 11788

Library of Congress Catalog Card No.: 96-26505

International Standard Book No. 0-8120-9718-1

Library of Congress Cataloging-in-Publication Data

Kenda, Margaret.
    Geography wizardry for kids / Margaret Kenda and Phyllis A. Sawyer (Williams);
        p.   cm.
    Summary: Introduces the world of maps and mapmaking.
    ISBN 0-8120-9718-1
    1. Maps—Juvenile literature. [1. Maps] I. Sawyer (Williams), Phyllis A.
    II. Title.
GA130.K325   1997
912—DC20
                                 96-26505
                                      CIP
                                        AC

PRINTED IN THE UNITED STATES OF AMERICA
98765432

CONTENTS

THINK LIKE A WORLD EXPLORER AND GEOGRAPHY WIZARD

*G*eography is your chance to explore the whole world, with all its mysteries and secrets.

You may think of a geography wizard as a very important mapmaker. And it's true. As a geography wizard, you don't just read maps. You make your own. For example, you can create a map to write on—and then erase when you want to write something else. Or you can design one-of-a-kind maps. Make your own cartoon map, a map you can wear, or an antique map that will look as if an ancestor of yours happened to be a famous explorer.

Of course, geography is much more than maps. Geography is the world, with all its people, plants, and animals, and being a geography wizard means you can work with it all.

You can do arts and crafts from all over the world—a model of an Inuit's igloo or a model bamboo house from Africa, a pirate's jolly roger, or Attila the Hun's mirror.

If you like to explore the world outdoors, you can plan your own hiking expedition, with everything you need from a special hiking map to a compass you make yourself.

If you like games, play a weird clues game, around-the-world tag, an ancient Mayan ball game, or world-sized marbles. Or try a Silk Road trading game from long ago or a modern import-export game.

Perform science experiments that show you something about the world. Find your own latitude, or prove for yourself that the world is not flat. Discover whether plants prefer to grow north, east, south, or west.

If you like the idea of making friends around the world, find a pen pal from another country. Or make an Olympic athlete's international friendship pin.

You might even like to design your own special gifts. Perhaps you want to create an explorer's round-the-world gift for Father's Day, a heart-shaped map for Valentine's Day, a paperweight that shows what's inside the Earth, or a spiced gift that once belonged only to rich people.

As a world explorer and geography wizard, you can give a world party, with food and games from all around the world.

After all, you're a wizard of the world. You can explore everywhere in the whole world.

GUIDELINES FOR WORLD EXPLORERS AND GEOGRAPHY WIZARDS

1. *Start a map collection.* Collect maps you like, or collect maps you make yourself. For example, design your own map overlay pages that picture the events of the world. Design layers that show bird, whale, and butterfly migrations. Or create unusual maps of world weather patterns.

2. *Keep a travel notebook.* Your own personal travel diary helps you remember vacations, school trips, or any trip that takes you more than a few miles from home. Be sure to write down the date, the distance from home, the weather and landmarks, the people you met, the animals and birds, and the trees and plants. Save a special entry for the best and the strangest things you see. (*Hint:* You might check a library to help you dream up a really important trip for the future.)

3. *Start collections from around the world.* You may like to collect postage stamps, postcards, letters from pen pals, sports cards, photographs, seashells, or pressed flowers. Your collection will help you learn about places you visit—and about the rest of the world, too.

4. *Explore with someone else.* When you go hiking and exploring, you'll have a better time if you go with adults and other friends—and you definitely will be safer than if you're on your own.

5. *Keep your projects organized.* Before you begin a project, read the steps all the way through. Make sure you understand everything you need to do. Then, as a first step, collect all the tools and materials you'll need. When you're finished, clean up, and put your tools and materials back where they belong. You know it's not fair to leave a mess for someone else to clean up.

6. *Keep your projects safe and clean.* To make things from all around the world, you'll sometimes use sharp or pointed tools, along with paints and other messy things that can spill. So you'll need to be responsible. You don't want to leave anything around that could hurt small children or pets. Be sure to use art materials with "nontoxic" labels.

7. *Stretch your imagination all around the world.* Plan what you want to see in the world and what you want to learn. To be a world explorer and geography wizard is to know about the mysteries and secrets in all the far corners of the world.

FOR
PARENTS
AND TEACHERS

Geography stretches to include just about everything—and all sorts of learning for children. It helps teach reading, reasoning, math, science, art, and imagination.

Geography is coming into its own. Many of us grew up without the concrete knowledge of geography that we needed in later life. Now for the first time in years, geography is a separate subject in schools. Indeed, educators have begun to define geography as one of the five basic academic subjects.

Children who are growing up in a safe environment (as we hope ours and yours are) are also growing up in a sort of necessary isolation. Yet our children will probably do more traveling around the world than any other generation. They will be doing business and dealing with the problems of people far away and much different from themselves. They will find the world an ever more crowded and complicated—and dangerous—place.

But studying geography helps children develop a sense of confidence in the world. They begin to grasp the interconnectedness of the physical and human world. They begin to feel confident about figuring out unfamiliar territory or strange ways of living. To the extent that they understand geography, our children will be more able to reach out to the world, to work to understand its multitude of problems, and to survive its dangers.

Here are some ideas for helping children to learn and love geography:

1. **Encourage hands-on experience with geography.** In a world of ready-made games, help children to create their own. Geography does not need to be a quiet study. Children can learn about the world by playing round-the-world variations of basketball, soccer, tag, and marbles. They can learn specifics about world places through board games and card games, even better if they design and create the game themselves. You may want to try a geography bee, especially if children do the research and design the "trivia" questions themselves.

2. **Save old maps and buy new maps.** Keep a globe where children can play with it and learn from it. Maps and globes are the language of geography. A child who learns to read, make, and enjoy maps will begin to understand something important about the world. A child who has designed and created a map is developing a spatial skill that will help with reading maps in the future. You can cut out old maps into shapes and create holiday cards from them. You can plan a family or school trip on maps (and figure out the distances ahead of time).

3. **Start a year-long mapmaking venture with children.** Once a week or so, make a transparent overlay page to go on top of a map of the world or a map of your country. Use these pages to show birds migrating in the fall or spring, where the president or prime minister is traveling, and where earthquakes, fires, floods, or hurricanes may be happening. Or you can help youngsters develop a sense of history by making layered maps that show ancient empires and the routes of famous explorers.

4. **Plan quality time to help children with projects, map-making, hiking, and exploring the world.** You'll probably have as much fun as they do.

5. **Keep track of directions—and of latitudes and longitudes, too.** Ask children to figure out the direction classroom windows face or whether a car is traveling north, east, south, or west. When you discuss a place or consult a map, make a point of looking up the latitude and longitude. Your children can be among the lucky few who grow up with a good concept of the addresses and crossroads of the world.

6. **Keep materials for spur-of-the-moment art, craft, and recipe projects.** You may particularly want a supply of construction paper, paper plates, and coloring pens and markers, along with a ruler, a drawing compass, and a directional compass for each child.

7. **Start a collection with and for your children.** A collection does not necessarily have to be serious and expensive in order to build a child's curiosity about the world.

8. **Talk to your children about your own dealings and travels around the world.** How are children's school days, homework, clothes, music, games different in Tokyo or Paris—or across your own country? Even if they don't travel around the world, children grow up to feel less isolated if they constantly hear about the rest of the world.

9. **If you use the Internet with children, you can help them keep up with the world's news.** You can find news that you don't see on the front page of your local newspaper or on TV. If you wish, you can look at news in English, Spanish, French, Japanese, or more than 50 other languages. For example, if you would like to see current pages from *The Hong Kong Standard,* look at this site:

http://www.hkstandard.com. Or you can choose among a list of newspapers from around the world at a site provided by Auburn University in Alabama: http://www.lib.auburn.edu. (Neither of these services charges a fee, and both were reachable as of the beginning of 1997.)

10. **Encourage each child to keep a personal travel diary and observation journal.** As an adult, don't you wish you still had a travel diary from when you were a child? Children can write and picture the world in their own unique styles—and all the time, they'll be learning how to look sharply at the world.

11. **Don't be reluctant to expose children to difficult (and sorrowful) concepts.** Make charts and graphs with your children so that they understand the war, poverty, famine, and drought that afflicts so much of the world. (You might like to try the wheels of life and wheels of survival in "Find Out About People Around the World." For a lighter note, you can compare the world's favorite foods and sports with your children's own favorites.)

12. **Dream with geography.** Plan a dream trip of places you'd like to go around the world—and encourage your children to design their own dreams into creative picture maps (including routes and each child's own favorite methods of transportation). The children's dream maps could range from the world's fastest plane circling the planet to a cruise ship slowly (and happily) drifting across oceans to a school bus on its way to the local amusement park.

Our children can be the first to learn geography "hands on," by exploring, discovering, and creating for themselves. Then they will make their way into the world with joy and confidence.

DISCOVER YOUR WORLD ADDRESS

*I*f you expected a visitor from outer space, how would you give directions? If you could dig all the way through the center of the Earth to the other side, where would you be? Would you come out in ocean, or would you arrive in the middle of a city?

Your world is not just a small, simple thing. It's the whole wide world of the planet Earth—and maybe beyond. You can find out about your world, your planet, your place. You can create your own artistic passport or design your own flag. You can create your own stamp of honor. You can explore the world on your own special maps.

Here's how to get to know your own world, with all its wonders.

· · · · · · · · · · ·
DISCOVER YOUR REAL ADDRESS
· ·

You already know the address that the post office assigned to your home. Here's how to find your address, beyond your street, expanding wider and wider into the universe. You can make writing your cosmic address into a work of art. Draw and design it to be just as fancy as you want. This is your cosmic address, your place in the universe.

Here's what you need:

Paper

Coloring markers or pens, in colors you choose

A map of your region

A globe, atlas, or world map

Here's what you do:

1. Write your name, street, and town on your paper with coloring markers or pens.

2. Consult a map of your region, and find all the names you live under (your district, township, county, state, province, island, or region) and write them down.

3. Write the full official name of your country. Now you have your political address, the names that people invented for your homeland. Draw or decorate this address, if you wish.

4. Find your address on your planet, and write the name of your continent.

5. Use your globe, atlas, or world map to check and write out the names of your two hemispheres. If you divide the world into north and south, then you live in either the Northern or the Southern Hemisphere. At the same time, you live in either the Western or the Eastern Hemisphere. (Here's a puzzle. The dividing line between the Northern Hemisphere and the Southern Hemisphere is the

. . . .

DISCOVER YOUR REAL ADDRESS

continued

Equator. What is the hemisphere for someone who lives in a country directly on the Equator?)

6. Now write directions to tell a visitor from outer space how to find your planet. Your planet Earth is the third planet from the sun. Then there's your solar system, a set of nine planets (that people know about so far) and the many asteroids bound by gravity to the sun. Your galaxy is the Milky Way, since the sun and its solar system are bound by long-distance gravity to the Milky Way. The Milky Way is part of this universe. Could there be other universes? Many astronomers think so. Perhaps some day you'll need to name your own universe as part of your address. You may want to draw a diagram for the visitor from outer space. However friendly they might be, those visitors might not be able to read your address in any human language.

> IMAGINE YOUR ADDRESS
> EXPANDING DEEP INTO OUTER
> SPACE, BEYOND THE POINT
> THAT ANYONE ON EARTH CAN
> SEE, EVEN WITH THE BEST
> TELESCOPES. GO ON TO FIND
> OUT MORE ABOUT WHERE YOU
> FIT INTO THE WORLD.

· · · · · · · · · · ·

FIND WHERE YOU FIT INTO THE WORLD

· ·

Think about where you really are when you are in your own home place. You want to know how to fit into your world.

Here's what you need:

A globe, atlas, or world map
A string, ruler, or straightedge
An almanac or geography book,
 if you wish
Paper
A pen or pencil

Here's what you do:

1. Use your globe, atlas, or world map to look up where you are. A string, ruler, or straightedge will help you find the places you want to see. An almanac or geography book can help you find facts about where you are.

2. Write about where you are. Look for:

• The nearest large river

————————————————

• The nearest large lake

————————————————

• The nearest ocean

————————————————

• The nearest island

————————————————

• The nearest desert

————————————————

• The nearest high mountain or mountain range

————————————————

• The nearest volcano, active or dormant

————————————————

• The nearest large earthquake fault line

————————————————

• The distance to the capital of your region, district, state, province, or island

————————————————

• The distance to the capital city of your country

————————————————

• The nearest really big city

————————————————

• The nearest agricultural area

————————————————

• The closest arctic or antarctic area

————————————————

• If you went directly to the nearest border of your country, where would you be?

————————————————

• If you went to the border of your country farthest away from you, where would you be?

————————————————

• If you went directly due south or north for as long as you could before you came to an ocean, where would you be?

————————————————

· · · · · · · · · · ·

FIND WHERE YOU FIT INTO THE WORLD

continued

- If you went directly due east or west for as long as you could before you came to an ocean, where would you be?

  ———————————————

- If you went straight across the ocean to the country opposite, where would you be?

  ———————————————

YOU COULD WRITE THE NAMES AND DRAW PICTURES OF SOME OF THESE PLACES AS PART OF YOUR OWN ADDRESS IN THE UNIVERSE. YOU MAY NEED TO LOOK IN AN ALMANAC OR A GEOGRAPHY BOOK TO FIND THE LOCATION OF THE NEAREST VOLCANO OR THE NEAREST LARGE EARTHQUAKE FAULT LINE.

. . . .

MAKE YOUR OWN PASSPORT

. . . .

When you travel to other countries, you need an official passport to say who you are and where your homeland is. The government issues you the passport in your own country. Then when you enter other countries, government officials there often stamp your passport with an official seal. That says that you are legally allowed to enter that country.

Some people are proud to have a passport with stamps from countries all over the world.

You can design your own personal passport. You can picture adventures all over the world. This is a project for a creative person with a strong imagination.

Here's what you need:

A ruler

A sheet of construction paper, in a dark color

Several sheets of paper or construction paper, white or light-colored

Scissors

A stapler

Gold or silver paper, wrapping paper, or foil

Household glue, paste, or tape

A small bit of ribbon in gold, silver, or another color you choose

Small gold or silver sticker letters of the alphabet, if you wish

Gold or silver pens or markers, if you wish

Pens or markers in other colors you choose

A small color photograph, such as a school photo, that clearly shows your face, about $1\frac{1}{2} \times 2$ inches (4×5 centimeters) or smaller

. . . .

MAKE YOUR OWN PASSPORT

continued

Here's what you do:

1. Use a ruler to measure a rectangle on the dark-colored construction paper, 7 × 10 inches (16 × 24 centimeters). Measure carefully, and make sure your rectangle is straight on all sides.

2. Repeat step 1 with several sheets of white or light-colored paper or construction paper. You decide how many pages you want in your passport.

3. Use your scissors to cut out each rectangle.

4. Fold each rectangle in half so that it is 3½ × 5 inches (8 × 12 centimeters).

5. Make a small book of the pages. The construction paper rectangle is the cover. The white papers are the inside pages.

6. Staple the pages of your book together along the center fold. Make sure the sharp points of the staples are safely on the inside. Use your scissors to round the corners of the pages slightly.

7. Design an important looking seal for the front cover out of gold or silver wrapping paper or foil, no larger than 2 × 3 inches (5 × 7 centimeters). You can get an idea for your design by looking at a symbol for your country of the sort used on passports, or you can create your own symbol. Glue, paste, or tape the seal in the middle of the front cover of your passport. Cut two small flat bits of ribbon to fit at the bottom of the seal. Glue, paste, or tape the ribbon in place.

8. If you wish, use gold or silver sticker letters to spell the word PASSPORT just above the seal. Or use a pen or marker to print the word in gold, silver, or another color you choose. Add the name of your country just below the seal.

9. On the first inside page of your passport, glue, paste, or tape a small photograph of your face. On that same page, use colored pens or markers to write in facts: your full name, the date and year of your birth, male or female, state or province or region of your birth, the country of your birth, the date and year you issued your passport.

10. At the top of each inside page, write PASSPORT in English and then PASSEPORT in French or PASAPORTE in Spanish. Or choose another language you like. Then on one side of each page, write ENTRIES, ENTREES, or ENTRADAS. On the other side, write DEPARTURES, SORTIES, or SALIDAS.

· · · · · · · · · · ·

MAKE YOUR OWN PASSPORT
continued

11. Now is your chance to use your imagination. Write in the names of foreign countries you have visited or foreign countries you want to visit. Beside each name, write a date, real or imagined, for when you arrived and when you left. Design and draw in a symbol for each place. If you wish, add a sticker or a picture you cut out from a magazine.

12. To enter some countries, you need to apply ahead of time for a visa or a special permit. You can design a few of those, too.

YOU CAN'T GO EVERYWHERE WITH A REAL PASSPORT, ESPECIALLY IF YOUR COUNTRY HAS UNFRIENDLY RELATIONS WITH SOME OTHER COUNTRIES. WITH YOUR OWN PERSONAL PASSPORT, HOWEVER, YOU CAN GO ANYWHERE, EVEN TO COUNTRIES THAT DON'T EXIST. YOU CAN PUT IN FUNNY AND ODD NOTATIONS FROM THE CUSTOMS OFFICIALS OF FARAWAY PLACES. YOU CAN PUT NOTES AND STAMPS IN YOUR PERSONAL PASSPORT THAT HINT OF STRANGE AND WONDERFUL ADVENTURES ALL OVER THE WORLD. YOU MIGHT EVEN WRITE IN VISITS TO MYSTERIOUS ISLANDS AND HIDDEN CITIES WHERE NO ONE ELSE HAS EVER TRAVELED.

· · · · · · · · · · ·

DESIGN YOUR OWN STAMP

· ·

Postage stamps show that you paid to mail a letter or package, and they usually show how much you paid.

But a postage stamp is also a miniature work of art. You can create your own stamp. You can choose as your subject an important place or event, a discovery or invention, holidays, animals or birds, a world-famous person, or even someone who is not famous. If you wish, you can make a block of four to six stamps to show different pictures of the same subject.

Here's what you need:

A pencil

Scrap paper

Paper, construction paper, or posterboard

Pens or markers, in colors you choose

Scissors

Household glue or paste

Here's what you do:

1. Use a pencil with an eraser to sketch your designs on scrap paper. Since these are stamps for decoration, you decide whether to write in a price and the name of a country.

2. If you want to display your design, you can take up as much space as you want on paper, construction paper, or posterboard. Color your designs with pens or markers. Border your design with scallops or dots.

3. If you want to use your stamps to decorate letters and cards, make small versions. Design them on paper or construction paper $1\frac{1}{4} \times 1\frac{1}{2}$ inches (about 3×4 centimeters). As long as you use that small size, you can turn your design around either way you want, horizontally or vertically. Use the scissors to cut the stamps out, and use glue or

· · · · · · · · · · ·

DESIGN YOUR OWN STAMP
continued

paste to attach them. Of course, you can't use your own stamps in place of the post office stamps, but they do make creative decorations. You could even design special stamps for holiday cards.

CALL YOUR POST OFFICE TO FIND OUT HOW TO SUBMIT STAMP DESIGNS FOR CONSIDERATION. SOMETIMES POST OFFICES DISPLAY STAMPS THAT CHILDREN DESIGN. YOU MAY WANT TO LOOK ON PAGE 303 ABOUT HOW TO BEGIN A COLLECTION OF YOUR POSTAGE STAMPS. A STAMP COLLECTION IS ESPECIALLY FUN IF YOU WRITE TO PEN PALS IN OTHER COUNTRIES. A PERSON WHO COLLECTS STAMPS IS A PHILATELIST.

. . . .

DESIGN YOUR OWN FLAG

. . . .

Flags once helped soldiers to survive in battle. In the heavy smoke of a battle, they could look for the bright colors of their own flag and know where their own troops were positioned. Now national flags serve as symbols for a country—and often they show something about love for a homeland and pride in a country.

Before you begin a flag design, you may want to look at a book that shows the flags of many countries. Or go to a store that sells flags. You'll probably get good ideas. Your own personal flag can show something about where you live, who you are, and what interests you. It can represent a family, a club, a sport, or a team. It can celebrate a special event, a holiday, or a season. It can be just for fun.

Decide whether you want a paper or felt flag. Then decide on basic colors. Flag colors hold symbolic importance. For example, in many places, red stands for liberty and courage. Blue can stand for equality, and white can stand for peace and for unity among the people of one land. (The symbols are not always the same. As just one example, the flag of the Solomon Islands features blue for the ocean, yellow for the sun, and green for the land. Colors in other national flags may stand for a religion, race, heritage, or a natural resource.)

Make big bold designs for your flag. The designs should not be too complicated and should not have too many details, so that your flag leaves a strong impression on people. If you decide on words for your flag, keep them short and simple.

Then decide on the size and shape you want. Almost all national flags are rectangular. (Countries sometimes change their flags because of ongoing political changes. Right now, however, only one country in the world has a nonrectangular flag. That's Nepal in the Himalaya mountains, between India and Tibet. Nepal's flag is a banner.) Your own flag can be a banner with streamers. It can be square, the shape of flags that sailors use to send signals from one boat to another. Your flag can be an unusual shape. Think about a tree, an animal, a house, a baseball player. This is your chance to be creative.

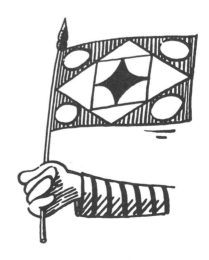

· · · · · · · · · · ·

DESIGN YOUR OWN FLAG
continued

Here's what you need:

Scrap paper and pencil

For a paper flag:

Paper, construction paper, or poster-board, in a background color you choose

Paper, construction paper, or poster-board, in other colors you choose

Scissors

Household glue or paste

For a felt flag:

> *Caution: Decide on the size and shape flag you want before you buy felt. Then buy a little more than you think you need.*

Felt in a background color you choose

Sewing pins

Sewing scissors

Felt in other colors you choose for the decorations on the flag

Fabric glue, preferably in a squeezable container

A small sponge or cloth

Yarn, if you wish

Here's what you do:

1. For either a paper flag or a fabric flag, use a pencil with an eraser to sketch your designs on scrap paper. Try cutting out practice designs on scrap paper before you make your final decisions.

2. For a paper flag, use paper, construction paper, or poster-board in the background color you prefer. Use your scissors to cut the background paper to the size you prefer. Then cut out your designs from papers of other colors you choose. Glue or paste the decorations onto the background of your flag, and get it ready for display.

3. For a felt flag, use felt in the background color you choose. Outline the shape you want with pins, and use sewing scissors to cut out the felt piece. Cut out designs or letters from felt of other colors. Arrange them on the basic flag, and be careful to pin them just where you want them. Use fabric glue to attach them. Keep a moist sponge or cloth handy to wipe up any glue that goes wrong. If you wish, you can use yarn to make letters or decorations. Spread squeez-able fabric glue in the form of the letters. Then attach twisted yarn on over the glue.

4. Display your flag on a bulletin board or in another good place. You can even fly your flag out-side when the weather is good.

· · · · · · · · · · ·

DESIGN YOUR OWN FLAG

continued

PERHAPS YOU WANT TO PUT YOUR SIGNATURE ON YOUR FLAG. YOU CAN GLUE ON YOUR NAME OR OUTLINE YOUR HANDPRINT WITH YARN. OR YOU CAN PUT ON A SECRET SIGNATURE THE OLD-FASHIONED WAY. WEAVE A SMALL STRAND OF YOUR HAIR INTO ONE OF THE TWISTED PIECES OF YARN.

LONG AGO, PEOPLE WHO MADE QUILTS CREATED THAT SECRET SIGNATURE. SINCE THEN, FLAGMAKERS HAVE SOMETIMES DONE THE SAME. MAYBE NO ONE WILL KNOW BUT YOU. IF YOU GET A CHANCE, LOOK AT THE STATE FLAG OF ALASKA. A 13-YEAR-OLD BOY DESIGNED IT.

· · · · · · · · · ·
Map the World As You See It
· ·

You may think of maps as serious business, full of exact measurements and precise shapes. Maps, however, are also often artistic creations, full of imagination and emotion. Can you imagine, for instance, how your ancestors would have mapped the world? What would you think of the world if you had lived thousands of years ago before anyone could travel very far around the world? How could you draw a map of a world you had not seen?

You would likely see your home as the center of the world, with a canopy of sky overhead. At the edges of your homeland, you might see boundaries of dangerous forest, forbidding desert, or a sea full of monsters. Your ideas about the world would probably come from stories the elders told you, from vague maps, or from your own imagination.

You can stretch your imagination right now and draw your own map of the world as you see it. This is your map for you only.

Here's what you need:

Paper or construction paper

A pencil

A ruler or straightedge

A protractor or artist's curve, if you wish

Pens, markers, or pencils, in colors you choose

Here's what you do:

1. Think about what parts of the world you have actually seen, your home and the places you have visited. Decide what is important enough to put in the middle of your map.

2. Begin with paper or construction paper. Use a pencil, a straightedge or ruler, and (if you wish) a protractor or artist's curve to sketch in maps. Then color and decorate your sketches with pens, markers, or pencils in colors you choose.

3. Draw a sign on your map to show the direction of north, east, south, and west. This is your own personal map, so you can put north at the bottom or side of the map rather than in its usual place at the top. Just remember to locate east, south, and west at points of your map clockwise from north.

4. Think of your feelings about home as the focus of your map. When you think of home, do you think of one building, a neighborhood, a landscape, or a whole town? What you think of then becomes the center of your map. This is not an exact map. Draw in shapes and colors that remind you of home.

· · · · · · · · · · ·

MAP THE WORLD AS YOU SEE IT

continued

5. Draw places you know beyond your home. Show cities, farms, and waterways. Use shapes and colors that show your feelings. For instance, you may think of large red blocks if you think of a city with lots of red brick. Or you may think of green for a farm, brown or gray for factories, a flash of silver for sun, on green-blue for a river. You may think of different shapes for mountain peaks and prairie. You may show a swirl for the wind you remember or hazy reflections for the heat. Remember how travel has seemed to you. If you flew across an ocean, you may remember the ocean as small and far below. Or you may remember it as long and dreadful. You may remember a car trip as an adventure, taking you through exciting places. Or you may remember it as a long, flat, shimmering road.

> MAKE THIS MAP AS BEAUTIFUL AND MEANINGFUL AS YOU CAN. THIS IS THE MAP OF THE WORLD AS YOU SEE IT WITH YOUR OWN EYES. GO ON TO EXPLORE THE WORLD WITH OTHER SORTS OF MAPS.

. . . .

EXPLORE THE WORLD OVER BREAKFAST

. . . .

Here is how to make a placemat map. You can use this map to explore the world. You can write on this map, too. For example, draw on the route of your favorite explorer. Then wipe off the map when you want to track another favorite explorer.

You can use this map for other routes, too. You can write in current events around the world. You can mark volcanoes or earthquakes. You can plan your own trips just about anywhere.

You can write in different colors and track several routes at once.

If you use plastic backing, you can even have breakfast on this map.

What you need first for a placemat map is a printed paper map. To track a world famous explorer, you will want a map of the whole world. You may also want a map of your hemisphere, your country, your state or province or district, or a local map.

You may want to make one placemat map after another, with all different sorts of maps. That's all right because they're fun to make.

Here's what you need:

A printed paper map of your choice

Posterboard, other heavy cardboard, or rigid plastic such as the kind used to make stencils, as large as your map or slightly larger, to use as backing. (You can find plastic of this sort at a hobby store or in the hobby section of a large department store.)

A pencil, if you wish

Rubber cement

A large dry sponge, if you wish

A helper, if you wish

A clear plastic sheet, large enough to cover the map and its base. Ask for laminating plastic when you buy it. For a placemat map larger than 8½ × 11 inches (21 × 28 centimeters) use a rolled clear plastic laminate.

Scissors

Washable markers, in colors you choose

A damp sponge

Here's what you do:

1. Place the map in the center of the posterboard, cardboard, or plastic backing. If you wish, use a pencil to trace a light mark around the map to know how it is supposed to fit.

2. Remove the map, and cover the base with rubber cement.

   Caution: Be careful with rubber cement. Do not leave it around small children, and don't use it anywhere near heat or flame.

3. If the backing and map are already the same size, cover the back of the map with rubber cement. If the map is smaller than the backing, then apply cement only to the backing. That way if you don't get the map on just right the first time you try, you can peel it off and try again.

EXPLORE THE WORLD OVER BREAKFAST
continued

4. Carefully center the map over the base without touching the base. Place one edge of the map in contact with the edge of the base. You may want a helper to hold up the other end. Smooth the map carefully with your hand or with a large dry sponge. Push slowly and evenly from the spot where you have placed the map toward the other end of the base. The smoothing will help to keep the map straight, and it will get rid of air bubbles. Take your time.

5. Use your finger to roll up any excess rubber cement that may have squeezed out from under the edges of the map. Now you know why it's called "rubber" cement.

6. Allow the map to dry for about 15 minutes.

7. Use the scissors to cut the clear plastic laminating sheet to a size just a little larger than the placemat. Peel back about ½ inch (about 2 centimeters) of the backing. Beginning at one edge of the map, slowly and carefully continue peeling off the laminate backing as you smooth the laminate over the surface of the map. Use scissors carefully to trim away the overhanging edges of the laminate.

8. When you want to use your map, write on it with markers. Use a damp sponge to wipe off the markings when you want to use it again.

YOU'LL FIND LOTS OF USES FOR PLACEMAT MAPS. YOU CAN EAT BREAKFAST AND LEARN THE COUNTRIES OF SOUTH AMERICA, THE PARTS OF EUROPE, THE STATES OF THE UNITED STATES, THE PROVINCES OF CHINA OR CANADA—OR ANYTHING ELSE YOU WANT TO KNOW ABOUT THE WORLD. YOU'LL PROBABLY LIKE YOUR OWN PLACEMAT MAPS MUCH BETTER THAN THE KIND YOU CAN BUY IN STORES.

· · · · · · · · · · ·
EXPLORE THE WORLD LAYER BY LAYER
· ·

Here is how to make another kind of placemat map, one with a layer—or perhaps more than one layer. You can use a layered map to track all sorts of different sets of routes and travels. You can make a layered map just as colorful, complicated, and interesting as you want.

You can even use a layered map to show how a land changes over time. For example, put a basic map outline for the first layer. Then on the next layer, show something about where the dinosaurs lived and how they looked. Go on to show the animals from a later era and the first human settlers. On the top layer, you could show symbols and pictures of the modern era.

First, you'll need a printed paper map. You may want a map of the whole world, or you may want a map of one continent or district.

Here's what you need:

A printed paper map of your choice

Tracing paper (colored or white) or a sheet of clear colored plastic

A marker or pen, if you are using tracing paper

A black indelible marker or pen, if you are using clear colored plastic

Clear plastic sheets, as large as your map or slightly larger. (You can find clear plastic by the foot or meter at an arts and crafts store or a hardware store. If your map is 8½ × 11 inches,

21 × 28 centimeters, then you can use overhead transparencies of the same size. Or you can cut apart clear flexible plastic file folders.)

Markers or pens, in colors you choose. (Use the type of pens made for overhead transparencies or any other marker that works well on plastic.)

Cut-out pictures or other small decorations, if you wish

Household glue or paste, if you wish

Removable tape

Double-sided tape

EXPLORE THE WORLD LAYER BY LAYER

continued

Here's what you do:

1. Make an outline of your map on tracing paper or a sheet of clear colored plastic. If you are using tracing paper, use any marker or pen you wish. If you are using plastic for your outline, use a black indelible pen. Make an outline that leaves out most of the detail.

2. If you are using tracing paper, go back to Explore the World over Breakfast page 25, step 7, to see how to laminate it. You are laminating it just as you would a placemat map. If you use plastic, you do not need to apply plastic laminate.

3. Decide what features you want to show on each layer of your map. Then decide the order you want for your layers.

4. Place a clear plastic sheet over the original map. Use your marker or pen to trace one feature that you want to emphasize for the first layer.

5. Place another clear plastic sheet over the original map, and trace another feature. This is a good chance to think creatively. For example, to show what grows in each region, you may want to draw an ear of corn, a sheaf of wheat, or a potato. On the top layer, you may want to paste cut-out pictures or other decorations as symbols. For instance, you could use a small piece of cotton to show an area that produces cotton.

6. To attach the layers permanently, first plan the order in which you want them. Carefully align the first layer. Secure the laminate sheet with removable tape along one edge. Lift the opposite side of the laminate sheet. Place double-sided tape along the edge of that side of the map, and carefully smooth the laminate into place. Lift off the removable tape. Now you have a layer fixed to your map, one that you can fold back from the basic map. Add the other layers, one by one.

YOU'LL FIND LOTS OF GOOD USES FOR A MAP WITH LAYERS. YOU CAN ADD AND CHANGE LAYERS AS YOU WISH. BE JUST AS CREATIVE AS YOU WANT.

. . . .

TRACK WORLD EVENTS ON A BULLETIN BOARD MAP

. . . .

This is a good way to keep track of world events. Put your favorite map on a bulletin board. Then use push pins of different colors and map symbols to show what's happening all over the world or track several events at once. Or make your own stick-on map symbols to stick on your map.

This is exactly how government leaders, army generals, and business executives keep track of events. You may even see a district map at the local firehouse to show where fires have been.

Here's what you need:

Plain lightweight paper or removable sticky note papers such as Post-it™ notes

Scissors

Markers, in black and other colors you choose

Push pins, in colors you choose

Rubber cement, a glue stick, or removable tape, if you wish

Here's what to do:

1. Decide on a code, a simple drawing that will stand for whatever you want to plot. For example, you could show a flame on a tree outline to stand for a forest fire, a running foot to show a marathon, or crossed swords to show battles or wars.

2. If you wish to use plain lightweight paper, use scissors to cut it in small shapes. If you use removable sticky note papers, use markers to draw on each code.

3. If you wish, use push pins, rubber cement, a glue stick, or removable tape to attach the symbols to the map.

4. Follow the news, and decide what world events you want to show on your map. Place a sticker at the place where the news is happening. Update your map at least once a week. Another way to use your map symbols is to track events from your social studies or history classes.

IN MOVIES YOU SEE MILITARY COMMANDERS OR SECRET AGENTS WITH MAPS LIKE THIS. THAT'S HOW THEY KEEP TRACK OF THEIR MISSIONS. THINK ABOUT OTHER WAYS YOU CAN USE A PLACEMAT MAP, A LAYERED MAP, OR A BULLETIN BOARD MAP.

TRAVEL WITH THE FIRST, THE BEST, THE BRAVEST WORLD EXPLORERS

*I*magine the first people to venture out in boats. They stayed in sight of their own land. They didn't know what lay beyond. Perhaps, if they strayed too far, they would fall into the hands of angry gods or fearsome creatures. Perhaps they would arrive at the land of the dead.

Why did the first explorers of ancient times go out into the great unknown seas? Sometimes it must have been by accident. Imagine a fishing boat blown out to sea. The boat comes upon a beautiful island, and suddenly the people in the boat feel like explorers instead of just frightened fishermen.

Sometimes it must have been force. In hard times, people left their homes to find food or to escape their enemies. They had to find new lands, whatever the danger.

Often, we hear that the first explorers went out of greed. They wanted the wealth they imagined in faraway places. They wanted fame for being the first and the best.

Sometimes they must have traveled just out of curiosity. To be curious is to be human.

When you hear about the great explorers, you may wonder who are the real discoverers.

Think what was happening thousands of years ago. A few brave people crossed from Asia to America. You can look at a map to see how they could have crossed from Siberia, across the Bering Straits, and into the land that is now Alaska and Canada. These ancient people are the ones who discovered America, long before the Viking expeditions or the voyages of Christopher Columbus.

Ancient Polynesian travelers left accounts of mysterious gods who forced them to leave their home islands. Perhaps those powerful gods were tyrannical human rulers. The Polynesians built outrigger canoes, plunged into the vast unknown Pacific Ocean, and went on to find new islands. The Polynesians may have gone on to discover South America, and in different generations, the South Americans, in their turn, may have discovered the Polynesian Islands.

Almost anywhere that European explorers arrived in the world, they found people already in residence, and those people could say they were discovering the Europeans.

Would you like to follow some of these great explorers and the others who came after them?

You can find where they went and see the dangers they faced. You can make devices to help them. You can prove the world is not flat. You can celebrate with the explorers and eat unusual food with them. You can see the impossible people and improbable places of the explorers' imaginations. You can play an explorer's game. You may even want to drink from the Fountain of Youth.

This is your chance to explore the world with the best and the greatest of them all.

CHOOSE YOUR FAVORITE EXPLORER

If you like adventure stories, you'll really like stories about explorers.

Perhaps you like explorers from your own country or explorers who were among the first to tell the world about your country. If you live in Canada, you may like stories of Samuel de Champlain, David Thompson, George Vancouver, or Alexander Mackenzie. If you live in the United States, you may like to read about Davy Crockett, Lewis and Clark, Kit Carson, and the many native Americans who were among the first to reach new territories.

But what about the whole rest of the world and much earlier times?

- The Viking chiefs, who sailed their dragon ships across the North Atlantic 1,000 years ago. Imagine being an Inuit in Greenland and watching those fearsome ships coming closer and closer.

- The legendary Polynesian sailor Hawai'i Loa, who may have crossed the Pacific on an outrigger canoe to discover the Hawaiian islands. Or Hui-te-Rangi-roa, another Pacific sailor who may have gone all the way to Antarctica.

- Ibn Batuta, the colorful Middle Eastern traveler who covered huge distances on foot across Africa and Asia.

- Ferdinand Magellan, the Portuguese captain of the first ship to sail all the way around the world. Or Captain James Cook, the first European seaman to cross the Antarctic Circle and to attempt friendship with the peoples of the Polynesian Islands, Australia, and New Zealand. Or Vasco Núñez de Balboa, the first European to set eyes upon the great Pacific Ocean.

. . . .

CHOOSE YOUR FAVORITE EXPLORER

continued

You'll like the stories of Juan Ponce de León, who went to Florida to discover the Fountain of Youth or of Christopher Columbus, who thought (and hoped) that Cuba was very near Japan or perhaps at the edge of China.

If you like Arctic or Antarctic stories, you'll like Raold Amundsen, who was the first to reach the South Pole. You'll want to know about the first people to leave reliable records of reaching the North Pole, an ambitious team, Robert Edwin Peary, Matthew Henson, and four Inuits whose names you may like. They were Ooqueah, Ootah, Egingwah, and Seegloo.

OR PERHAPS ALL THE EXPLORERS WILL BE YOUR FAVORITES. IF YOU WANT TO TRACK THE ROUTES OF YOUR FAVORITE EXPLORERS, MAKE A WORLD PLACEMAT MAP. YOU CAN FIND OUT HOW IN EXPLORE THE WORLD OVER BREAKFAST, ON PAGE 24.

MAKE AN EXPLORER'S MAP-READING TOOL

. . . .

Each of the world navigators had to perform an extremely difficult feat, getting around Cape Horn at the southern tip of South America. Even before they began their long period of starvation as they crossed the Pacific Ocean, Magellan's ships encountered dreadful and dangerous storms at Cape Horn. The sailors were further confused by their constant search for a river that would give them a short and easy way through. The passage took more than a month and killed many of Magellan's sailors. The not-very-brave sailors of one ship deserted and, without a word to their fellow seamen, sailed back to Spain.

These days, sailors traveling around Cape Horn can call for help by satellite communication. They can send an electronic signal that reaches a satellite circling the Earth. Then the satellite sends the signal to tracking computers. The electronic signal gives rescuers a close idea of the location of the ship. The signal lasts for several days, sending its message again and again, while the rescuers search.

Yet still the search can fail. The rescuers, often expert teams from Chile, go through storms and cold. They look and look across the vast distances of the ocean. Sometimes they never find the doomed ship. The Cape is still a dreadful and dangerous passage.

To find one reason, make a map-reading tool that explorers took along on board ship.

You'll find this tool useful for your own map reading. Some explorers and geographers created fancy dividers made of precious metals. Yours won't be nearly so expensive.

Here's what you need:

2 plastic drinking straws
A two-pronged paper fastener
A straight pin
Scissors
A globe or world map

Here's what you do:

1. Hold the two plastic drinking straws together. About ½ inch (2 centimeters) from the top, make a hole in each straw. Use a straight pin to begin the hole and then use scissors to enlarge the hole. Put the fastener through the hole. When you insert the fastener, don't flatten the plastic straws. Make sure the two straws move easily, and then turn the prongs outward.

. . . .

MAKE AN EXPLORER'S MAP-READING TOOL
continued

2. Use scissors to cut the tips of each straw to a point.

3. Now you can use your dividers to measure distances on maps. The dividers will give you a better idea of distance than just using your fingers or a pencil.

Here's one way to use your dividers:

1. Put one end of the dividers at the tip of South America. Put the other at the Antarctic Circle.

2. Hold the dividers steady, and put one end at the tip of Africa, the Cape of Good Hope. Does the other end reach the Antarctic Circle from that position? You'll find that the continent of South America reaches much closer to the Antarctic Circle than does the African continent. The journey around

Africa may be risky, but that voyage is not nearly as dangerous as the trip around South America.

3. Now use your dividers to find the Panama Canal in the country of Panama, in Central America. If you hold the dividers steady, you can see about how much distance sailors save by going through the Panama Canal instead of sailing all the way around the tip of the South American continent.

USE YOUR DIVIDERS WHENEVER YOU READ A MAP OR A GLOBE, BUT DON'T EXPECT THEM TO GIVE YOU PERFECT ACCURACY. MOST MAPS DON'T SHOW EVERY TWIST AND TURN IN A ROAD, AND FLAT MAPS CAN'T SHOW THE RIGHT PROPORTIONS AS THE EARTH CURVES.

MAKE AN EXPLORER'S ANTIQUE MAP

Even though the antique maps were usually far from correct, they were interesting and often very beautiful. Today people collect them as works of art. You can make your own fancy antique map. Then treat it so that it looks as if Christopher Columbus or Vasco da Gama handed it down to your family centuries before you were born.

Before you begin, you may want to find some pictures of old maps as inspiration.

You may want a compass rose on your antique map and perhaps some wind cherubs and imaginary beasts. Making an antique map can be fun. Choose any part of the world you like. Perhaps you want to sketch in the general shape of China, Australia, Africa, North or South America. Perhaps you want to invent a country or land never seen before. Inventive mapmakers of the past often had no idea of the shape or size of the land, so don't worry about accuracy too much. You may even want to follow in the footsteps of the old mapmakers by creating a shape that looks like something significant. For instance, you could make China in the shape of a large dragon, or Scandinavia in the shape of a looming beast.

Here's what you need:

Scratch paper and pencil

Paper in gray, ivory, cream, or tan

A ruler or straightedge

Pens, markers, or pencils, in colors you choose

A cup of tea

Paper towels

Posterboard, if you wish

Household glue or paste, if you wish

Here's what you do:

1. Sketch your map on scratch paper before you begin the real map. Use a pencil with an eraser, along with a ruler or straightedge.

2. Select an off-white paper color that could look old, such as gray, ivory, cream, or tan. Use pens, markers, or pencils in as many colors as you wish, but remember to use dull, non-bright colors. A map fades over time, and you want your map to look faded. If you are making a valuable royal map, try gold and silver colors. Leave plenty of room at the edges.

MAKE AN EXPLORER'S ANTIQUE MAP
continued

4. Decide what you want on the edges of your map. Here are suggestions:

• You may want a cartouche. A cartouche is a fancy scroll that gives the title of the map and its date, the name (and perhaps even a portrait) of the important person to whom you are presenting the map, and the name of the mapmaker.

• You may want a beautiful and complicated compass rose, giving the directions of your map. If you would like to see how to make a compass rose, look at page 106.

• You may want cherubs at the edges to show the directions of the winds. The cherubs must have their mouths open, cheeks puffing, blowing wind with all their might.

• You may want fearsome sea beasts, waiting to swallow up sailors who stray off the route.

5. When you finish your drawings, tear off bits around the corners and edges of the map.

6. Dip the edges of the map in a cup of tea for a finishing antique touch. Then the map will look weathered and worn from hundreds of years of use. Dry the map on paper towels.

7. If you wish, mount your map on a piece of posterboard. Use glue or paste.

DISPLAY YOUR ANTIQUE MAP WITH PRIDE. NOT EVERYONE IS A CLOSE FRIEND OF PRINCE HENRY THE NAVIGATOR OR AMERIGO VESPUCCI.

PROVE THE WORLD IS NOT FLAT

The story is that when Christopher Columbus sailed on his first voyage in 1492, people warned him that he would fall off the edge of the flat Earth. That story is not true. A few people thought that the Earth was flat, but most people who had studied the question agreed with Columbus that the Earth had to be a sphere or round shape.

Actually, more than 2,000 years ago, great thinkers like Aristotle and Plato knew that the Earth is a sphere. You can look at the question the way they did. You may have to wait until you're in the right place at the right time.

Here are three ways to see for yourself that the earth is not flat:

1. When you are near an ocean or a large lake, stand on shore and watch a ship sail toward the horizon. Notice that the hull of the ship disappears from your view first. Then gradually, the masts and sails disappear. If the Earth were flat, you could watch the entire ship sail away until your eyes could no longer see that far.

2. When you are riding in a car across flat land, look ahead toward the next buildings. You may see a tall building, a church steeple, or a tower. Notice that at first you see only the top. Then gradually, you see the rest, as it appears over the curve of the Earth.

· · · · · · · · · · ·

PROVE THE WORLD IS NOT FLAT
continued

3. Consult an almanac or a calendar to see when to expect the next eclipse of the moon. If you have a clear night at the time of the eclipse, go outside to watch. During an eclipse, the shadow of the Earth falls across the surface of the moon. Look for the curve of the shadow. A round object casts a curved shadow. If you can't look directly, you can go to a library and look at photographs of an eclipse.

AN ECLIPSE IS SO BEAUTIFUL THAT IT'S WORTH SEEING EVEN IF YOU ALREADY KNOW YOU LIVE ON A ROUND PLANET. PLATO AND ARISTOTLE WOULD HAVE LOVED TO SEE SPACE PHOTOGRAPHS OF OUR BEAUTIFUL ROUND EARTH. ACTUALLY, OUR PLANET IS NOT A PERFECT SPHERE. IT BULGES AT THE EQUATOR AND IS A BIT FLAT AT THE NORTH AND SOUTH POLES.

· · · · · · · · · · ·

PLAY A GAME OF MYSTERIOUS MESSAGES

· ·

Imagine that explorers come to your home. They talk a strange language. Their alphabet is not like yours. They use signs and gestures, but those are not like yours, either. The only gestures you have in common are smiles and frowns.

This game is somewhat like charades. You can't say words. You must figure out signs and gestures.

Play this game with two teams, the explorers and the people. Explorers must use sign language to get their messages across. The people must guess the message. Then turn it around. The people use sign language to get their messages across, and the explorers guess.

For this game, make up your own short messages. Your message could be the title of a movie, book, or TV program that you want to recommend to your friends. The message could be a homework reminder. It could be a plan for the weekend.

Set up a timer. Each player has no more than 3 minutes to get the message across.

GO ON TO SEE REAL MESSAGES THAT EXPLORERS AND THE PEOPLE THEY VISITED TRIED TO GET ACROSS TO ONE ANOTHER. SOMETIMES THESE MESSAGES HAD SERIOUS CONSEQUENCES. SOMETIMES THEY WERE A MATTER OF LIFE AND DEATH.

. . . .

SOLVE THE RIDDLE OF MYSTERIOUS MESSAGES

. . . .

Think of yourself as the citizen of another land. Imagine how to answer these messages from the very strange explorers who come to your home. Imagine what action you will take. These are real messages that real explorers tried to get across to the people they visited.

1. The explorers tell you they are gods.

2. The explorers tell you they are hungry. They don't seem to like the food you offer them.

3. The explorers demand that you show them directions to the Seven Cities of Gold. If you don't, they threaten to kill you. Yet there are no Seven Cities of Gold.

4. The explorers want you to take them to your king or queen. You never heard of a king or queen.

5. The explorers seem like kind and good people. They bring food and gifts. But then they pat the heads of the children.

6. The explorers tell you they are dirty and hot, and they certainly look as if they need baths.

7. The explorers are wearing fancy red coats, embroidered with elaborate designs. They have socks on their feet. You've never seen such wonderful things.

8. The explorers want you to lead them to the North Pole, across the shifting ice of the sea. You know it's far too dangerous.

IMAGINE THAT YOU LIVE ON A SOUTH PACIFIC ISLAND, ON THE COAST OF SOUTH AMERICA, OR IN THE ARCTIC. HOW WOULD YOU ANSWER THESE STRANGE EXPLORERS? IF YOU WANT TO SEE WHAT HAPPENED IN REAL LIFE, TURN TO PAGE 55.

. . . .

CELEBRATE WITH THE EXPLORERS

. . . .

When you visit someplace special for the first time, you really ought to celebrate—and celebrate with your pets, too.

Captain James Cook's men celebrated crossing the Equator by dunking every first-time crosser into the sea. That meant everybody, even cats and dogs. The men constructed a mechanical sea-dunking chair for the ceremony. There were only two ways you could escape the dunking. You could give a generous gift to the crew (and another gift if you didn't want wet pets). Or you could show proof that you had already crossed the Equator.

The next time you visit someplace special for the first time, you can bring home a display that proves you were really there. This is a good project for a creative person, and it helps you remember the special places you visit.

Caution: Some parks and beaches do not allow taking anything at all.

Here are ideas for collecting souvenirs:

- Take care when you look for nature's souvenirs, especially around water. Take a friend with you.

- Find a flower blossom, fern, or unusual leaf that you like. Use blunt scissors so you can cut off a part of the plant without injuring the whole plant.

- Don't collect insects, snails, or other live creatures. Be sure to inspect natural things like seashells or sea weed to make sure you're not stealing a creature's home.

- Collect small seashells, sand dollars, jewel-like sea urchin shells, or a bit of seaweed. You can even collect interesting sand or colorful soil in a small plastic container. (The legend is that if you take home some sand, you will get to return another time.)

· · · · · · · · · ·

CELEBRATE WITH THE EXPLORERS

continued

- Take only a very small number of any of nature's souvenirs. Water creatures find homes inside old shells, and all sorts of creatures need the plants. You want to leave beaches and other natural wonders undisturbed.

- Look for interesting rocks. If you're really lucky, you may find a fossil imprint in a rock. Fossils were once living plants or animals that have left an imprint in soft mud or clay. Then the clay hardens over time and preserves a print. Look carefully. Sometimes fossils are very small.

- Make sure to dry out anything from a beach. A complete drying may take several days. If you want to display seashells, soak them in a half-and-half mixture of water and bleach. Then scrub them with cotton swabs or an old toothbrush.

- You may want to take home photographs, postcards, pictures, brochures, or postage stamps from the place you visit.

- Take home signatures and messages from the people you meet. You can collect autographs from people you like, even if they're not famous.

Here's what you need for a display:

Posterboard or cardboard or a scrapbook with plastic fold-over pages
Household glue or paste, if you wish
Plastic ties, if you wish
Scissors, if you wish
Egg cartons, if you wish
Pens or markers, in colors you choose

Here's what to do:

1. Lay your posterboard, cardboard, or scrapbook on a flat surface, and see how you want to arrange your souvenirs. Leave room for titles and labels.

2. After you decide on a final arrangement for a poster, use household glue or school paste to attach souvenirs. Or use long plastic ties. Poke holes in the posterboard with scissors. Thread the plastic tie through, and then tie on the souvenir. Or just fold over the plastic pages of a scrapbook to protect your collection. Keep seashells and rocks in an egg carton.

· · · · · · · · · · ·

CELEBRATE WITH THE EXPLORERS

continued

3. Ask someone to help you identify your findings. Then you can label them with names and the place and date you found them.

4. Make your display as creative and interesting as you can. Use pens and markers to make the titles and labels. Be sure to sign and date your poster or scrapbook. You may need it as proof some day.

THESE DAYS, WHEN YOU CROSS THE EQUATOR, YOU MAY HAVE TO KNEEL IN FRONT OF SOMEONE DRESSED AS NEPTUNE, KING OF THE OCEAN, AND GET A BUCKET OF SEAWATER TOSSED OVER YOUR HEAD. IF YOU CROSS THE ARCTIC CIRCLE, YOU MAY FIND IT'S A BUCKET OF ICE WATER TOSSED. KEEP A RECORD, A DIARY OR JOURNAL, OF TRIPS YOU TAKE, EVEN SHORT TRIPS. ALL THE GREAT EXPLORERS DO THAT.

PACK FOR A JOURNEY OF EXPLORATION

How would you pack if you were sailing around the world? Of course, your plans for a journey of exploration would be different from those of the early explorers.

Can you imagine how to pack supplies for an early explorer who doesn't even have a map? Or for an explorer who has no idea what lay beyond the horizon? Think what packing would be like if you had no modern equipment or conveniences. You would probably have severely limited space. Yet what you take could make the difference between life and death.

When you make plans for a family or school trip, or a hiking or boating adventure with friends or a club, you'll want to figure your supplies as wisely as the great explorers.

. . . .

PACK FOR A JOURNEY OF EXPLORATION
continued

Here are supplies to consider:

Food and water, possibly dried foods and nonperishable fruits and vegetables

A canteen or water bottle

Utensils, such as a pot, fry pan, cutlery, dishes, camping stove, grill, reflector oven

Shelter, such as a tent, ground cover, sleeping bag

Matches in waterproof, air-tight container

Clothing, including a poncho in case of rain and backup clothes in case the weather changes

Emergency supplies, such as a first aid kit, water purification tablets, any necessary medications, sunscreen, insect repellent

A directional compass

Maps, perhaps waterproof or in a plastic bag

Rope and twine

A sewing kit with safety pins, needles, thread

A jackknife

A hatchet

A light folding shovel

A fishing line and hooks

Soap, toothbrush, comb, towel

Money for supplies you plan to purchase along the way

Pocket field guides (for plants, birds, animals, fish), as you wish

A camera and film

A notebook, diary, or sketchbook and pen or pencil to record your trip

Here are guidelines to help you with packing:

1. Learn all you can about where you are going. Ask people who have been there. Read books and guides. Many early explorers did not have this opportunity.

2. Know who and how many people will be going on the trip.

3. Plan your route. Will you be able to restock along the way? Where will you spend the night? On the trail, in a camp, or on a boat?

4. What type of clothing will you need? The rule of thumb is that you need at least one outfit to wear, one to be washed, and one in reserve. You need to plan for changes in weather, too. Depending on the weather, you may need two or three changes of clothing in reserve. If you're walking, how many pairs of shoes will you need and what types? Decide if you need a swimsuit or an extra warm jacket.

5. Think about the poisonous snakes, biting insects, black flies, or mosquitoes that you are liable to meet. You may need special clothes, coverups, and insect repellents.

· · · · · · · · · · ·

PACK FOR A JOURNEY OF EXPLORATION
continued

6. Figure the amount of food and water you need ahead of time. You may be able to acquire more along the way, or you may need to carry it all with you. Take into account how you will be traveling. Plan the meals, and figure the amount needed per person for the trip. If you are traveling with animals, such as a dog, horse, or donkey, you must be especially careful to provide enough food and water for them. On a sea voyage, you will have to take enough fresh water and food to last until you reach port plus some extra in case you get off course or sail into calm waters.

7. For backpacking or a small boat, keep your packing light. Take everything you need, but think about how much space each item takes and how much you can carry and store.

8. Figure on changes in weather and plan for the unexpected. For hot weather journeys, wear clothes of natural fabric and light colors. For cold weather trekking, remember that layers of clothing provide the best insulation. Layers of clothes help when weather changes. As temperatures go up and down, you can remove and add layers.

> GREAT EXPLORERS PLAN AHEAD FOR MORE THAN JUST BASIC NECESSITIES. REMEMBER TO TAKE A CAMERA, BINOCULARS, NOTEBOOK OR SKETCHBOOK, AND WHATEVER ELSE YOU NEED FOR SHARP OBSERVATION. YOU'LL WANT TO LOOK AT SEA AND STARS, THE LAND, AND THE LIVING CREATURES, AND SEE ALL THAT YOU CAN SEE.

. . . .

EAT DINNER WITH THE EXPLORERS (WITHOUT THE WORMS)

. . . .

If you are an explorer, you have to explore new foods. In Australia, you might join the explorers for a meal of kangaroo. You might partake of a giant turtle. On board ship, you might be happy to catch a crow or an albatross for dinner. Out in the Arctic, you might join the Inuit people to dine on seal intestines and whale blubber.

Mostly, though, you would dine on hardtack. Hardtack is a sort of cracker or biscuit, made without flavoring and usually without yeast. On a ship or in a polar land, you could easily run out of fresh food, even fish. You made do with giant sheets of hardtack.

"Tack" is slang for inferior food, and of course, these giant sheets could get very hard after long storage. If hardtack stayed in the hold of the ship long enough, it also ended up full of maggots and worms. You'd have to pick out the worms.

Here's how to make your own hardtack. Only yours will be good and tasty—and without worms. The explorers would envy you.

Here's what you need:

2 cups (500 milliliters) white or whole-wheat flour

1 teaspoon (5 milliliters) salt

1 teaspoon (5 milliliters) shortening

About ½ cup (125 milliliters) water

Here's what you do:

1. In a large bowl, mix flour and salt. Add shortening, and work it in with your fingers. Stir in just enough water to make a very stiff dough.

· · · · · · · · · · ·

EAT DINNER WITH THE EXPLORERS (WITHOUT THE WORMS)

continued

2. Knead the dough over with the palms of your hands. Or else beat the dough with a wooden mallet or a piece of clean wood. Fold, knead, and beat until the dough is stretchy. The more the dough is folded and beaten, the better the hardtack will be. For long voyages, too, the explorers wanted the dough very flat, with no bubbles of air in it. That meant fewer worms and bugs getting into it.

3. Push the dough with your hands or use a rolling pin to roll the dough out to about ½ inch (2 centimeters) thickness.

4. Use a knife to cut the dough in squares of about 2 to 4 inches (5 to 10 centimeters). Or use a biscuit or round cookie cutter to make circles.

5. Place the dough shapes on a greased baking sheet. Bake at 325°F (162°C) for 30 minutes or until brown.

6. Remove your biscuits from the baking sheet. Cool on wire racks. Store in a tightly covered container (or in the hold of your ship).

7. Serve with other long-lasting treats, such as jam or jelly.

THE EXPLORERS NEEDED FRESH FOOD. WITHOUT VITAMIN C AND OTHER NUTRIENTS, THEY DEVELOPED PAINFUL DISEASES. THE MOST FEARED DISEASE AMONG THE ARCTIC EXPLORERS AND THE WORLD MARINERS WAS SCURVY. SCURVY MADE THEIR TEETH GET LOOSE AND EVENTUALLY FALL OUT. THEIR JOINTS SWELLED PAINFULLY, AND SORES FORMED ALL OVER THEIR BODIES. SCURVY KILLED MANY BRAVE EXPLORERS IN THE END. GO ON TO SEE DELICIOUS WAYS TO PREVENT TROUBLE AND GET THE GOOD NUTRITION AN EXPLORER NEEDS.

DRINK FROM THE FOUNTAIN OF YOUTH

When Juan Ponce de León came to Florida, he found a lush land, with flowers in bloom everywhere. At his home in Spain that spring, people would be celebrating the Easter season and what they called the Pascus Florida, or the Feast of Flowers. So he called this flower-filled land Florida.

He wanted to find the Fountain of Youth. Take one drink, and you could live forever as a young, healthy person.

Why did Ponce de León believe in something so impossible as the Fountain of Youth? Perhaps the native people told him legends about the Fountain of Youth.

Possibly he did not believe the stories, but told them to King Ferdinand of Spain anyway. Queen Isabella, who had given Columbus money for his voyages, had died by then, and her husband, King Ferdinand, was a frail old man in poor health. The king might give money for a voyage that would bring him back such a precious drink. There had been miracles from the New World already. Why not one more?

Ponce de León searched Florida in 1513 and again in 1521. Before he could find the magical Fountain, the native Indians of Florida killed him in battle. He was not yet 50 years old.

Here is a recipe for a sparkling Fountain of Youth drink. It may not make you live forever, but it will definitely help prevent malnutrition—or thirst. Ponce de León would have liked it.

. . . .

DRINK FROM THE FOUNTAIN OF YOUTH
continued

Here's what you need:

1 quart (1 liter) orange juice

1 quart (1 liter) cranberry juice drink

1 pint (0.5 liter) mango juice drink

1½ quarts (1.5 liters) sparkling water

Ice cubes or crushed ice, if you wish

Mint, basil, or strawberries, if you wish

Here's how to stir up the recipe:

1. In a large pitcher, stir together orange juice, cranberry juice drink, and mango juice drink.

2. Add sparkling water just before serving.

3. Pour into glasses full of ice cubes or crushed ice. If you wish, top each glass with a sprig of mint or basil or with a strawberry.

THIS RECIPE MAKES 4 QUARTS, JUST OVER 4 LITERS, OR ABOUT 16 GLASSES. YOU CAN MAKE MORE OR LESS. YOU MAY WANT TO EXPERIMENT WITH OTHER TYPES OF JUICES, TOO. THIS IS A GOOD RECIPE FOR PEOPLE WHO LIKE TO EXPERIMENT ON A HOT SUMMER DAY.

EAT LUNCH WITH CAPTAIN COOK (OR TAKE A WHIPPING)

You had to be careful if you sailed with Captain Cook. He ordered 12 lashes for any sailor who refused his ration of nutritious foods.

Captain Cook was a fanatic about good nutrition. It was his pride that none of his men suffered from scurvy or other types of malnutrition. Scurvy destroyed many other crews, but not Cook's.

Cook got his ideas about nutrition from a British naval surgeon, Dr. James Lind. Dr. Lind recommended fresh food, especially citrus fruits and other forms of vitamin C. Cook took with him orange and lemon syrup, onions, "sellery" (celery) to be made into soup, and live cattle for fresh beef.

He especially liked to store barrels of sauerkraut. The men hated it. Sometimes they'd rather take the 12 lashes. They especially hated sauerkraut when it had sat in the barrels a few too many months. Cook ordered the officers to set a good example to the crew and pretend they liked sauerkraut.

You could eat this sauerkraut every day and never worry about getting a whipping. You'd be too busy eating.

To make sauerkraut, you need to create a chemical change in cabbage. You need to make the cabbage ferment or cure before you cook it. For this recipe, the chemical change takes nine days. Be sure to plan ahead.

· · · · · · · · · ·

EAT LUNCH WITH CAPTAIN COOK
(OR TAKE A WHIPPING)

continued

Here's what you need:

Grater
Canning jar with lid
Dish
Plastic wrap
Large cabbage, enough for about 2
  pounds (1 kilogram) shredded cabbage
2 teaspoons (10 milliliters) salt
Water

Here's what you do:

1. Grate the cabbage.

  : *Caution: You need an adult to*
  : *help you shred the cabbage.*

2. Pack the shredded cabbage tightly in a 1-quart (1-liter) canning jar until it is half full. Then add one teaspoon (5 milliliters) salt. Pack in the rest of the cabbage very tightly until the jar is filled to the shoulder. Add 1 teaspoon (5 milliliters) salt. Fill the jar with cold water until it is overflowing. Set the jar on a dish to catch the overflowing water. Cover the jar loosely with plastic.

3. Keep the jar at room temperature for 9 days. Once a day, add cold water so that the jar stays full to overflowing.

4. At the end of nine days, when the chemical changes of fermentation have stopped, screw the lid down tightly and store. Sauerkraut keeps very well, but Captain Cook's sailors could tell you that you might be happier with it if you didn't keep it in the hold of your ship for months and months.

5. To cook and serve the sauerkraut, fill a large pan with water or juice from the sauerkraut and boil the sauerkraut for about 15 minutes.

  : *Caution: You need adult help*
  : *with boiling water.*

6. If you wish, mix in pieces of apple. Or serve with a roast pork and potato dinner.

  : TO PREVENT SCURVY, THE
  : BRITISH SAILORS BEGAN EATING
  : LIMES AS A SOURCE OF
  : VITAMIN C. THAT'S WHY
  : PEOPLE STILL CALL BRITISH
  : SAILORS "LIMEYS."

MAKE AN EXPLORER'S AROUND-THE-WORLD GIFT

You can make a one-of-a-kind present for the next birthday or holiday. Take a clue from the explorers and make your own personal gazetteer. A gazetteer is a dictionary of geographical names. You can put your own list of funny or odd or important names into a book.

This is a good project for an artistic and creative person.

First, choose the subject for your gazetteer.

Here are ideas for a gazetteer:

- Look for place names that have something to do with Christmas or another world holiday. Decorate and draw pictures on your list, and you'll have a one-of-a-kind holiday present.

- Find funny or peculiar place names. You'll have a funny birthday present. (You may find some good stories behind the strange place names, too.)

- Find place names from your own heritage. If you are Native American, for instance, look for places that your own society named in the United States or Canada.

- Find family names all over the world. Or find the place names that are the same as the personal name of someone you especially like.

Here's an example:

Suppose you want a decorated gazetteer for your father, and your father's name is one of the most popular names on Earth, David. Your gazetteer could tell your father all about how important David is around the world.

Look in a dictionary of place names or in the index of an atlas, and find *Davids* and variations of *David*.

In the United States, your gazetteer could list Camp David, the Presidential retreat in the mountains of Maryland as well as David City (actually a town) in eastern Nebraska, David Island in New

· · · · · · · · · · ·

MAKE AN EXPLORER'S AROUND-THE-WORLD GIFT
continued

York's Long Island Sound, Davidson Counties in both North Carolina and Tennessee, both Davies County and Davidstown in North Carolina, and mountains named Davidson in both Nevada and Alaska (plus a Davidson glacier). There's the town of Davidson in Saskatchewan, Canada. In England, you could find Davidstow, and in Scotland you could find Davidson's Mains. In Russia, there's David-Forodok, and Panama has its own David River.

You could keep going until you find all the *David* names you want for your gazetteer.

Here's what you need:

A dictionary of place names

An atlas of the world or any part of the world you choose, with an index of place names

Scrap paper and pencil

Paper or construction paper, in colors you choose

Pens, markers, or pencils, in colors you choose

A paper punch or scissors

A length of colored yarn or string

Here's what you do:

1. In a dictionary of place names or in the index of an atlas, find the place names that interest you, and find where these places are located.

2. Use scrap paper and a pencil to plan your gazetteer. Decide how you want to list and decorate the names. Perhaps you want to sketch in maps. Perhaps you want to draw cartoons or color decorations for each page.

3. Make the gazetteer on paper or construction paper. Use pens, markers, or pencils to create your names, maps, pictures, and decorations. Make special decorations for the front cover.

4. Fit the pages of your gazetteer together. Use a paper punch or scissors to make two or three holes along the left margin of each page.

5. Thread a length of colored yarn or string through the holes. Tie the pages of your book together.

A GAZETTEER CAN BE A ONE-OF-A-KIND PRESENT. YOU MAY EVEN WANT TO MAKE ONE JUST FOR YOURSELF.

SOLUTIONS TO MYSTERIES

Solve the Riddle of Mysterious Messages, page 40: Here's what sometimes happened in real life. You may want to read about the explorers and find out the complete stories.

1. The explorers who let people think they were gods were foolish. Often, they paid with their lives. The people were frightened of these gods and their guns. They might honor them for a time. Then the celebration ended forever.

2. The explorers were often desperately hungry, and kindly native people helped as best they could. In the Arctic, the Inuit people saved lives by offering their nutritious food—seal intestines and whale blubber. The peoples of Polynesia generously offered roast dog. The people of the Caribbean Islands gave Columbus fried iguana, corn, and a bitter chocolate drink. (He liked the corn.) Perhaps you would like to share a favorite banquet food of the generous Hawaiians, coconut saturated with saliva from the mouth of the chief.

3. In the 1540s, the Spanish explorer Francisco Vásquez de Coronado made just such a threat to the native American people. Perhaps wisely, they indicated that he should travel far, far away to the northwest. He thought he had failed when he found no gold. But his men were the first Europeans to see the Grand Canyon, the Rio Grande, California's Mojave Desert, and portions of what is now Arizona, New Mexico, Texas, Oklahoma, and Kansas.

4. When Captain Cook asked to see their king or queen, the people of Tahiti found just the right woman, Purea. Captain Cook may have asked to see a tall person, and Purea was tall. They thought he may also have asked to see an important person. Purea came from an important family, and besides, everybody liked Purea. Being liked makes a person important.

5. The Maori people of New Zealand were not sure what Captain Cook meant by patting the heads of the children. He could be taking their spirits, touching their spiritual power, or working a magic spell on them. Of course, he intended only to be kind to the children.

6. The European mariners were often quite a shock when they landed after months at sea. Polynesian and Hawaiian people felt they had a lot to teach the Europeans about how to stay clean and cool. There was water all about, and the islanders liked to swim as well as bathe, as often as three times a day. The

SOLUTIONS TO MYSTERIES

continued

native Americans of what is now Virginia also thought the new settlers needed a good cleaning. They even offered to do laundry for them.

7. Captain Cook liked the Tahitian people, but he soon discovered they had little idea of private property. Once, a clever fellow stole the good captain's socks right out from under his pillow as he lay in bed. The naturalist, James Banks, was sorry to lose his fine embroidered coat. The Tahitians said they were only curious and interested in beautiful things.

8. Of course, the Inuit people knew that venturing out onto the icy sea toward the North Pole was far too dangerous for any human being. Wisely, the Arctic adventurers, Robert Peary and Matthew Henson, lived with the Inuits for years and learned their ways of coping with the Arctic climate. Even then, they found it difficult to persuade four Inuit men to go with them on their expedition to the North Pole.

BARGAIN, TRADE, AND NEGOTIATE ALL AROUND THE WORLD

*T*he first people of ancient times to venture far from home may have been traders. They probably wanted to buy and sell. Many of the explorers sailed around the world not only to see what was out there but to see what they could trade or buy or take.

Now the world runs on a complex system of trade routes. Your clothes and food, your furniture and television set or radio or CD-player, your books and magazines and the printing inside them, a car and all its parts, everything you own or see may come from different parts of the world.

Some of your possessions may travel through the world to you on ancient trade routes. You can play a game of traveling the centuries-old Silk Road, staying wary of the bandits. Explorers searched for routes to the fabled Spice Islands. Now you can create foods and perfumes with spices that were once only for a few very rich people. You can grow a plant that turned out to be better than gold.

You can make a pirate flag or barbecue the favorite pirate food.

This is your chance to trade, bargain, and negotiate all around the world.

. . . .
PLAY A TREASURE-HUNTING GAME
. . . .

Perhaps when you think of hidden treasure, you think of pirate coins buried under ground for hundreds of years and just waiting for someone to find the secret map. Perhaps you think of a ship sunk in a long-ago storm and still laden with gold and jewels.

Or you can find not-very-hidden treasure by looking around you. Here's how to play a treasure hunting game. You can play at home or at school. Or, if you have an adult with you and everyone is very well behaved, you can look around in a store. You can play this game with your mother, your father, or a friend. If you are at home, you can even look by yourself.

Here's how to play:

1. The goal is to find treasure in the form of food, clothes, toys, games, books, electronics, cars, and other products imported from around the world. The goal is to find the places of origin, where products were built or manufactured and where food was grown.

2. Choose a territory. Perhaps you can look at things at your home, in your classroom, on people's clothes, or in a grocery store.

Caution: You must have an adult with you in a store. Don't be in too much of a hurry. Be sure your hands are clean. Don't touch breakable things. If you do touch something, put it back just as it was.

3. Choose clues. You need to have evidence about the place of origin for a product. The evidence can be a label ("Made in Taiwan"), a store sign ("Israeli Oranges for Sale"), or a statement from a store employee or someone else you can trust ("Dad says he bought that sweater in Scotland"). Look at

· · · · · · · · · · ·

PLAY A TREASURE-HUNTING GAME

continued

the copyright page of a book or magazine to see where it was printed. You won't find a label or sign on every product, and you won't always find evidence about where parts were made. A car, for instance, may contain parts from a dozen different countries, but you won't find signs or labels that tell you that. Sometimes you can find a label on packaging for a product, even if there is no label on the product itself.

Caution: In a store, don't take anything out of its packaging.

Here's what to find, if you can:

- Find something from your own country.
- Find a product that was made by the original native people of your country.
- Find something from a country that borders your country.
- Find something from a country that does not border your country.

- Find something from your own town or local farm.
- Find a product from as many of these continents as you can: Africa, Asia, Europe, North America, or South America.
- Find a product from Australia or from an island. (Look on a map if you're not sure which places are islands.)

KEEP YOUR EYES OPEN FOR PRODUCTS FROM ALL AROUND THE WORLD WHENEVER YOU TRAVEL, VISIT A FACTORY, OR SHOP IN A STORE. YOU MAY WONDER HOW WE GET PRODUCTS AND PARTS FROM JUST ABOUT EVERYWHERE.

· · · · · · · · · · ·

FIND WHAT HOLDS THE WORLD TOGETHER

· ·

From the beginnings of time, people have wanted to trade. They want to sell what they have and buy what someone else has. Perhaps trade is what holds the world of people together.

The trade of products around the world helps people get to know one another and learn to cooperate. Sometimes, trade promotes peace instead of war.

Choose a product, and make symbols for it so you can see where the product comes from. This is a good use for a world map you make yourself, such as a layered map, placemat map, or a bulletin board map. For example, draw and color tiny television sets for the 15 countries that export electronics.

Here's where to put symbols for three interesting kinds of products:

- Flowers. Most countries trade flowers, seeds, and bulbs locally or perhaps to one or two other countries. Here are some countries that export around the world.

- Chocolate and cocoa. Here are 15 nations to find on a map and attach symbols for chocolate lovers.

  In Africa: Sierra Leone, the Cote d'Ivoire, Ghana, Togo, Benin, Nigeria, Cameroon, Equatorial Guinea, the Congo, and the nation of Sao Tome and Principe.

  In South America: Bolivia and Ecuador.

  In the Pacific Ocean: Vanuatu, 80 islands joined as one nation.

  In Europe: Switzerland and France, with fine chocolates.
  (Import and export is always complicated. Switzerland and France import cocoa and other ingredients from several countries and then export the finished chocolates.)

In North and South America: the United States, Canada, El Salvador, and Colombia.

In Europe: the Netherlands with famous Dutch tulip bulbs.

. . . .

FIND WHAT HOLDS THE WORLD TOGETHER
continued

- Electronics such as television sets, CD players, radios, and computers. As more and more people want to buy electronics, more and more countries design, produce parts, and assemble.

In North America: the United States, Puerto Rico, and Canada.

In Asia: India, Japan, Taiwan, Singapore, the Philippines, Malaysia, South Korea, and China.

In Europe: France, Germany, Italy, and the Netherlands.

FIND OUT WHAT PRODUCTS YOUR OWN TOWN, DISTRICT, OR COUNTRY MAKES. MAKE SYMBOLS FOR YOUR OWN LOCAL PRODUCTS AND PUT THOSE SYMBOLS ON YOUR OWN MAP.

. . . .

PLAY THE SILK ROAD GAME

. . . .

For more than two thousand years, generations of Chinese traders moved shipments of silk along a road that led from eastern China all the way to the Mediterranean Sea. The road split into several routes at one point, and altogether went on for more than 4,300 miles (6,900 kilometers). The traders walked, rode horses, and rode in camel trains to get from one end to the other.

Besides silk, the Chinese traders brought jade and other gems, fine porcelain, and spices. They returned from the Middle East, Arabia, and Europe with gold, silver, and horses.

After the traders left their home territory, bandits and warlords awaited them. The traders had to pay a tax to warlords who offered to protect them from the bandits, and then pay the bandits to protect them from other bandits. If they survived, they'd meet at the Kunlun Mountains, with peaks 25,000 feet (7,620 meters) high. (Look for them on the border between Tajikistan and Xinjiang Province in China, at 35°N, 88°E.)

Then they crossed the Taklimakan Desert. It's 600 miles (965 kilometers) wide, and its name means go in and you won't come out.

You can play your own Silk Road game, with two or more players.

Here's what you need:

A pencil

Paper, construction paper, or poster-board

Markers or pens, in colors you choose

Coins, buttons, pebbles, or board markers from another game, one for each player

A pair of dice

Here's how to make your Silk Road game board:

1. Use a pencil to construct a road on a piece of paper, construction paper, or posterboard. Make the road curvy and with 31 steps from beginning to end. Number each of the steps from 1 to 31. In a corner of the paper, draw a compass rose showing north to the top, east to the right, south to the bottom, west to the left. Your road should run from east to west.

2. Color and decorate your road with colored markers or pens.

63
•

PLAY THE SILK ROAD GAME

continued

3. Label the beginning of the road "Anxi." Label the end "Tajikistan." In between, note the stops: "Swamps" at about step 9, the "Karim Basin" at about step 14, "Dunes" at about step 21, the "Kunlun Mountains" at about step 29.

Here's how to play the Silk Road game:

1. The goal of each player is to lead a trading caravan along the first 1,000 miles (1,600 kilometers) of the Silk Road from Anxi in central China to Tajikistan. Play by taking turns with the dice. Then move your marker along the steps of the road. Remember that all kinds of good and bad things can happen.

2. If you roll an even number on the dice, go west one space.

3. If you roll an odd number, match it to the list below:

3—Five of your camels and horses escape during the night. Lose one turn while you round them up.

5—You rescue a Mongol guide from bandits. He helps you go west two extra spaces.

7—You must detour around a war zone. Go east one space.

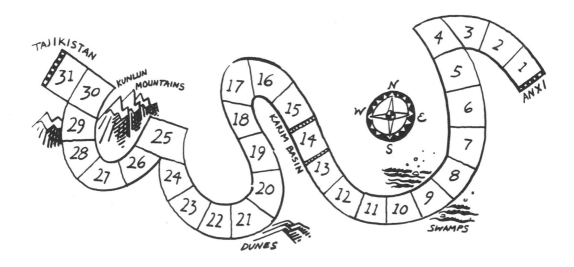

· · · · · · · · · · ·
PLAY THE SILK ROAD GAME
continued

9—A warlord stops you and wants taxes. You lose one turn while figuring out how to pay.

11—You discover an oasis with fresh water and fruit trees. Go west one extra space.

4. The first player to cross over the Kunlun Mountains into Tajikistan (and space 31) wins. The winner meets traders who have come east from the lands that are now Iran and Afghanistan. They get the silk, and the game winner gets brass and carpets to take back to China.

YOU MAY WANT TO DESIGN YOUR OWN GAME FOR THE ENTIRE SILK ROAD—OR FOR THE JOURNEY BACK TO CHINA. TODAY IN CHINA, YOU CAN STILL TRAVEL PARTS OF THE SILK ROAD. BY THE SEVENTEENTH CENTURY, HOWEVER, THE SILK ROAD DID LESS AND LESS BUSINESS AS A TRADING ROUTE. THE SEA ROUTES AROUND THE WORLD WERE BEGINNING TO OPEN TO TRADERS, AND SHIPPING BY SEA BROUGHT IN HIGHER PROFIT THAN DID THE OLD LAND ROUTES WITH ALL THEIR DANGERS.

. . . .

EAT LIKE A RICH PERSON

. . . .

The Europeans (and a few other people) loved spices with a passion that led them to world exploration for trade routes—and to dark deeds committed in pursuit of their spice dreams.

On the spice routes from Asia, the spices changed hands again and again. Each change provided a profit to one more trader, bandit, or warlord. Often, the trade routes were broken for years at a time, as battles raged over the wealth that was changing hands. By the time the spices reached their goal, they had become extremely expensive. Only rich people could afford them.

The most coveted of all spices was black pepper from the Malabar coast of India. About a quarter of all the spice trade worked to bring pepper to Europe and the Mideast. (Look for the Malabar coast at 18°N, 72°E.)

The traders also hoped to bring back the other favorite spice, cinnamon or its more strongly scented form, cassia. In the Biblical Book of Exodus, God ordered Moses to consecrate the temple with sacred myrrh, cinnamon, cassia, and olive oil.

Suppose you are a very wealthy European of about 500 years ago. You can afford these spices, no matter how much they cost. You can pamper yourself.

You may have eaten something like this before in the form of cinnamon toast. This is different.

You're in for a taste treat.

· · · · · · · · · · ·

EAT LIKE A RICH PERSON

continued

Here's what you need:

A slice of bread
Butter or margarine
Pepper
Cinnamon
Knife
Toaster

Here's what you do:

1. Toast the bread. Spread it with butter or margarine.
2. Sprinkle on lots and lots of pepper and cinnamon together.

THE TRADE IN SPICES AROUND THE WORLD CREATED THE IDEA THAT YOU COULD ENJOY EATING. THE PEOPLE WHO COULD NOT AFFORD SPICES MADE DO WITH ROUGH FOODS, OFTEN BARELY EDIBLE AND WITH NO VARIETY OF TASTES. OF COURSE, WHAT PEOPLE ENJOY EATING DOES CHANGE CONSIDERABLY OVER THE YEARS. NOW THAT ANYBODY COULD MIX PEPPER AND CINNAMON, NOBODY PARTICULARLY WANTS TO.

. . . .

MAKE YOUR OWN SPICED FRAGRANCES

. . . .

This is your chance to be a fragrance scientist. Combine spices you find in your kitchen, and see what creates the best smells. (Make sure you have permission. Spices are no longer terribly expensive, but your parents may want to keep some for cooking.)

When you create spice combinations, you can imagine that you are very wealthy and powerful, with magic spices that few other people have ever seen. That's how spices seemed to people hundreds of years ago.

The mysterious and exotic taste of Asian spices disguised ordinary foods. You could almost stand to eat spoiled meat, if spices covered the taste. Even kings and queens sometimes ate meat that would have smelled and tasted very bad—except for the spices.

Northern European farmers of long ago could not grow enough hay and oats to get their livestock through the winter. The farmers were not rich enough to keep their cattle, sheep, and pigs alive over a long, hard winter. So most of the time, they slaughtered their animals in the fall. Then they smoked, dried, or pickled the meat. Pepper and other sorts of spices made the meat taste a little better as the months went on.

Spices were practical for people who didn't have refrigeration. But spices also had mysterious powers. They were flavoring, but they were also perfume, medicine, and cosmetics. Sometimes people used them in religious ceremonies. Nutmeg oil was said to create wonderful dreams. Cloves were an ancient perfume and bath salt. For thousands of years, Chinese people who could afford cloves used them as breath sweetener. (The oil of cloves, eugenol, is still used as an ingredient for mouthwash.) Cloves also soothed minor pains and toothaches.

The most expensive and exotic spice of them all was saffron. Saffron created enticing fragrances in foods. (You may taste it sometime in French or Spanish cooking.) It is still used for perfume and exotic yellow dye.

· · · · · · · · · ·

MAKE YOUR OWN SPICED FRAGRANCES
continued

Here's how to experiment with what combines for the best fragrances. In a bowl, mix just a very small amount at one time. Sniff before you add a spice, and then add no more than $\frac{1}{8}$ to $\frac{1}{4}$ teaspoon (one milliliter) at a time. Try a few of these for fragrance:

Cloves

Nutmeg

Ginger

Dried orange and lemon peel

Cinnamon or a cinnamon stick

A bayleaf

Dried mint leaf

Basil

Dill

Marjoram

Rosemary

Thyme

Rosehips

Lavender

Allspice

Herbal tea leaves

GO ON TO MAKE YOUR FRAGRANCE COMBINATIONS INTO A SWEET-SMELLING GIFT.

· · · · · · · · · · ·
MAKE A SPICED GIFT
· ·

Make your favorite fragrance combination into a gift. Plan ahead two weeks so your gift will be just right.

A potpourri is a jar with a mixture of flower blossoms and spices, made to smell nice. A sachet is a small pillow or square of fabric filled with spices, usually used for keeping clothes smelling fresh.

Here's what you need:

Flower blossoms or clover or juniper berries that you pick yourself

2 pieces of cardboard

2 heavy books

Spice combinations you create yourself

A small jar with a lid or handkerchief or square of cotton fabric with a ribbon

A notecard and pen

Here's what you do:

1. Pick flower blossoms, clover, or juniper berries.

2. Press the flower blossoms or clover between two pieces of cardboard. Then press the cardboard between two heavy books. Keep the flowers pressed for about two weeks. If you're using juniper berries, set them aside to dry.

3. When you decide on a combination of spices and fragrant leaves you like, put a small amount of the mixture into a jar. Or fold a small amount into a handkerchief or small square of cotton.

4. Fill the rest of the jar or fabric square with the pressed flower blossoms, clover, and juniper berries.

5. Put a lid on the jar, or tie the fabric square tightly with a ribbon.

6. Use your pen to write greetings and then note the meaning of the scents inside your gift on a notecard.

Here are the ancient meanings attached to some scents and spices:

• Basil: Money is attracted to you. It comes to you easily.

. . . .

MAKE A SPICED GIFT

continued

- Chamomile (as in tea): You will be free of colds and flu.
- Dill: You cast a spell on people, and they have to love you.
- Lavender: You have good friends, and I am your friend.
- Marjoram: You make people happy, and you make me happy.
- Rosemary: You stay young. People always remember you, and I won't forget you.
- Thyme: You are strong and brave. You keep away sadness.

You may not really believe these meanings, but they make people feel good.

ONCE UPON A TIME, YOU WOULD HAVE HAD TO GO ALL OVER THE EARTH AND TRADE YOUR MOST VALUABLE POSSESSIONS TO GET THESE SPICES. NOW PEOPLE WHO ARE NOT EXTRA WEALTHY CAN HAVE THEM. BUT SHIPS AND AIRPLANES STILL IMPORT THEM FROM THE SAME PLACES IN INDIA, THE MOLUCCAN ISLANDS, AND THE REST OF INDONESIA.

· · · · · · · · · · ·

GROW A PLANT THAT'S BETTER THAN GOLD

· ·

Columbus and the other explorers hoped to find exotic wealth in new lands. They wanted gold and spices. While they were searching for valuables, though, they brought back a few curiosities, souvenirs that didn't seem to have much value.

One of their souvenirs of the New World turned out to be better than all their gold.

That was their sample of sweet potatoes. The sweet potato and, later, the potato became major crops in the Old World. They were new foods that rescued people from starvation.

These basic foods provide good nutrition and lots of vitamins. They grow almost anywhere, even in poor soil or bad weather. They store well to provide food during a long dry season or a long winter.

Potatoes and sweet potatoes are in the same tuber family, vegetables that grow underground on roots. (Don't confuse sweet potatoes with yams. They look somewhat similar, but they're not in the same plant family.)

Usually, sweet potatoes grow best in hot climates. The people of Central America had depended on sweet potatoes for thousands of years, and the Polynesians may have grown sweet potatoes long before the Europeans discovered them. Soon after Columbus brought sweet potatoes to Europe, traders took them to almost all of Europe, Asia, the Philippines, and Africa.

Potatoes, on the other hand, grow best in cold climates. The Incans had grown potatoes in the mountains of South America for thousands of years. Soon after Spanish traders brought them to Europe, potatoes

became a major food in northern climates such as Britain and Ireland. Potatoes came to the United States and Canada not through South America, as you might expect, but from Britain and Ireland.

Now people almost all the world over eat potatoes and sweet potatoes. There are even new potato farms in China, where a few farmers hope to convince the Chinese people that potatoes are as good to eat as rice or sweet potatoes.

GROW A PLANT THAT'S BETTER THAN GOLD
continued

Here's how to grow your own sweet potatoes, better than gold. Although sweet potatoes were once tropical and subtropical plants, new varieties grow well in temperate and northern climates. You can grow a sweet potato plant in almost any sunny garden space.

Here's what you need:

Sweet potato seedlings or small plants, available at a garden center

A hoe

Gardening gloves

Organic material such as peat moss or compost from a garden

A watering can or hose

A fertilizer, the low-nitrogen type recommended for vegetables, available at a garden center

Dry grass clippings from mowing a lawn, hay, or mulch in bags available at a garden center

A trowel or small spade

Here's how to plant your sweet potatoes:

1. As soon as the ground is warm in spring or summer, prepare the soil. Your sweet potato plant will grow in almost any kind of soil, but it does best in somewhat sandy soil. When you're ready to plant, get out a hoe and put on your gardening gloves. Get a bag of organic material and hoe it into the soil until you have about one-third organic material and two-thirds soil. Pile up the mixture to make a hill that is about 2 feet (about 60 centimeters) at the bottom and 1 foot (about 30 centimeters) at the top. If you're planting several sweet potato plants, make a long mound instead.

2. Make holes for the plants along the top of the hill or mound. The plants need to be 15–18 inches (40–45 centimeters) apart. Fill the holes with water from your watering can or hose. Let the water drain.

3. Then set in the seedling plants. Use your hoe to firm the soil so each plant is held securely. Water once again.

4. Around each plant, spread on a mulch, such as dry grass clippings from mowing a lawn, hay, or mulch from a bag. The mulch helps to keep in moisture and prevent weeds.

5. Water every few days, especially during hot weather.

. . . .

GROW A PLANT THAT'S BETTER THAN GOLD
continued

Here's how to harvest your sweet potatoes:

1. Let the plants grow as long as possible into the fall. In late fall before the weather turns cold, use a trowel or a small shovel to dig out your sweet potatoes. Be careful not to damage them as you dig. (If you wish, you can dig out a sample in early fall, just to see how they're doing.)

2. Keep them in a box in a warm place for about 2 weeks.

3. Now you can eat your sweet potatoes or store in a cool place to use later in the fall or winter.

Here's how to bake or boil your sweet potatoes:

1. To bake: Scrub the potatoes and cut off any damaged or woody parts. Poke a few holes with a fork or knife. In a microwave oven, bake at full power for 15 minutes. Or bake in an oven at 350°F (175°C) for 1 hour. Your sweet potato is done when you can squeeze it and it feels soft. Serve with butter.

2. To boil: Peel your sweet potatoes and boil them until they are soft enough to eat.

> ***Caution: You need adult help with boiling water.***
>
> **YOU CAN ALSO MAKE YOUR SWEET POTATOES INTO A CANDIED CASSEROLE, A SWEET POTATO PIE, OR FRITTERS. THEY'RE GOOD IN LOTS OF RECIPES ALL AROUND THE WORLD.**

· · · · · · · · · · ·
DRINK NEW WORLD COCOA
· ·

In 1502, Christopher Columbus returned from his fourth voyage with a new curiosity, the cocoa bean. The native Americans prized cocoa beans so highly that they used them as a form of money. Columbus and his crew, however, disliked the bitter taste. Try a taste of unsweetened cocoa or baking chocolate some time, and you'll agree. The Aztec word for cocoa was *xocolatl*. (Do you see our word *chocolate* in that?) The word meant bitter water.

The Aztecs liked the bitter water, though, and they had been drinking it for thousands of years before the rest of the world found out about it. Cocoa became the favorite drink for the rest of the world—but usually with some sweetener.

The next time you make a cup of hot cocoa, make it the Aztec way, with real Aztec spices (but without the bitter taste). As you fix your cup of hot cocoa, just add a dash of allspice and ¼ teaspoon (1 milliliter) of vanilla extract.

SOON AFTER COLUMBUS' VOYAGES, COCOA BEANS, VANILLA BEANS, AND ALLSPICE—AND OTHER NEW WORLD FOODS—WERE TRADED AROUND THE WORLD.

GROW A HELPFUL PLANT

Usually, when you think of trading and bargaining around the world, you think of big ships and trucks full of major cargo like oil or wheat. But traders also bargain to sell whatever is unique for their part of the world. For example, the rain forests of Central America, South America, and other places grow unique plants. These plants are often valuable because they provide ingredients for medicine. A liquid inside the stem of a rain forest plant treats eye disease. Another plant seems to hold the key to a new kind of antibiotic to cure infections.

These are wonderful plants, and the world needs to know more about them.

Even if you don't live in a rain forest full of miracle plants, you can grow a helpful plant of your own. This is an aloe. Every home ought to have one. Break open a leaf from this plant, and you find a sort of lotion inside it. You can soothe a small burn, rash, or rough spot on your skin. In a store, you'll see commercial lotions that advertise aloe as an ingredient. Drug companies use aloe for other kinds of medicine, too.

You can buy an aloe from a garden center that sells house plants. (Ask for a small variety, since some types eventually grow as tall as small trees.) Or you can grow your own from another aloe plant. For all the good they do, these plants are easy to grow.

You'll need a sunny window for your aloe. Or you can grow it in indirect sunlight, such as it would get through a curtain or window blind.

. . . .

GROW A HELPFUL PLANT

continued

Here's what you need:

An offshoot from the base of an aloe plant

A small knife to cut the offshoot

A 4- to 6-inch (10–15 centimeters) plant pot with an underdish

Pebbles

Potting soil

Peat moss

Perlite or sand

Standard liquid house plant fertilizer

Water

Here's what you do to get your aloe started:

1. Choose an offshoot from the base of another aloe plant. Look for an offshoot right at the bottom or low on the stem. If you can, find one large enough to have its leaves already forming into a rosette shape. (That's a circular cluster of leaves radiating from the center so that they look somewhat like a rose). If you're really lucky, you may find an offshoot that already has little roots growing. Cut the offshoot along with the solon or stem that attaches it to the big plant.

   : *Caution: You need adult help*
   : *with using a knife.*

2. Cover the bottom of the pot with the pebbles.

3. Mix together a potting mixture: about one-third potting soil, one-third peat moss, and one-third perlite or sand. (Perlite is a kind of glassy gravel that began inside a volcano.)

4. Fill the pot about halfway with the potting mixture. Plant the offshoot. Then cover with more potting mixture. Gently pack down the mixture so the plant is firm. Sprinkle a little perlite or sand on top.

5. Mix standard liquid house plant fertilizer with water, according to the directions. Water the plant lightly, and set in a window.

6. Water about twice a week. Keep the soil slightly moist, but don't let water collect on it. You don't want your aloe to rot.

7. Add the fertilizer every two weeks, except during the winter.

8. Let the plant rest without fertilizer, and water it only once a week during the three winter months. After the winter, you may find blooms most of the rest of the year.

   : YOU CAN GIVE AN ALOE AS A
   : USEFUL GIFT. IT'S LIKE HAVING
   : YOUR OWN SOOTHING LOTION
   : ON HAND ALL THE TIME. AN
   : ALOE IS HELPFUL, BUT BE
   : CAREFUL WHEN YOU TOUCH IT.
   : SOME TYPES HAVE SPINES AND
   : EVEN HOOKED TEETH. THAT'S
   : ONE WAY THE PLANTS PROTECT
   : THEMSELVES AGAINST ANIMALS
   : THAT MIGHT WANT TO EAT
   : THEM.

. . . .

MAKE A PIRATE'S MAP

. . . .

Pirates once roamed the Earth, conducting their own sorts of trade, bargaining, and rough negotiating. Each of the infamous pirate captains had a special method of trade.

A few well-known pirates really did have wooden legs, fearsome eye patches—and maybe parrots on their shoulders. But you can't always imagine them that way. Two vicious pirate captains who have come down in history supposedly began life as well-behaved women. Other pirates were famous for their politeness in trading and bargaining—although the politeness could have a nasty edge to it, when you realized your life was at stake.

Each pirate had a land base, often in the Caribbean or on the island of Madagascar off the east coast of Africa. So many of the old-time Spanish pirates lived in the islands of the Caribbean that the Caribbean Sea itself came to be called the Spanish main. Some pirate captains owned their own islands. They had fortresses and cities at their command. They were the bosses everywhere they went. (There are still pirates around the world, and they are still well organized and very dangerous. But they don't have quite the same traditions and methods as the old-time pirates.)

Like every other sailor, the pirates needed maps. They had maps of hidden treasure, maps of hideaways, and maps with the latest information on the movements of trading ships across the seas.

You can make a pirate map of your own. This is a fun map to make, because you can let your imagination run wild.

· · · · · · · · · · ·

MAKE A PIRATE'S MAP

continued

Here's what you need:

Pencil and paper
Markers or pens, in colors you choose
A ruler

Here's what you do:

1. Make up a name for your pirate. The pirates went by names like Blackbeard or Devil Jack. They didn't want too many people to know their real identities. Then make up an island to call your own. Your island will need an interesting shape and contours, with plenty of good hiding places.

2. Use a pencil at first to draw your island on paper. Then plan to fill it in with colored markers or pens.

3. Choose a scale. Perhaps on your map, 3 inches (about 8 centimeters) represent 1 mile (or 1 kilometer).

4. Choose directions. In one corner, draw a compass rose showing north, east, south, and west. Then decide heights, the hills, mountains, and slopes of the island.

5. Choose symbols and colors for your map. You'll want to use symbols for the pirate's special hiding places, with weapons, treasure, and secret food supplies. Perhaps you'll have lookouts along the shore to keep a watch on the pirate's enemies. Or perhaps you'll have a seclud-

· · · · · · · · · · ·

MAKE A PIRATE'S MAP

continued

ed place for a campfire hidden from the sea. Choose colors to tell a story. Perhaps you'll use green for forest hideaways, light yellow for the flat land, and a range from light brown to dark brown as the hills and mountains rise from the sea. You may want a range of light blue to dark blue colors to show depths in the ocean and island ponds.

6. In the corner of the map, put a key to show scale and the meanings of your symbols and colors.

7. With light pencil, draw a grid across your map. Use your ruler to make the lines exactly the same distance apart. Across the top of the map, label the vertical (up and down) lines as A, B, C, and so on. Down the side of the map, label the horizontal lines (across) as 1, 2, 3, and so on. Then when you want to state one of your map locations, you can write something like C2. Map readers will know where to look.

8. Decorate your map with coloring markers and pens. The pirates were colorful characters, and they liked creative sorts of maps.

> A PIRATE'S MAP WAS EXTREMELY VALUABLE. THE PIRATES SOMETIMES WEIGHTED THE EDGES OF THEIR MAPS WITH LEAD. THEN IN CASE OF ATTACK, THEY COULD THROW THE MAPS OVERBOARD AND BE SURE THEY WOULD SINK. THE PIRATES DIDN'T WANT ENEMIES TO GET THEIR HANDS ON ONE OF THESE SECRET MAPS. TODAY IF YOU WANT TO KNOW ABOUT THE LOCATION OF hidden TREASURE, BUY A MAP. THERE ARE MAPS THAT SHOW MORE THAN 3,000 LOCATIONS OF SUNKEN SHIPS, MANY OF THEM IN THE CARIBBEAN AND SOME OF THEM LONG-AGO VICTIMS OF PIRATE ATTACK.

. . . .

DESIGN YOUR OWN JOLLY ROGER

. . . .

A Jolly Roger is a pirate's flag, the sort with skull and crossbones or some other fearsome symbol. (If you have a pirate's sense of humor, you can see that the skull looks rather jolly with its grinning jaws, and for some reason the skulls on pirate flags came to be named Roger.) Each of the pirate captains had his or her own specially designed flag.

The Jolly Roger was not the only flag pirates used. Often, pirates carried a supply of flags from many countries. If they saw a Spanish ship in the distance, for example, they hoisted their Spanish flag. Then some of the pirates disguised themselves as Spanish women. They'd lean over the side of the ship and call out in Spanish. The Spanish sailors probably yearned for mail and news of home. They might fall for the trick and turn their ship around—and sail right toward their doom.

Suddenly, they'd see a new flag on the mast, the dreaded pirate flag. The Jolly Roger was supposed to frighten the sailors, but it was also an invitation. Join us, it said. Come over to our side as pirates, and we will spare your life. Some sailors fought bravely, but others accepted the invitation. For them, it could mean a transformation from a life of poverty and misery to a life of freedom and perhaps even wealth.

The flag to be feared was plain red. It meant that the pirates would show no mercy. They intended to kill everybody.

Here's how to design a paper Jolly Roger of your own. The pirates preferred simple, dramatic flags in black and white.

. . . .

DESIGN YOUR OWN JOLLY ROGER
continued

Here's what you need:

Scrap paper and a pencil with an eraser
White construction paper
Scissors
Black construction paper
Household glue or paste

Here's what you do:

1. Use scrap paper and a pencil to design your flag. Make a scary symbol such as a skeleton, swords, or the figure of a pirate (maybe even a skeleton pirate). Make the outlines bold and dramatic.

2. When you are happy with your design, sketch it onto the white construction paper. Use scissors to cut out the design.

3. Arrange the white design on the long side of the black construction paper. Use household glue or school paste to attach the white design onto the black paper.

4. Display your flag on a bulletin board. If you'd like to make your flag in felt, look on page 20.

SOME PIRATES BEGAN AS TRADERS AND SEA CAPTAINS WORKING WITHIN THE LAW— OR AT LEAST WITH THE KNOWLEDGE OF A LEGAL GOVERNMENT. SIR FRANCIS DRAKE OF SIXTEENTH-CENTURY ENGLAND PROUDLY FLEW THE BRITISH UNION JACK. HE WASN'T STRICTLY A PIRATE, BECAUSE THE QUEEN (SOMETIMES SECRETLY) APPROVED HIS ATTACKS ON THE SPANISH SHIPS. QUEEN ELIZABETH I IS SAID TO HAVE INVESTED HEAVILY IN HIS RAIDS ON THE SPANISH. SUPPOSEDLY, DRAKE BROUGHT HER BACK A 1,400% PROFIT. (COMPARE THAT TO YOUR SAVINGS ACCOUNT AT A BANK WHERE YOU MIGHT MAKE 3% INTEREST.) NO WONDER SHE GAVE DRAKE A KNIGHTHOOD SO HE COULD BE CALLED SIR WHEREVER HE WENT! DRAKE'S ODD METHOD WAS HIS UNFAILING COURTESY. HE TOOK HIS VICTIMS CAPTIVE, GAVE THEM DINNER, AND PRESENTED THEM WITH GIFTS—AS HIS HELPERS TOWED AWAY THEIR SHIPS AND TOOK EVERYTHING OF VALUE.

MAKE A PIRATE'S BEST-SELLING BARBECUE

Some of the pirates of the Caribbean began as good businesspeople. They had a highly desirable product for sale, and they traded it for what they needed, either in money or goods.

Here's how it happened. In the seventeenth century, the Spanish settlers moved away from Haiti. (Look for Haiti at 19°N, 72°E.) They left behind their cattle, oxen, and pigs, who ran wild across the island. Meanwhile, trading ships from France, England, and Holland often stopped in Haiti for supplies before they entered the open ocean on their way back home.

Sailors of the time had a hard life. They made very little money, and they were often cruelly treated. They were certainly not used to good food. Some of them saw the beautiful island, with all its cattle and pigs. They deserted their ships. Deserting the ship was a crime punishable by death, so the minute they deserted, they were outlaws.

These former sailors became hunters. The native people of Haiti taught them how to prepare the meat they hunted, making a form of corned beef and then grilling the meat so that it was wonderfully delicious.

Soon the former sailors were in business. When the European ships came to Haiti, the former sailors sold them the delicious corned beef. It could keep for weeks on ship, and everyone liked the taste. In return, they received money, clothing, gunpowder, and bullets.

· · · · · · · · · · ·

MAKE A PIRATE'S BEST-SELLING BARBECUE

continued

And they received a new name. The French name for that sort of corned beef was "bukan." The former sailors were *boucaniers* or meat-curers. In English, the word became *buccaneers*. The buccaneers went on to new adventures. Remember that they were already outlaws. So to this day, pirates are often called buccaneers.

Here's how to make your own delicious corned beef, the pirate's favorite best-selling food. You can buy corned beef, or you can make your own. If you decide to make your own, plan ahead at least 2 days. (Corned beef has nothing to do with corn. The word refers to the whole grains of salt, "corns," that people used to preserve meat.)

This recipe gives the distinctive corned beef flavor, but it can't preserve the meat for weeks. The buccaneers preserved meat with lots more salt than people use now—and the result was extra dry and hard beef, probably more tasty to them than it would be for us.

Here's what you need:

1½ lbs. (70 kilograms) boneless
  beef sirloin, brisket, round, or chuck

To corn the beef:

4 cups (1 liter) water
½ cup (125 milliliters) salt
1 bayleaf
6 peppercorns

To prepare the beef for grilling:

⅔ cup (170 milliliters) water
⅓ cup (80 milliliters) brown sugar
1 tablespoon (15 milliliters) salad or
  cooking oil
1 teaspoon (4 milliliters) ground ginger
¼ teaspoon (1 milliliter) minced garlic

To serve the beef:

Your favorite barbecue sauce

Here's how to make the beef into corned beef:

1. Slice the beef into strips. Each strip should be about 2 by 6 inches and about ⅛ inch thick (about 5 by 15 centimeters, and about 3 millimeters thick).

   Caution: You need adult help with cutting the strips.

2. Arrange the beef strips in a shallow glass pan.

3. Pour the water into a medium bowl. Stir in salt until it dissolves and pour over the beef strips. Add bayleaf and peppercorns.

4. Cover the pan lightly with plastic or foil. Refrigerate for 36 to 48 hours.

· · · · · · · · · · ·

MAKE A PIRATE'S BEST-SELLING BARBECUE

continued

Here's how to grill the corned beef strips:

5. About a ½ hour before you want to grill the strips, marinate (or soak) them. In a large bowl, mix together soy sauce, brown sugar, salad or cooking oil, ground ginger, and minced garlic. Put the beef strips into the mixture for 20 to 30 minutes.

6. Thread the beef strips onto barbecue skewers. Grill the strips on a hibachi or a charcoal grill over low-burning charcoal. Turn often, and grill until the beef strips are well done, without too much pink in the middle.

Caution: You absolutely must let an adult do the grilling.

7. Serve with your favorite barbecue sauce. Makes about four servings.

WHAT'S THE DIFFERENCE BETWEEN PIRATES AND BUCCANEERS? USUALLY, THE BUCCANEERS ATTACKED ONLY SPANISH SHIPS. THE PIRATES ATTACKED SHIPS FROM SPAIN AND ANY OTHER COUNTRY— AND EVEN SOMETIMES OTHER PIRATE SHIPS.

CONQUER THE WORLD

*P*erhaps you don't want just to read about the conquerors and soldiers who once ruled large parts of the world. You may want to find out what happened to them and the people they conquered.

You can play a game from the great empire of the ancient Mayans, a game that was the ancestor of our own team sports. You can make a necklace that Attila the Hun would have killed for. You can build a Roman villa, suitable for a Roman army officer, with family and slaves.

You can find out the secret plan of a Viking chief sailing through the North Atlantic. You can sail your own message out into the world.

CHOOSE YOUR FAVORITE
(OR LEAST FAVORITE) CONQUEROR

If you like to send chills up your spine, read about people who tried to conquer the world.

You can hear about terrible people like Attila the Hun, Ghengis Khan, or Tamerlane—and the bloody sweeps of their armies through Asia and parts of Europe. You can picture the murders and tortures. In Persia, Tamerlane cut off the heads of thousands of people and then piled the heads into giant towers. He wanted to spread fear and terror across the other lands he intended to conquer.

In the Americas, the Spanish *conquistadores* behaved as brutally, murdering thousands of the native people as they pushed through deserts and jungles to find El Dorado—an imaginary land, supposedly covered with gold.

But no matter how much land they seized and how much suffering they caused, none of the conquerors really even began to take over the entire world. Sometimes the invaded people fought back—and fought fiercely and beat them. Sometimes they accepted the conquerors, gave them some of what they wanted, made what peace they could, learned from them—and then went on with their lives.

CHOOSE YOUR FAVORITE
(OR LEAST FAVORITE) CONQUEROR
continued

Even the Spanish conquerors of the Americas settled down finally. They married native Americans and blended the two races and cultures into a new race and culture. Now, on Columbus Day on October 12, Latin American countries celebrate the Day of the Race.

The simple size of the world often defeats conquerors. In 325 B.C., Alexander the Great claimed power over the entire known world. The story is that he wept because there were no worlds left to conquer. He did have the power he claimed—but only in the small part of this one world he could reach after 11 years of marching his armies overland from Greece toward India. The faraway Chinese, Incans, and all the rest of the people in the world had never even heard of him.

The Greeks of Alexander's time had a very general idea of about a quarter of the Earth's land mass. But all they knew in detail were the lands that Alexander and his father Philip of Macedon had invaded, mostly on foot. Their lands extended from Greece as far as Egypt in the south and ancient Persia in the east. After his 11 years of conquering, Alexander turned back at the mountains of the Hindu Kush in Persia, now the border between Afghanistan and Pakistan. (Look for the Hindu Kush at 35°N, 69°E.)

Alexander had built his empire—and spread Greek culture—far and wide to Asia Minor, North Africa, Egypt, and Rome. He died the conqueror of world as he knew it. He was still a young man when he died at age 33. Life was short in those days. Soldiers suffered one wound after another, and deadly illnesses could strike at any moment.

Look at a map, this time at Eastern Europe and Russia, about 1,150 miles (1,850 kilometers) north of Greece. That's where another emperor, Napoleon Bonaparte of France, tried to expand his control more than 2,000 years later. He had decided to march east from France, deep into Russia.

Napoleon had accurate maps, thousands of cannons pulled by horses and oxen, and an army of 600,000 as he began to push east in June of 1812. He defeated the Russians in the "one good battle" he wanted at Borodino and marched ahead steadily. He reached Moscow by mid September. (Look for Borodino at 53°N, 35°E, and for Moscow at 56°N, 36°E.)

But look at the immense land still ahead of him—and partly behind. Was he taking it over, or was it slowly surrounding him as the months of fighting wore on?

. . . .

CHOOSE YOUR FAVORITE
(OR LEAST FAVORITE) CONQUEROR
continued

The Russians kept retreating in front of him, but they were also burning their grain fields and moving livestock away, to make food the biggest problem they could for the invaders. Then winter came on. Slowly Napoleon's army turned from an irresistible force into a shrinking column of hungry men and animals, struggling through the snows. Finally, in December of 1812, Napoleon had to give up and retreat back toward western Europe.

Napoleon had been conquered himself—by the fierce resistance of the Russians, and by the size and climate of the geography he'd invaded.

YOU MAY WANT TO READ ABOUT YOUR FAVORITE CONQUEROR. OR PERHAPS YOU WANT TO CHOOSE YOUR LEAST FAVORITE CONQUEROR, SINCE THEY WERE OFTEN CRUEL AND EVIL. YOU'LL SEE WHAT THEY THOUGHT THE "WHOLE WORLD" WAS. YOU'LL SEE THAT THEY FACED VERY BIG OBSTACLES—TIME, DISTANCES, CLIMATES, SEASONS, OCEANS, MOUNTAIN RANGES, AND TOUGH DEFENDERS—AND ALSO SEE WHY WE DON'T ALL LIVE TODAY IN ONE GIANT EMPIRE.

DESIGN THE KNOWN WORLD

When we say the known world, we may mean a very small place. The ancient conquerors may have thought they conquered all there was, but that was only within their own ideas of the world. Often, the Europeans showed the world as a T shape inside a circle. The T divided Asia, Europe, and Africa, the only three continents that Europeans knew. The circle was the ocean surrounding all.

Here's how to create a plate of the world as an early European artist saw it. The artist, like others of the time, showed the world as small and ringed with dangers. Soldiers or bandits from a foreign land could arrive at any time and take over, and where could the people flee? Most people lived surrounded by wilderness, with thick, dangerous forests on all sides. Or else they lived bounded in by a sea or lake. Most people did not travel much, and when they did the travel was so slow and dangerous that they might not want to go again.

This is a design of the world that you might see in a museum. The picture of the world is a fine painted plate that shows the known world of that time and place, about 1,000 years ago.

· · · · · · · · · · ·

DESIGN THE KNOWN WORLD
continued

Here's what you need:
A large paper or plastic plate, with a smooth border

A pencil

A ruler or straightedge

Coloring markers, pens, or poster paints, in colors you choose

Here's what you do:

1. Use a pencil and a ruler or straightedge to draw a line down the center of the plate.

2. Draw a line around the border of the plate.

3. On one half of the inner circle of the plate, draw a village crowded with people. Use markers, pens, or poster paints to color the village.

4. On the other half of the inner circle of the plate, draw and color a wilderness full of trees, with monster animals peering out.

5. On the top half of the border, draw and color a night sky with large stars.

6. On the bottom half of the border, draw and color an ocean with monster fish in it.

> YOUR DESIGN SHOWS A WORLD THAT MAY BE BEAUTIFUL BUT ALSO FRIGHTENING. PERHAPS THE WORLD IS NOT SO DIFFERENT TODAY.

SAIL WITH A VIKING CHIEF

Imagine that the year is 880, and you are Floki Vilggerdarson, a daring Norse chief in the Faeroe Islands. Your longboat raids on Ireland and central Britain have made you rich. Now you want to sail to Iceland. (Look for the Faeroe Islands at 62°N, 7°W. Look for Iceland at 64°N, 22°W.)

Floki planned to sail about 400 miles (640 kilometers) in the cold and stormy weather of the North Atlantic. He had no map. He knew other Norsemen had reached Iceland, and he had a general idea of the direction. That knowledge, however vague, gave him an advantage over some navigators.

His Viking ship was long and fearsome, with a huge curved dragon head and a dragon tail. Floki, like the other Vikings, intended to frighten the people he met.

Plus Floki had a secret plan. His 30 crewmen must have wondered what was happening when Floki brought cages of ravens on board ship.

Here's how to make a model of one longboat for 30 Viking warriors. You can use a walnut shell. Your walnut boat may not be as fearsome as the dragon boats of the Vikings, but you can use it to see the problems of a Viking voyage to Iceland—and how Floki solved those problems.

Here's what you need:
Walnuts

A knife suitable for splitting a walnut

Scissors

Paper

A pencil or marker

Toothpicks

Regular household glue, paste, or modeling clay

A map that shows the North Atlantic and Iceland

Paper, pencil, and a calculator, if you wish

· · · · · · · · · ·

SAIL WITH A VIKING CHIEF

continued

Here's what you do:

1. For each longboat you want to make, split a walnut along the seam at the middle.

   : *Caution: You may need adult*
   : *help to split the walnut.*

   Hollow out each half, and eat the nut inside. It'll give you strength.

2. Make a sail for each walnut boat. Use scissors to cut out a ¾ inch (about 2 centimeters) paper square. If you wish, use a pencil or marker to draw a war design on it.

3. Make a mast for your sail. Stick a toothpick through the sail at two points in the middle.

4. Use glue or school paste to attach the sail to the center of the shell. Now you have a scale model of a Viking longboat.

5. Try sailing a walnut boat in a bathtub or large pan of water, to get an idea of Floki's problems.

Remember that Floki had no maps, and no real instruments; he could not turn back. How would he even know where he was?

That's when Floki unleashed his secret weapon—the ravens. In the first part of his journey, Floki released a raven. The raven flew east toward the Faeroes and did not return. Floki knew he wasn't yet far into the voyage. The second raven flew off and then returned to the ship. Floki knew he was not near land at all, either the Faeroes or Iceland. The third raven flew west toward Iceland and didn't return. Floki knew he was getting close, and he knew he could follow the raven's direction to land.

: **FLOKI LIKED ICELAND WHEN HE**
: **GOT THERE. THE AMAZING**
: **PART IS THAT HE DIDN'T MAKE**
: **WAR. HE STAYED IN ICELAND**
: **AND SETTLED DOWN FOR 2**
: **YEARS. HE WAS NOT KNOWN**
: **AS FLOKI THE BLOODY OR**
: **MIGHTY FLOKI BUT RATHER**
: **RAVEN FLOKI.**

· · · · · · · · · · ·
BUILD ROME IN A DAY

· ·

The saying is that you can't build Rome in a day. You can't do a difficult job too quickly. But here is an elegant Roman house that won't take you too long to build.

The actual Roman Empire of the Caesars took 800 years to build. Sixty million people lived in it, in a huge rectangle with Britain, Morocco, Israel, and Georgia as the corners. (On a map, look for Britain at 54°N, 0°, the Prime Meridian. Look for Morocco at 30°N, 10°W. Look for Israel at 32°N, 35°E. Look for Georgia in Russia at 42°N, 42°E.)

The center of the Empire was Rome, filled with the temples, monuments, stadiums, and theaters, some of which still stand today. It was the richest city ever seen in the ancient European world, with many of its people living in large, cleverly designed houses and apartment blocks. (Look for Rome at 42°N, 12°E.)

Here is how the Roman architects and builders laid out a house. If you give it a try yourself, you'll wind up with a model of a real Roman house. This is the sort of house that one of Caesar's best generals might have built for family and slaves.

You can find some of the materials for your model outside.

· · · · · · · · · · ·
BUILD ROME IN A DAY
continued

Here's what you need:

Heavy cardboard to use as a base, 12 × 24 inches (30 × 60 centimeters)

A set of small wooden or plastic building blocks

A piece of aluminum foil, 2 × 7 inches (5 × 17 centimeters)

2 handfuls of the smallest pebbles you can find

A small bucket of sand

A dozen of the smallest green leaves you can find

A dozen small twigs

A directional compass

Here's what you do:

1. Set up a cardboard base for your house. Make marks on the base for north, east, south, west. The Romans wanted each part of their houses to face particular directions. (When you are finished, you can turn the base toward the right direction.)

2. Use small wooden or plastic building blocks to build the outside walls of the house, three layers high. Build the house in a rectangle 12 × 24 inches (30 × 60 centimeters). Leave openings for doorways at the northwest and southeast corners of the outside walls. (Each opening should be ¾ inch or 2 centimeters.) Also leave a gap in the south wall for your solarium or sunroom. (That opening should be 7 inches or 17 centimeters.) The solarium faces south to take in as much daylight as possible at Rome's latitude. Use your foil to show where the solarium is. Lay it down flat inside the wall.

3. Use your blocks to show where the interior walls and doorways would be for the kitchen, living rooms, bedrooms, and dining room. (You may need to put some of the blocks in sideways or on end.) The very small bedrooms are for the slaves. The dining room is open, to face the solarium and the inside garden during meals.

4. Reserve the central area (about 9 ×14 inches or 23 × 36 centimeters) for the major feature of the house, the garden. Use your smallest pebbles to mark off a border. Then carefully pour in a layer of sand as a bottom for the garden. Arrange small leaves and twig pieces in the sand to decorate the garden.

5. A raised portico or porch usually ran along one side of the garden as a place to sit and relax. Build it with one extra row of blocks inside the house.

6. When you display your Roman house, don't forget to turn it in the right direction, so that the solarium faces south and the doorways face northwest and southeast.

BUILD ROME IN A DAY

continued

ROMAN DESIGN WAS BOTH ELEGANT AND PRACTICAL, WITH THE SOLARIUM FOR DAYLIGHT, THICK WALLS TO KEEP THE HOUSE COOL, AND THE INSIDE GARDEN FOR DECORATION. OUTSIDE WERE THE PAVED STREETS, BRIDGES, PLAZAS—AND CROWDS—OF AN IMPERIAL CITY AT THE HEIGHT OF ITS POWER. BY THE YEAR 50, WHEN ROME CONTROLLED ALL OF THE KNOWN WORLD BETWEEN BRITAIN AND THE MIDDLE EAST, ALMOST 6 MILLION PEOPLE LIVED IN THE CITY— AND THAT WAS JUST 10% OF THE POPULATION OF THE TOTAL EMPIRE.

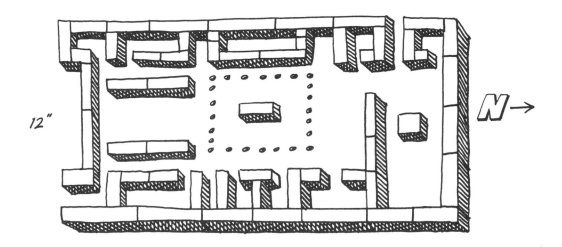

12"

N →

. . . .

MAKE A DARK AGES MIRROR
WITH ATTILA THE HUN

. . . .

Powerful as it was, the Roman Empire came under constant attack during the years 100 to 500. Raiders called the Vandals and Visigoths swarmed in from northern Europe.

The Huns attacked from east and north of the Black Sea, and they won so many battles by the year 460 that their cruel chief—Attila the Hun—could demand and get 2,000 pounds (about 907 kilograms) of gold from the Romans as yearly tribute. (Look for the Black Sea at 46°N, 39°E.)

But today, we know very little about the Huns as people. They left behind no buildings or written history, just gravesites and armor fragments—and thousands of mirrors. Each mirror found has been a small, highly polished, strangely marked disc, made to be worn around the neck as either insignia or jewelry.

Perhaps you would like to wear a design that is 1,500 to 2,000 years old. Here's how to make one for yourself.

Here's what you need:

A piece of locker mirror, 6 inches (or about 15 centimeters) square. (Locker mirror is a soft, cuttable material that's shiny on one side. You can get it at a craft store or at the store where you buy school supplies.)

A drawing compass

A pencil

Scissors

A paper punch

Coloring markers or pens, in colors you choose

A 20-inch (50-centimeter) length of string or cord

Here's what you do:

1. On the back of your locker mirror, pick out a point in the middle. Then use the drawing compass to construct a circle 3 inches (or 8 centimeters) in diameter.

2. At the top of the circle, draw a ⅝-inch (2-centimeter) square box. Then use the scissors to cut out the combined circle and square as one piece.

3. Use the paper punch to make a hole in the center of the box.

4. Now you're ready to design the shiny side with markers or

. . . .

MAKE A DARK AGES MIRROR
WITH ATTILA THE HUN

continued

poster paint. You can copy the Hun designs, change them, or combine them in any color.

5. When the art is done, thread your string or cord through the hole so you can wear the mirror around your neck.

THE HUNS USED HAMMERED BRASS AND TIN INSTEAD OF GLASS TO GET A SHINY SURFACE. EXPERTS ON ANCIENT ART ALSO THINK THAT THE HUNS PROBABLY COPIED THEIR

MIRROR DESIGNS FROM CHINESE ORIGINALS. THAT'S ONE REASON WE THINK NOW THAT THESE MYSTERIOUS RAIDERS MAY HAVE RIDDEN INTO EUROPE FROM VERY FAR AWAY. THEY LIKELY CAME FROM THE AREA AROUND TODAY'S BORDER BETWEEN KAZAKHSTAN AND MONGOLIA, ABOUT 3,000 MILES (4,800 KILOMETERS) FROM EASTERN EUROPE. (LOOK FOR MONGOLIA AT ABOUT 49°N, 105°E.)

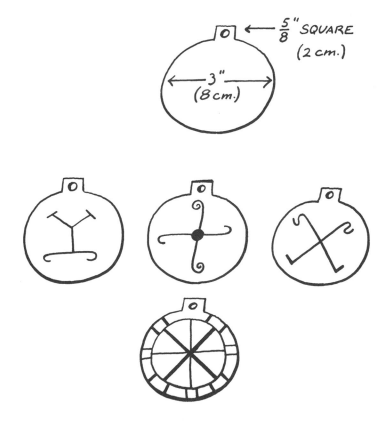

PLAY POK-TA-POK WITH THE ANCIENT MAYANS

T hough history books tell us about the rise and fall of empires, it's also true that empires do live on. Their languages, religions, science, and art can remain important for centuries, long after the old rulers are gone.

Sometimes even sports survive—like pok-ta-pok, a ball game that the Mayans first played 1,500 years ago. The Mayans lived on the Yucatan Peninsula in Mexico, and played the game on huge stone plazas near their temples. (Look for the Yucatan Peninsula at 21°N, 87°W.)

Give pok-ta-pok a try. It's one of the ancestors of modern sports like soccer, volleyball, lacrosse, hockey, and basketball. You'll need two teams of five or six players each, plus a scorekeeper.

Here's what you need:

A beachball, volleyball, or soccer ball
2 cardboard boxes or milk crates
Paper and pencil to keep score

Here's how to play:

1. In a yard or park, lay the boxes or crates down as goals about 50 yards (46 meters) apart. That's about half the length of a football field. You can pace off the distance or measure it. The distance does not have to be exact.

The open sides of the boxes should face toward each other, like hockey or soccer goals. Assign one goal to each team.

2. The basic rule is that the ball can't touch the ground.

3. In the middle of the field, one team starts with the ball, going toward the goal by passing or kicking it in the air to one another. The other team tries to intercept the ball and head toward their goal.

. . . .

PLAY POK-TA-POK WITH THE ANCIENT MAYANS
continued

4. The team with the ball gets one point for each time they make four passes. Shout "1, 2, 3, 4" as your team makes each successful pass.

5. The only time the ball can hit the ground is when there's a shot at the goal. If one team lets the ball hit the ground, then that team must turn the ball over to the other team.

6. Getting the ball into the goal wins the game. Scoring a goal is difficult, so just one goal wins the game. If nobody can score a goal, the higher point total from passing wins.

WHEN THE MAYANS PLAYED POK-TA-POK, SCORING A GOAL COULD BE DRAMATIC. THE PLAYER WHO DID IT GOT THE RIGHT TO TAKE ALL THE JEWELRY FROM THE SPECTATORS—IF HE COULD CATCH THEM.

TAKE OVER THE WORLD IN YOUR OWN GOOD WAY

The early European explorers had the strange practice of claiming a land as the property of their own king or queen—but without telling the people who already lived there.

You can picture Christopher Columbus landing in the New World, kneeling on the beach, lifting his sword, and announcing that all this now belonged to him and to Queen Isabella of Spain. If the people already in the New World had understood, they would have been shocked and horrified. (The New World was not the least bit empty. Possibly 40 million people already lived in the Americas when Columbus first landed in 1492.)

For some would-be conquerors, claiming a land was simple. You could bury a bottle with a note in it, or you could leave a note under a rock. The idea was to tell the other Europeans who might arrive next that your country held the first legal rights.

What were those supposed rights? All too often, those rights were to conquer the land, to take anything of value, and to exploit, kill, and enslave the people.

You can send your own message in a bottle. This time, perhaps, it will be a good message. If you're really lucky, your message will arrive in a wonderful distant part of the world.

Here's what you need:

Clear plastic bottles with screw-on tops,
 such as disposable soft drink or juice
bottles

Dry sand

Marker or pen

Cards

Modeling clay

101
•

. . . .

TAKE OVER THE WORLD IN YOUR OWN GOOD WAY

continued

Here's what you do:

1. Fill each clear plastic bottle about one quarter of the way full with dry sand. The sand will help the bottle float so people can see it. (Try floating the bottle in water, to see if you need to add or subtract some of the sand.)

2. Use a pen or marker to write messages on cards. Be sure to include your name and address.

3. Put the lid on tight. Waterproof your message bottle by molding modeling clay all around the lid.

4. Take the bottle to the ocean or a lake shore and float it away. If you can, release it from a boat, a bridge, or the end of a dock. If you are at an ocean, see if you can arrange to throw the bottle in just as the tide turns after high tide. You want to do everything you can to make sure the bottle floats far away and doesn't just come back to the same beach.

PEOPLE SAY THE CHANCE OF AN ANSWER TO YOUR MESSAGE IS ABOUT ONE IN TEN. SO PERHAPS YOU WANT TO SEND MESSAGES IN AT LEAST TEN BOTTLES.

FIND YOUR WAY AROUND THE WORLD AND DON'T GET LOST

*P*erhaps you would like to find directions with a compass you make yourself. Perhaps you'd like to find directions by the stars.

You can try a north, east, south, west science experiment. You can make your own directions stone, something beautiful for a garden or a playground.

Here's how to find your directions all around the world.

A MAGNETIC STORY

The legend is that the first person who discovered a magnet was a shepherd guarding his sheep. The shepherd was guiding the flock around dangerous rocks. Suddenly his metal crook flew from his hand. A large magnetic rock had pulled it away.

Perhaps the shepherd and his friends discovered that magnetic rocks are fun and make good toys. Perhaps they dreamed of practical ways to use their special rocks.

One specially magnetic rock is a lodestone. A lodestone is a type of iron ore. It pulls metal, and it can make other metal take on magnetic qualities. Since a lodestone can help find directions, the name means "stone that shows the way."

Here's how to prove that a lodestone can help find directions. Tie a bar magnet to a piece of string and let it swing freely. Then check its direction with a compass. One end turns north, and at the same time, the other end turns south.

Before long ancient sailors were taking their lodestones with them wherever they went. We can guess that perhaps those first ancient sailors who knew about lodestones were Chinese. About 2,000 years ago, Chinese writings began  referring to the lodestone as a "south pointer," and by 270 B.C. Chinese sailors were using the first magnetic compasses.

(Of course, a magnetic lodestone points north as well as south. The direction it points just depends on how you look at it.)

You may be surprised to learn that a compass needle does not point exactly toward north. Magnetic forces deep inside the Earth pull a compass needle toward north. That's magnetic north, though, not the exact North Pole. The forces that pull a compass needle can shift from time to time, so magnetic north can be as much as 1,000 miles (1,610 kilometers) from the North Pole.

Don't be concerned. For almost all purposes, an ordinary compass is close enough and will lead you in the right direction.

GO ON TO SEE HOW TO MAKE A COMPASS WORK FOR YOU.

· · · · · · · · · · ·
MAKE A COMPASS WORK FOR YOU
· ·

You can make a compass work to find directions for you. You'll like having a compass in your pocket when you're outdoors, hiking, camping, or traveling.

You can even put your compass in the dog house. (That's a hiker's phrase that has nothing to do with dogs.)

Here's how to use a directional compass:

1. Orient your compass so that the needle points north. You may need to push a button or loosen a screw at the top of the compass so that the needle can float.

2. Hold the compass flat at about waist level. Wait until the needle stops moving.

3. Turn the compass until the magnetic needle points to the north arrow on the compass. (That's putting the dog in the house. The magnetic needle is inside the printed arrow of the compass.) Now your compass needle is oriented toward magnetic north. You can use it to find north, east, south, and west.

4. Try to find other directions, like south southwest (SSW) or north northeast (NNE). Unless you have a fluid compass, you need to orient again each time you want to find a new direction.

IF YOU HAVE A LARGE COMPASS, THE 360° OF A CIRCLE WILL BE PRINTED ALL AROUND IT. IF SO, YOU CAN USE IT TO FIND 360 DIFFERENT DIRECTIONS. GO ON TO FIND HOW TO MAKE YOUR OWN MAGNETIC COMPASS AND A FANCY PAINTED COMPASS AS WELL.

MAKE YOUR OWN COMPASS ROSE

Sometimes you see signs pointing north, east, south, and west. They can even tell you the directions to cities all over the world, all at once.

But are you quite sure about your own directions? Which way does your favorite sunny window face? If you could fly directly like a bird, which way would you head to your friend's house or to school? What direction are you facing right now? You may not be able to tell, especially when you are inside.

You can go outside and find directions by the sun rising in the east and setting in the west. Or you can use a compass for precise directions, and it will work just as well indoors as outdoors.

The early explorers kept a compass rose. This was not a working compass but rather directions painted on wood. After the sailors used instruments to find their direction, they pointed the painted compass rose in the right direction and kept it there until time to consult their instruments again. Even though a compass rose could not tell direction automatically, sailors could use it to read exact degrees of direction.

You can look for a compass rose on both old and new maps.

A compass rose is supposed to be decorated in a creative and artistic way. You can make your own and use it to remind you of directions.

. . . .

MAKE YOUR OWN COMPASS ROSE

continued

Here's what you need:

A drawing compass

A pencil

Construction paper, posterboard, or cardboard, in a color you choose

A protractor

A ruler or straightedge

Coloring markers or pens, in colors you choose

A directional compass

Here's what you do:

1. Use a drawing compass and pencil to draw a large circle on the construction paper, posterboard, or cardboard. Leave some space around the circle.

2. Use a protractor to help you divide the circle into 16 equal segments. Place the protractor so that its exact center is over the center mark of the circle. Starting with 0 at the top, make pencil marks around the outside rim at these degrees: 0, 22.5, 45, 67.5, 90, 112.5, 135, 157.5, 180, 202.5, 225, 247.5, 270, 292.5, 315, 337.5.

3. Use a ruler or straightedge to draw straight lines at each mark through the center and extending beyond the rim of the circle.

4. Outside the circle, mark the segments in order like this: N (for north), NNE, NE, ENE, E (for east), ESE, SE, SSE, S (for south), SSW, SW, WSW, W (for west), WNW, NW, NNW.

5. Use the drawing compass and pencil to make fancy circles and pointers inside the large circle. Your decorations may look just a bit like a rose. On an antique compass rose, you might expect an especially fancy pointer for north.

6. Use the markers or pens to decorate the circle, pointers, lines, and directions. Cover up your pencil marks, and make your compass rose just as colorful and artistic as you wish.

7. Use a directional compass to find north. Turn the compass rose so that N points toward north. If you want to use your compass rose to help remember directions, display it on a flat surface just as if it were a real compass. If you wish, you can add signs telling the directions of your favorite places, near or far.

: GO ON TO MAKE A COMPASS
: THAT WORKS.

MAKE YOUR OWN REAL COMPASS

You can make your own directional compass. It can almost seem like magic as the needle turns north again and again.

You probably want to own a modern compass to find directions for you. Make your own, though, and you'll have a compass similar to the type that very early explorers took with them on voyages. When you make your own compass, you'll see the difficulties an explorer would have taking the compass along on a voyage. Early sailors actually had to float their needles all around the world.

Here's what you need:

A magnet, preferably a bar magnet

A needle, preferably a large darning or carpet needle

A metal paper clip or pin

A non-metallic dish or bowl

Water

A cork large enough to float the needle

A directional compass to check your homemade compass

Here's what you do:

1. Stroke the magnet over the surface of the needle a number of times, always in the same direction. As you rub, you are imparting a magnetic quality from the magnet to the needle.

> *Caution: Magnetizing a needle takes many strokes. Be patient. Count to 50 before you stop to test your needle.*

2. Test the needle to see if it's magnetized. Try to pick up a metal paper clip or pin with it, and see if you can feel the magnetic pull.

3. Fill a nonmetallic dish or bowl with water.

4. Place the needle on the cork, and float the cork. The cork ought to move until it comes to rest with the blunt end of the needle pointing at magnetic north.

5. Use another compass to check it.

> *Caution: Don't set your compass close to metal objects. The needle will turn toward the metal instead of turning toward north.*

NOW YOU HAVE AN EXPLORER'S COMPASS. YOU CAN DISPLAY IT NEXT TO A COMPASS ROSE POINTED IN THE SAME DIRECTION, JUST AS THE EARLY EXPLORERS DID. THE EXPLORERS WOULD LIKE YOUR MODERN METHODS.

MAKE A NORTH, EAST, SOUTH, WEST GARDEN STONE

You can make your own garden stone. You can use it to remember north, east, south, west, and no one else will have one like it. Put the stone in a garden, by a walkway, or in another pleasant place. People will feel happy to see it.

Your garden stone is not really stone. It's plaster of Paris, with your own special artwork to show directions.

Here's what you need:

Paper and pencil

A square or round disposable pan, such as a foil or light plastic cake pan

Plaster of Paris

Water

A paper towel

Shortening

A putty knife

A pointed knife or a wooden stick, such as a chopstick or wooden barbecue skewer

Scissors or a craft knife

Old newspapers, if you wish

Acrylic paints or brushes

Clear polyurethane

A trowel

Here's what you do:

1. Practice with paper and pencil first, so you can design the arrows, pointers, and direction markers you like best for your garden stone.

2. When you're ready to make the garden stone, choose a foil or plastic pan of a size you like. Use a paper towel to rub shortening over the pan.

. . . .

MAKE A NORTH, EAST, SOUTH, WEST GARDEN STONE

continued

3. Mix plaster of Paris with water according to directions on the bag. You'll need about 6 cups (1.5 liters) of plaster of Paris with about 4 cups water (about 1 liter), depending on the size of the foil pan.

4. Fill the pan with the plaster of Paris mixture.

5. With the putty knife, level off the surface of the plaster of Paris so that it is even with the edges of the pan.

6. Use a pointed knife or a wooden stick to carve in arrows or pointers and to mark each direction, north, east, south, and west. Be sure to carve in your signature and a date.

7. Set the mold to dry for a day or more, until it no longer feels damp.

8. Remove your garden stone from the pan. Use scissors or a craft knife to help cut away the pan. Do this work on old newspapers or else take the job outside.

> *Caution: Be careful not to damage the stone. You may need adult help with using a craft knife. Use the knife or stick to clean off any bubbles or rough edges.*

9. Use acrylic paints and brushes to paint the garden stone, arrows, and direction marks, in the colors you choose. Let the paint dry completely.

10. Cover the paint with clear polyurethane to protect it from the weather. Also use the clear polyurethane to cover the unpainted underside of the stone. Let dry for several hours.

11. Decide on a good place to set your garden stone. Use a directional compass to find north and decide exactly how to orient the garden stone. Clear a space for it and make the place level and clean. Use the trowel to dig a shallow hole the exact size, and carefully set in the garden stone. Make sure you have the arrows and markers pointing the right directions.

12. If you want to keep your garden stone outdoors all the time, clean it once a year and paint it again with clear polyurethane.

> NOW YOU HAVE AN ARTISTIC GARDEN STONE. PEOPLE WILL LOOK AT IT TO FIND NORTH, EAST, SOUTH, AND WEST. IF YOU WISH, YOU CAN PLANT FLOWERS AROUND IT AND MAKE IT LOOK AS BEAUTIFUL AS POSSIBLE.

DO A NORTH, EAST, SOUTH, WEST EXPERIMENT

Find out what directions flowers like best: north, east, south, or west. Experiment on four plants by growing them with sunlight from four directions.

You must be a careful scientist to make this experiment work. Begin by making sure that everything that helps plants grow is the same for your four plants. Grow the plants from the same packet of seeds in the same sort of pot. Give them the same soil, the same water, and the same good treatment. If one plant does better than the others, then you'll know that the direction of sunlight made the difference.

Find four unshaded windows that face in four directions. Check that trees, bushes, or other buildings outside don't make one window darker than the others. The windows need to be as much the same as possible, except for the directions they face.

Here's what you need:

A directional compass

Gardening gloves

A small trowel or large spoon

4 4-inch (10-centimeter) plant pots, cans, or empty milk cartons, all the same, with an underdish for each

Potting soil

Flower seeds, (If you want seeds that grow rapidly, choose marigolds.)

Old newspapers, if you wish

Water and a measuring cup

4 white cards or pieces of paper

Scissors

An observation notebook and pen

A ruler

Here's what you do:

1. Use a directional compass to choose four windows that directly face north, east, south, and west (or in four other opposite directions). *Hint:* You can do this experiment with two or three windows that face different directions.

2. Use your gardening gloves and the trowel or spoon to fill each of the four pots with potting soil. If you are using cans or cartons, be sure to punch small holes in the bottom of each for drainage. Plant four or five seeds in each pot, according to the directions on the seed packet.

   : *Caution: Put old newspapers*
   : *under the pots as you work or*
   : *else take this job outside.*

   Set the pots or cartons on saucers to catch any water that drains.

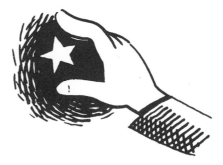

. . . .

DO A NORTH, EAST, SOUTH, WEST EXPERIMENT
continued

3. Measure out ⅓ cup (80 milliliters) of water to pour into each pot. Make sure each plant has exactly the same amount of water.

4. Set each pot in a different window. Cover each with a white card or piece of paper.

5. Water your plants every third day. Use exactly ⅓ cup (80 milliliters) water for each.

6. When the seeds begin to poke out of the soil, remove the cards or pieces of paper.

7. When the plants grow their first real leaves, use scissors to snip them off so that each pot has only two leaves.

8. In your observation notebook, note how the plants are different on the same day each week. Use the ruler to measure the plants each week, and write down the size of each plant. Also note other signs about how each plant is doing: the number and condition of the leaves and flowers, the colors, the strength of the stems.

9. After 4 to 6 weeks, decide which angle of sunlight is best for growing these particular plants.

> YOU MAY WANT TO RE-DO THIS EXPERIMENT WITH OTHER KINDS OF SEEDS. YOU CAN LEARN A GREAT DEAL ABOUT DIRECTIONS FROM WATCHING PLANTS.

FIND THE EXPLORERS' FAVORITE STAR

Explorers and navigators look for the North Star. It appears always in the same direction, and it makes a wonderful guide.

You can see the North Star only when you are north of the Equator. (The North Star is also called Polaris or the Pole Star.) North of the Equator, you could still navigate by the same complex ways the ancient Polynesians did south of the Equator, but the North Star makes navigation clear and easy in comparison.

Here's how to find the North Star:

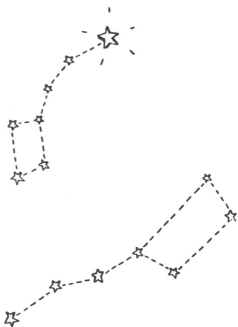

1. Go outside on a starry night, and look for the seven stars of the Big Dipper. Take a guide book if you wish, but you can probably find the Big Dipper on your own. It is one of the brightest and most distinct shapes in the northern sky. (The Big Dipper is part of the star constellation of Ursa Major or the Great Bear.)

2. Look for the two stars on the body of the Big Dipper just opposite the handle of the Big Dipper. Those two stars point directly at the bright North Star. The North Star is at the end of the handle of the Little Dipper.

(The Little Dipper is the northernmost constellation and is part of the Ursa Minor or Little Bear constellation. You can trace both those constellations from a guidebook sometime and see if they look like bears.)

USE THE NORTH STAR TO FIND YOUR OWN LATITUDE. YOU CAN EVEN MAKE YOUR OWN OUTSIDE LATITUDE FINDER. YOU CAN FIND OUT ALL ABOUT THE CROSSROADS AND ADDRESSES OF THE WORLD, THE LATITUDES AND LONGITUDES OF THE WORLD.

FIND THE CROSSROADS AND ADDRESSES OF THE WORLD

*I*f you look at any globe or almost any map, you see the world crossed round and round, and up and down, with latitudes and longitudes. They are imaginary lines, but they are important. They show the addresses of the world.

Every place in the world is at a crossroad of latitude and longitude. You can find the crossroads where you live—or exactly opposite where you live. You can find all sorts of odd and curious world addresses.

You probably want to play ping-pong on the International Date Line, or find what time it is all around the world. You can make your own latitude.

This is your chance to find out all about the addresses and crossroads of the world.

MAKE YOUR OWN LATITUDE FINDER

Here's an instrument to help you find out how far north of the Equator you are. You can use it to find your latitude at home or wherever you are, as long as you are in the Northern Hemisphere.

Here's what you need:

Heavy cardboard or posterboard, at least 13 inches (33 centimeters) long

A ruler or yardstick

A pencil

A paper punch or awl

Scissors or a craft knife (depending on the thickness of the cardboard)

A two-pronged paper fastener

A protractor

A piece of string about 18 inches (45 centimeters) long

A weight such as a nail

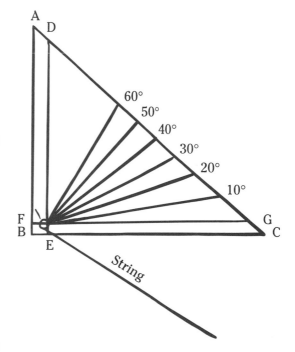

Here's how to make a latitude finder:

1. From a corner of the cardboard or posterboard, use the ruler to measure 13 inches (33 centimeters) down the side of the board. With a pencil, make a mark at that point. From the same corner, measure 13 inches (33 centimeters) to the other edge and make a mark.

2. Use the ruler to draw a straight line between the two marks.

3. Use scissors or a craft knife to cut out the triangle.

> **Caution: You need adult help with the craft knife. Keep it out of the reach of small children.**

4. Draw lines 1 inch (2 or 3 centimeters) in from the corner, parallel to each side. (Look at the diagram to see how.)

5. Where those lines intersect, make a small hole with a paper punch or awl.

> **Caution: You may need adult help to punch the hole.**

6. Set the protractor on your latitude finder so that the center mark or hole of the protractor is over the hole you have punched.

. . . .

MAKE YOUR OWN LATITUDE FINDER

continued

Trace the edge of the protractor, and mark the first 60°. Draw lines outward from the center mark at the degree marks for 0°, 10°, 20°, 30°, 40°, 50°, and 60°. Draw dots for the individual degrees (one through nine) in between.

7. Insert a two-pronged paper fastener through the hole in the triangle.

8. Tie one end of the string under the head of the paper fastener.

> NOW YOU HAVE AN INSTRUMENT TO HELP YOU FIND LATITUDE. GO ON TO SEE HOW TO USE IT.

. . . .

FIND YOUR OWN LATITUDE

. . . .

Take your latitude finder outside on a starry night. See if you can find your own latitude, and then check it on a map or globe.

Here's what you need:

Your latitude finder
A helper
A pencil or an erasable marker
A ruler or straightedge
A map to check your latitude

Here's what you do:

1. Find the North Star. (To do that, look at Find the Explorers' Favorite Star, on page 113.)

2. Stand at a level place, and hold your latitude finder to your eye at the level of the paper fastener. Have a friend check to be sure that the bottom of the finder is parallel to the ground.

3. Close one eye, and pull the string taut. Hold the string so that it points to the North Star.

4. Have your helper make a small mark with a pencil or erasable marker at the point that the string crosses the finder.

5. Hold a ruler or straightedge between the mark and the protractor markings to find the degree of latitude.

6. Check your latitude on a map or globe.

NOW LOOK AT OTHER PLACES ON THE MAP THAT SHARE THE SAME LATITUDE. YOU'LL FIND THAT PLACES THAT SHARE A LATITUDE DO NOT NECESSARILY SHARE THE SAME CLIMATE. YOU CAN PROBABLY FIGURE OUT WHY. THINK ABOUT ALL THE FACTORS THAT INFLUENCE CLIMATE BESIDES LATITUDE: HEIGHT ABOVE SEA LEVEL, THE WINDS AND AIR CURRENTS, OCEAN, LAKES, AND RIVERS.

· · · · · · · · · · ·

REMEMBER THE DIFFERENCE BETWEEN LATITUDE AND LONGITUDE

· ·

Here's an easy way to remember the difference between latitude and longitude, the imaginary lines that run round and round the Earth.

The word *latitude* comes from the Latin word for *wide* or *side*. You can use Latin to remember that latitudes go from side to side, worldwide.

Longitude comes from the Latin word for *long*. You can use Latin to remember that longitudes are long, up and down from top to bottom on the Earth.

TOP AND BOTTOM WORK ONLY IF YOU LOOK AT A GLOBE OR A WORLD MAP WITH THE NORTH POLE ON THE TOP AND THE SOUTH POLE ON THE BOTTOM. THERE IS NO UP AND DOWN IF YOU LOOK AT THE EARTH FROM OUTER SPACE.

. . . .

TAKE APART AN EARTH ORANGE

. . . .

You can see something about directions around the world from an orange. You can find out about latitudes and longitudes, the imaginary round-the-world lines that people use to tell directions.

There are 360 major latitude divisions around the Earth (with smaller and smaller divisions inside those major divisions). Count latitudes north all the way from 0° at the Equator to 90°N at the North Pole. Count latitudes south from the Equator all the way to 90°S at the South Pole.

There are 360 major longitude divisions around the Earth (with smaller and smaller divisions inside those major divisions). Longitude 0° runs through England at the Greenwich Observatory near London. That's called the Prime Meridian, since it's the meridian (or longitude) where you start counting. Count the longitudes east from Greenwich half way around the world, and you come to longitude 180°E at the International Date Line. Count the longitudes west from Greenwich half way around the world, and you come to the same place, longitude 180°W (and 180°E) at the International Date Line. Think of the International Date Line as the place where west meets east.

Here's what you need:
Two oranges

Knife

Cutting board

: **Caution: You may need adult**
: **help with using a knife.**

Here's how to cut two oranges into latitudes and longitudes.

1. To cut the first orange into latitudes; picture the orange as if it were the Earth, with the top (where the stem of the orange was attached to its tree) as the North Pole and the bottom (the navel) as the South Pole. Slice the orange exactly at its Equator. Then cut the orange into slices, each slide parallel to the Equator. (That's slicing the orange with the lines all going in the same direction as the Equator. Parallel lines never meet or cross.) A latitude is also called a parallel. Now you can see why. Each line of latitude is parallel to the Equator.

2. To divide the second orange into longitudes, peel the orange into segments from top to bottom. You can see that the orange peel segments naturally curve and come together at the top and bottom of the orange. Since the Earth is a huge circle, you can picture it divided into 360 of these curved, up-and-down segments.

: **DON'T EXPECT TO GET 360**
: **SLICES OR 360 SEGMENTS FROM**
: **YOUR ORANGES. BUT YOU WILL**
: **GET SLICES AND SEGMENTS**
: **THAT ARE GOOD TO EAT.**

· · · · · · · · · · ·

LOCATE THE PLACE IN THE WORLD OPPOSITE YOU

· ·

Where in the world would you be if you dug straight down from where you live? If you could dig a hole right through the middle of the Earth, where would you end up? If you live in North America, do you really dig through to China? Here's how to use your latitude and longitude locators to find the place exactly opposite you on the Earth.

Here's what you need:

A globe or world map that shows latitudes and longitude

A detailed map of your home place and of the area opposite, if you want

A ruler

Here's what you do:

1. Look on a globe or world map to find the latitude and longitude of your town or area. An atlas or the index to an atlas may tell you your exact latitude and longitude, with the degrees and probably the minutes, too. Or you can look for the latitude and longitude marked at the edges of the map, with lines extending across the map. On most globes and maps, the lines of latitude and longitude are 15 degrees apart.

2. To find your exact latitude and longitude, you can measure the distance between those lines on a globe or world map. Suppose you live in Miami, Florida. On a globe or world map, you'll find that Miami's latitude is between 15°N and 30°N. Measure between the lines and you can estimate that Miami is about 25° north of the Equator.

3. Figure longitude the same way. For example, on a globe or world map, you'll find that Miami is between 75°W and 90°W. Measure between the lines, and

LOCATE THE PLACE IN THE WORLD OPPOSITE YOU

continued

you can estimate that Miami is about 80°W.

4. Check your answer in a detailed atlas or map, if you wish, and see how close your estimate is. For example, Miami is 25°N and 80°W. Now you can go on to use your latitude and longitude locators to find the exact opposite place.

5. Look at latitudes carefully and you'll see that the opposite is the same latitude but at the opposite side of the Equator and of the world. For example, the opposite of 25°N is 25°S.

6. Look at longitudes carefully and you'll see that the opposite longitude is not the same number. For example, the opposite of 80°W is 100°E. You can find the opposite place to Miami at 25°S, 100°E.

YOU OUGHT TO FIND THAT THE PLACE DIRECTLY OPPOSITE MIAMI IS A SPOT IN THE INDIAN OCEAN JUST SOUTH OF THE TROPIC OF CAPRICORN AND ABOUT 750 MILES (1,207 KILOMETERS) WEST OF AUSTRALIA. WHAT'S YOUR OPPOSITE SPOT?

· · · · · · · · · · ·

COUNT ON CURIOUS LATITUDES AND LONGITUDES

· ·

You'll need a world globe or map to look up interesting latitudes and longitudes. That's like looking at street corners of the globe. Then on page 130, you can check the parts of the world you discovered and see what's special about each latitude and longitude.

Remember that when people write locations, they put latitude first and then longitude.

Here are curious latitudes and longitudes to discover:

1. Latitude 0°.
2. Latitude 0° where it intersects with longitude °0. (Write that as 0°, 0°. You can't put in north, east, south, west this time, since 0° is where it all starts.)
3. Latitude 90°N.
4. Latitude 90°S.
5. Longitude 0°.
6. Longitudes 180°E and 180°W. (*Hint:* These longitudes are just the same.)
7. 0°, 180°.
8. Latitude 23°N. (*Hint:* Look for very large cities on this latitude around the world: Riyadh in Saudi Arabia, Muscat in Oman, Dhaka in Bangladesh, Karochi in Pakistan, Calcutta and Delhi in India, Guangzhou in China, Hong Kong, Taipei on the Island of Taiwan, Havana in Cuba.)
9. Latitude 23°S. (*Hint:* Look for the deserts at this latitude that cross Africa and Australia. Look for a few large cities, too, such as São Paulo and Rio de Janeiro in Brazil.)
10. Latitudes 30°N and 30°S.
11. The latitude and longitude address of your own home

GO ON TO LOOK FOR THE CITIES, OCEANS, MOUNTAINS, AND OTHER INTERESTING PLACES ALL ALONG YOUR OWN LATITUDE AND LONGITUDE LINES AS THEY CIRCLE THE GLOBE.

· · · · · · · · · · ·

A PRIZE LONGITUDE STORY

· ·

The first latitude has to be at the Equator. Where else could it be? The degree 0 of latitude is simple.

Longitude is not so simple. The first longitude could be anywhere. Throughout history, people have decided on all sorts of locations for it.

The brilliant Egyptian astronomer Ptolemy invented the idea of latitudes and longitudes. He ran the imaginary first longitude, the Prime Meridian, through the Fortunate Islands. Now they're called the Canary and Madeira Islands. Perhaps they were once Fortunate to hold the Prime Meridian. (Now look for them at 29°N, 16°W.)

At various times after that, astronomers moved the Prime Meridian through great cities: Rome, Jerusalem, St. Petersburg, Copenhagen, Pisa, Paris, Philadelphia. Today the Prime Meridian runs through the historic observatory at Greenwich, in England, just outside London. (Sometimes, a rebellious country draws its own Prime Meridian through its own land. But then, of course, that country is not figuring direction in keeping with the rest of the world.)

You can figure longitude by keeping time.

The Earth takes 24 hours to complete one full spin of 360°. That's a full circle. Divide 360° by 24 hours. That's 15, the number of degrees the Earth spins in 1 hour, or ¹⁄₂₄ of the Earth's full spin. Suppose a ship leaves its home port at 12 noon. It travels until it reaches a new time zone, 11:00 A.M. The ship has traveled through one degree of longitude or 1 hour of time change.

That's not the same as the distance the ship might have traveled. For example, a ship sailing on the Equator can travel a full 1,000 miles before it goes through 15° longitude. On the other hand, an explorer at the North or South Pole might walk just about zero distance to travel through 15° longitude.

To tell your longitude on an early ship, you needed to have precise knowledge of the hour in two different places at once. You could have a clock on board set to time in Greenwich. Then you could figure time where your ship was by the sun or by a second clock. If it's 3 P.M. in Greenwich and 12 noon where your ship is, you can figure you're 3 time zones west of the Prime Meridian. That's 45°. You're at about longitude 45°W.

A PRIZE LONGITUDE STORY

continued

The trouble was that early sailors could not keep accurate time. The clocks of the time wouldn't work on ship. A clock pendulum cannot swing regularly when it's tossed about on the sea. The salt air makes the metal pieces on the clock rust, and any number of other things can go wrong. Studying the sun hurt the eyes of the sailors, and besides, the sun could not tell them the time in some other place.

Finally, in 1714, the British government decided to offer a prize, a huge amount of money (the value of millions of dollars today). The astronomers went to work. They tried hard to figure longitude by observing the moon and stars.

Then a poor boy went to work, a young man who did not have all the advantages of wealth and schooling that the astronomers had.

His name was John Harrison. Later he was called John Longitude Harrison. He was born in 1693, the son of a poor carpenter and custodian. He studied all on his own, without school, and became a clock inventor. He determined to win the longitude prize by inventing a clock without a pendulum. He wanted a clock that was free of friction. His clock would need no lubrication, no oiling or cleaning that could make it stop working aboard ship. It would never rust. He spent years deciding on different metals that could expand and contract with temperature changes, but all the time keep the clock going at a constant rate.

His first clock had elaborate dials to tell the hours, minutes, seconds, and months. It weighed 75 pounds (about 34 kilograms). It worked well, but Harrison wanted a perfect clock. His next clock weighed 86 pounds (about 39 kilograms). The third clock took 19 years to build. It had 753 parts and weighed 60 pounds (about 27 kilograms).

Then suddenly, John Harrison had a different idea. The fourth clock weighed only three pounds (only about 1.4 kilograms).

Harrison had enemies, though. Some of the astronomers thought that because Harrison was just a poor man who hadn't been to school, he was not as important as the grand astronomers. They did everything they could to delay Harrison's work and to prevent him from winning the prize.

In 1773, John Harrison finally won the prize. The prize had taken him more than 40 years of hard work and struggle. He had solved the problem, though, and now sailors could figure both their latitude and their longitude. They were forever grateful to John Longitude Harrison.

IF YOU EVER TRAVEL TO LONDON, LOOK FOR HARRISON'S CLOCKS IN A MUSEUM. THEY'RE STILL IN GOOD WORKING ORDER.

· · · · · · · · · ·
Tell Time All Over the World
· ·

You've heard the phrase that time is money. That may be so, but you could also say that time is longitude. Time zone lines run right along longitude lines.

There are 24 time zones around the world, one for each hour around the clock. The time zone lines run up and down every 15° of longitude. When it is noon at the Prime Meridian in London, it is midnight on the other side of the world at the International Date Line. If you looked for the longitude of your home at 3:00 in the afternoon, you can imagine that at the opposite point, it's probably 3:00 in the morning.

A few countries change the rules, though, so you can't always be sure. For example, China is a huge country, and you'd think it would cross several time zones. But the government in China chooses to keep the whole country at just one time. Some countries, like India and Australia, change times zones at the half hour instead of the hour. Many countries have daylight savings time and push the time forward one hour during the summer season.

Here's how to make a time zone clock for the world. Turn it around whenever you want, and you can find out the time almost—but not quite—everywhere.

This is a clock with 24 hours all around instead of the usual 12 hours.

Here's what you need:

A piece of white or light-colored poster board

A pencil

A large white paper plate

A protractor

A two-pronged paper fastener

Markers or pens, in colors you choose

Here's what you do:

1. Find the center of the posterboard. Make a pencil mark, and use the pencil point to punch a small hole.

2. Find the center of the paper plate. Make a pencil mark, and use the pencil point to punch a small hole.

125
·

TELL TIME ALL OVER THE WORLD

continued

3. Use a protractor to divide the outside rim of the paper plate into 24 equal sections. Place the protractor so that its exact center is over the center mark of the plate. Starting with 0 at the top, make pencil marks around the outside rim of the plate every 15°. Your plate is like the world, with a new time zone line every 15° of longitude.

4. Pencil in the times all around the rim of the plate. Write the times on the plate, not on the posterboard. Begin with the first mark, and write the times like this. Of course, you want to write them clockwise around your clock: 12 noon (at the top of your clock), 1 P.M., 2 P.M., 3 P.M., 4 P.M., 5 P.M., 6 P.M., 7 P.M., 8 P.M., 9 P.M., 10 P.M., 11 P.M., 12 midnight (at the bottom of your clock, directly opposite 12 noon), 1 A.M., 2 A.M., 3 A.M., 4 A.M., 5 A.M., 6 A.M., 7 A.M., 8 A.M., 9 A.M., 10 A.M., 11 A.M.—and back to 12 noon.

5. Fasten your clock to the posterboard. Insert the two-pronged paper fastener through each of the small center holes. You ought to be able to move your clock easily.

6. Turn your clock so that 12 noon is at the top. Now you're ready to write names of cities and other interesting places around the world. Write the names on the posterboard, not on the plate. You'll be able to tell what time it is in each of those places just by turning your clock. Look on page 127 for some places and times.

7. Use markers or pens in colors you choose to decorate your world clock. You may wish to draw a nighttime half on your plate, with moon and stars. On the other half you could design a daytime half, with a sun shining. You may want to decorate the clock with flags and pictures you draw (or cut out from magazines) of places around the world. This is your chance to be creative.

IN MANY PARTS OF THE WORLD, TIMES ARE NOT DIVIDED AS A.M. FOR MORNING HOURS AND P.M. FOR AFTERNOON AND EVENING HOURS. INSTEAD, THERE ARE 24 HOURS AROUND THE CLOCK. THE TIME RUNS 1 O'CLOCK TO 12 NOON. THEN THE HOURS CONTINUE AS 13 (INSTEAD OF 1 P.M.), 14 (INSTEAD OF 2 P.M.), 15, AND SO ON ALL THE WAY TO HOUR 24. MILITARY AND AVIATION PEOPLE USUALLY COUNT TIME LIKE THAT, TOO. IT'S A PRECISE, CLEAR WAY TO TELL TIME.

. . . .

MATCH TIMES AND PLACES
AROUND THE WORLD

. . . .

Here are just a few of the places around the world, with their times. You'll want to write a few of them around your world clock:

12 noon London, England, at the Prime Meridian

1 P.M. Paris, France—Rome, Italy—Algiers, Algeria—Monrovia, Liberia—Bamako, Mali

2 P.M. Berlin, Germany—Athens, Greece—Cairo, Egypt—Jerusalem, Israel—Tripoli, Libya—Goma, Zaire

3 P.M. Helsinki, Finland—Moscow, Russia—Khartoum, Sudan—Ankara, Turkey—Mecca, Saudi Arabia—Doha, Qatar—Nairobi, Kenya—Mogadishu, Somalia

3:30 P.M. Teheran, Iran

4 P.M. Dubai, United Arab Emirate—Muscat, Oman

4:30 P.M. Kabul, Afghanistan

5 P.M. Karachi, Pakistan

5:30 P.M. New Delhi, India

7 P.M. Bangkok, Thailand—Phnom Phen, Cambodia

8 P.M. Beijing, China—Hong Kong, China—Singapore—Kuala Lumpur, Malaysia

9 P.M. Seoul, South Korea—Tokyo, Japan

10 P.M. Sydney, Australia—Port Moresby, Papua New Guinea

11 P.M. Solomon Islands

11 P.M. or 12 midnight The Pacific Ocean at the International Date Line

12 midnight Auckland, New Zealand

1 A.M. Honolulu, Hawaii, U.S.A.

2 A.M. Anchorage, Alaska, U.S.A.

3 A.M. Vancouver, Canada—Los Angeles, California, U.S.A.

4 A.M. Calgary, Alberta, Canada—Denver, Colorado, U.S.A.

5 A.M. Toronto, Ontario, Canada—Chicago, Illinois, U.S.A.—Mexico City, Mexico—Guatemala City, Guatemala—San Salvador, El Salvador

6 A.M. Montreal, Quebec, Canada—New York, New York, U.S.A.—Havana, Cuba—Bogota, Colombia—Quito, Ecuador—Lima, Peru

7 A.M. Halifax, Nova Scotia—Caracas, Venezuela—La Paz, Boliva

8 A.M. Rio de Janiero, Brazil—Buenos Aires, Argentina

8:30 A.M. St. John's, Newfoundland

11 A.M. Reykjavik, Iceland—the Azoran Islands—Cape Verde

127
•

. . . .

MATCH TIMES AND PLACES AROUND THE WORLD

continued

NOTICE THAT PLACES IN ASIA, AUSTRALIA, AND NEW ZEALAND ARE ON THE OTHER SIDE OF THE INTERNATIONAL DATE LINE. SO IT'S NOT ONLY A DIFFERENT TIME THERE, BUT IT'S ALSO A DIFFERENT DAY. AS YOU TRAVEL WEST, YOU HAVE TO TURN YOUR CLOCK EARLIER AND EARLIER. BUT WHEN YOU CROSS THE INTERNATIONAL DATE LINE, YOU ALSO GO TO THE NEXT DAY. SO IT'S BOTH EARLIER AND LATER. FOR EXAMPLE, IF IT'S SUNDAY IN THE UNITED STATES, IT'S ALREADY MONDAY IN ASIA, AUSTRALIA, AND NEW ZEALAND. YOU CAN SEE WHY THE INTERNATIONAL DATE LINE WAS PLOT- TED NOT TO RUN THROUGH THE MIDDLE OF ANY ISLANDS, TOWNS, OR HOUSES. GO ON TO SEE WHAT COULD HAPPEN IF YOU WERE CRUISING ON A SHIP RIGHT ALONG THE INTERNATIONAL DATE LINE.

Anchorage,
Alaska, U.S.A.

London,
England

· · · · · · · · · ·

Play Ping-Pong on the International Date Line

· ·

Look at a globe or a world map, and you'll see that the International Date Line is not straight. Look what would happen if it were straight. It could run across an island, right through the middle of a town, or directly through somebody's house. As it is, the line crosses only ocean.

Picture yourself on a cruise ship cruising the Pacific Ocean along the International Date Line. You're playing ping-pong with your friend Fred. It's December 30, 1999. Or is it?

You know a new year is on its way, the year 2000. A new century is also on its way. As the twentieth century ends, the twenty-first century is beginning. You're also very close to a new millennium. That's a span of 1,000 years. The millennium between the year 1 and the year 1999 is finishing. Now you'll start a new millennium.

If you want to celebrate with Fred, you're going to have to do some figuring. (If you wish, look for the answers on page 131.)

Here's how to figure it:

1. You're on the east side of the ping-pong table. You ping the ball to Fred at 11:59 P.M. on December 30, 1999.

2. Fred is on the west side of the line. He pongs the ball back to you 30 seconds later at 10:59 ½ P.M. on December 31, 1999. It's an hour earlier plus a day later for Fred on his side of the dateline than it is for you on your side.

3. At 12:01 A.M., you ping the ball to Fred. What date is it, and what year is it now on your side of the International Date Line? Remember the day has changed for both you and Fred, but it's still one day later on Fred's side.

4. You play for another hour. At 12:01 A.M. his time, Fred pongs the ball back to you. What date is it for Fred, and what year is it for him?

5. By the time it's January 1, 2000, for you, what date is it for Fred?

: **Now You And Fred Can**
: **Celebrate The New Year,**
: **New Century, And New**
: **Millennium.**
:

129
·

. . . .

SOLUTIONS

. . . .

Count on Curious Latitudes and Longitudes; page 122.

1. Latitude 0° is the Equator.

2. 0°, 0° is in the Gulf of Guinea, off the western coast of Africa. The nearest city is Lagos, on the southern coast of Nigeria.

3. Latitude 90°N is the North Pole.

4. Latitude 90°S is the South Pole.

5. Longitude 0° is the Prime (or the beginning) Meridian. It runs through England at the Greenwich Observatory just outside London.

6. Longitude 180°E and longitude 180°W are the same. Longitude 180° marks the International Date Line.

7. 0°, 180° is the intersection of the Equator and the International Date Line. That's in the Pacific Ocean, near the Gilbert Islands.

8. Latitude 23°N marks of Tropic of Cancer. That's an imaginary line that goes around the Earth and marks the northernmost part of the Torrid Zone, the part of the Earth near the Equator. It's called the Torrid Zone because all around the Earth, you can expect mostly hot or even really hot or torrid weather. This latitude marks where a constellation, the star formation of Cancer or the Crab, becomes visible in the sky every year on the first day of summer. Early explorers marked this line as the northernmost point of what seemed like the movement of the sun. (Now we know the Earth is moving around the sun rather than the sun moving around the Earth. But the Tropic of Cancer is still important.)

9. Latitude 23°S marks the Tropic of Capricorn. That's an imaginary line that goes around the Earth south of the Equator and marks the southernmost part of the Torrid Zone. This latitude marks where a constellation, Capricorn or the Goat, becomes visible in the sky every year on the first day of winter. Early mapmakers marked this line as the southernmost point of what seemed like the movement of the sun.

10. Latitudes 30°N to 30°S are the Horse Latitudes. The Horse Latitudes feature calm weather and light winds. That sort of weather sounds good when you're on land, but it could be bad for the early sailing ships that needed the wind so they could keeping going. No one really knows where the latitudes got their name. One story is that ships may have been stuck for so long in that part of the ocean that they had to lighten their loads in order to move on. In desperation, the sailors may have thrown the poor horses overboard, just so the horses wouldn't

· · · · · · · · · ·

SOLUTIONS

continued

weigh down the ship and keep it from moving on. Another, happier story is that Spanish soldiers traveling on the ships named the Horse Latitudes after their own horses. The soldiers thought that their horses were changeable and didn't always do as they should—and so were the winds. Within the Horse Latitudes and near the Equator are the Doldrums, where the air is almost always calm and quiet. If people speak of being in the doldrums, they mean that they feel dull and weary.

11. Here are some examples. If you live in the capital city of the United States, Washington D.C., you could write your latitude /longitude address at 38°N, 77°W. If you live in Canada in the city of Toronto, you are at 43°N, 79°W.

Play Ping-Pong on the International Date Line; page 129.

3. At 12:01 A.M., *east* of the international Date Line, it's now December 31, 1999.

4. At 12:01 ½ A.M., *west* of the International Date Line, it's now January 1, 2000.

5. At 12:01 A.M. on January 1, *east* of the International Date Line, it is 11:01 A.M. January 2, 2000 *west* of the line. Now both you and Fred are in the new year, new century, and new millennium.

·

HIKE AROUND THE WORLD

*Y*ou probably like to hike. Here's how you can plan a hike and make your own hiking map. You can make a bearing board of the sort that hikers and surveyors love to use. Then you can impress your friends with a little directions trick.

PLAN A HIKE

You probably like to go hiking. Perhaps you like long, complicated hikes. Here's how to plan a hike so it's fun and safe. The first part of planning a hike is to invite friends, including adults, to plan and hike with you. Having people with you automatically makes the hike more fun and safer.

You definitely should not go into unknown territory unless you have an adult with you who is familiar with the terrain.

Naturally, you need a good map.

Here's what to look for when you buy a hiking map:

1. Buy a map that shows contours, the ups and downs of the land. You may want to plan a route that avoids steep places. Unless you plan ahead and know how to climb a mountain, you would find a mountain in your way very inconvenient. On a good map, you'll find a legend, probably in a corner or on the first page of an atlas. A map legend describes symbols, scale, and other important details about the map. A legend, for instance, may show the colors and symbols so you can understand the distances and heights for the contour lines and the depths for lakes, waterways, and perhaps even the swampy places.

2. Look for a map that shows lots of detail. A scale you might like is 1 inch on the map to represent each 1 mile of territory. (That's about 2.54 centimeters to represent about 1.61 kilometers. Maps that use the metric system will have a somewhat different scale.) You can get maps with even more detail than that, too.

3. Make sure your map is up to date. Look for the copyright date, and also look for revised and field-checked dates.

4. You may want to buy a plastic or laminated map—or put a plastic overlay on it yourself. (To see how to do that, look at page 26.) Rain and bad weather won't damage a map with a plastic surface over it. And you may be able to write and erase right on the map itself.

PLAN A HIKE

continued

Here's how to read a hiking map:

1. Plan a route on your map; count miles or kilometers carefully so that you don't plan more than you can do, especially in the cold of the winter, in the heat of the summer, or in bad weather. Remember to figure time as well as distance. You need the time and energy not only to make your hike but also to get back to your starting point.

2. Look for a route that avoids problems, such as swamps or cliffs that you can't cross. Hikers call places like that stoppers. They can stop your hike.

3. Look carefully at the contour markings on the map, so you know the steep places. You probably want to avoid very steep rises or drops. Even if you don't mind climbing, you should know what's ahead. Contour lines on a map connect points that are on an equal level. Look for the map distances between the contour lines, like this:

   - If the contour lines are close together, that means steep ups and downs in the land.

   - If the contour lines seem to cross or run very close together, you'll find an abrupt drop such as a canyon or a cliffside.

   - If the contour lines are far apart, that means a gentle, slow rise or fall in the land.

   - If the contour lines are very far apart, the land is nearly flat.

   - If you see no contour lines, the land is quite flat.

4. Look for places that will help you know where you are, such as a brook or a highway at the edge of the woods. Hikers call places like that handrails. If you hike along the edge of a stream, for instance, it's like holding a handrail. You probably won't get lost. (But be extra careful when you travel along a stream. Streams may go through swampy areas, and you need to keep on dry ground.)

5. As you plan your route, look for the north, east, south, west directions. Even better, look for precise degrees of direction.

6. After you plan your route, mark it with a highlighter pen. (Then you can see your route in color. Yet you won't cover up map details that you want to know.) On a plastic map, you can probably erase highlighter markings when you want to plan another route.

· · · · · · · · · ·

PLAN A HIKE

continued

Here's what to take on a hike:

A canteen or bottle of water

Food (fruit or energy bars) and plenty of water, packed so it's all protected from the weather

Your map, with your route carefully marked

A directional compass, preferably one that shows 360° of direction

Very good hiking shoes and socks

Layered clothes that protect you from cold, heat, bug bites, and sunburn (plus you can change the layers if the weather changes)

Rain poncho and other rain gear

Sunscreen and bug repellent

Cellular phone if you like, so you can call for help if you need it

Here's how to use your map on a hike:

1. Leave a copy of your route, and tell someone your plans. If you get in trouble, someone will know where to look.

2. Use your map and directional compass to get your bearings as you begin your hike. As you hike, note how to return to your starting place.

3. Keep track of where you are all the time. Stay on a handrail or where you can see obvious land-marks.

4. Choose checkpoints along the way where you take your bear-ings and make sure you are stay-ing on your route, without getting lost. Hikers call the checkpoints their attack points. Attack points ought to be reason-ably close together and easily identified. At each attack point,

135
·

· · · · · · · · · · ·

PLAN A HIKE

continued

figure out your directions and make sure you're going just right.

5. You should have a waterproof watch with you. You or adults with you ought to know how to orient to the sun. You can tell by the position of the sun that you are walking in the generally right direction.

6. Keep track of the time. You need to start back in plenty of time so you don't run into sunset and darkness, or other problems that you didn't plan.

7. When you are on a hike, remember other ways to stay safe. Look at Pack for a Journey of Exploration, on page 44.

REMEMBER A GOOD MOTTO FOR HIKING: THE SHORTEST DISTANCE BETWEEN TWO POINTS IS A STRAIGHT LINE ONLY IF YOU'RE NOT HIKING OR CLIMBING A MOUNTAIN. THE BEST HIKING ROUTE MAY BE LONGER THAN A STRAIGHT LINE—AND A LOT MORE FUN AND INTERESTING. THE BEST ROUTE HAS A HANDRAIL PLUS ATTACK POINTS—AND NO STOPPERS.

MAKE A BEARING BOARD

You can make your own bearing board. Use it with a directional compass, and you can make all sorts of good maps. You can make your own precise hiking map. You can even make a hidden treasure map.

A bearing board shows you not just north, east, south, and west. It helps you find 360 degrees all around a circle. That's 360 directions you can find.

Here's what you need:

A ruler

White laminated foam board, about $3/16$ inch (4 or 5 millimeters) thick (available at craft and hobby stores, craft sections of department stores, and some office supply stores)

A soft pencil

A craft knife

A drawing compass

A protractor, full or half circle

A fine pointed black marker or fiber pen

A directional compass

Here's what you do:

1. Use a ruler and soft pencil to measure and mark a square 15 × 15 inches (38 × 38 centimeters) on the foam board. Carefully mark your measurings with a pencil.

2. With a craft knife, carefully cut the square from the board.

   Caution: You need adult help with using a craft knife, and you need a secure surface for cutting. Cut on a board or thick cardboard, so you won't damage a table surface.

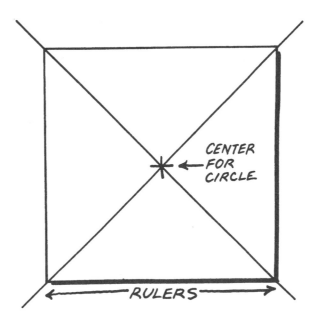

CENTER FOR CIRCLE

RULERS

· · · · · · · · · · ·

MAKE A BEARING BOARD

continued

3. To find the center of the square, put the edge of the ruler across the square from corner to corner. Make a light mark across the center point of the ruler. Then put the ruler corner to corner from the other direction. Make sure it crosses your mark at the center point of the ruler. Place the pointed edge of the compass on that point to draw the circle.

4. To draw a circle about 12 inches (30 centimeters) across, open the drawing compass to about 6 inches (15 centimeters). Place the point of the compass at the center of the square and draw the circle.

5. Put your protractor so that its center mark is at the center of the circle. Use a pencil to make a tick mark at each 10° all around the outside of the protractor. If your protractor is a half circle, mark every 10° around the half circle. Then move the protractor to mark the remaining degrees. Carefully match the edges of the protractor's half circle.

6. With a pencil and your ruler, draw lines from each 10° marking through the center of the circle and on to the opposite marking. Start at the top of the circle to line up the edge of the ruler with each of the two oppo-

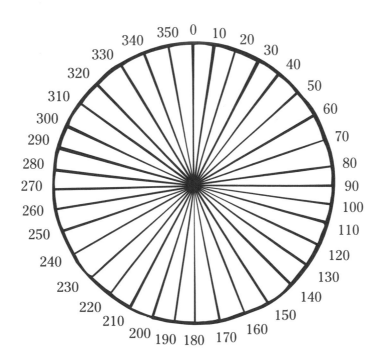

· · · · · · · · · ·

MAKE A BEARING BOARD

continued

site points you have marked. Continue around the circle until you have drawn 18 lines to connect the 36 points.

7. Starting at the top, label each point on the rim of the circle from 0° to 350°. (The circle is 360° around. When you come to 360°, you've gone all around the circle. The 360° mark falls right at the 0° mark.) If you make a mistake, you can always erase and try again. Make your markings large and distinct, especially at the 0°, 90°, 180°, and 270° marks.

8. Fill in your markings with a fine-pointed black marker or fiber pen.

9. Go outside with your bearing board and your directional compass. Use the compass to find north. Then hold the bearing board at about waist level, and point it toward north. Now you can see 360°, all the way around. You have the ability to find 360 directions.

YOU CAN SEE WHY SURVEYORS AND HIKERS LIKE BEARING BOARDS. NOW YOU HAVE YOUR OWN. GO ON TO SEE EVERYTHING YOU CAN DO WITH IT.

MAKE YOUR OWN HIKING MAP

You can use your bearing board to make your own hiking map. You can make a hiking map of forest trails. Or you can make a map of a field, park, or camp. With a bearing board, you can state exact directions. No one will get lost on your hiking route.

This is a good project for a class or a group of friends. Or you can make a map for a family, school, or club hiking trip.

You may want to begin with a short hiking route.

Here's what you need:

A yardstick or other measuring stick

A pencil with an eraser

Graph paper or plain paper

A directional compass

Your bearing board

A protractor and ruler, if you wish

Colored markers, if you wish

Here's what you do:

1. Walk a short distance and use a yardstick or other measuring stick to decide the average length of your pace. A pace is the normal length of your step or stride as you walk. People have different paces. Take 3 paces, and measure the total distance. Then divide by 3 for the average. Pencil in the average length of your pace in a corner of the paper.

2. Decide on a scale for your map. If you are using graph paper, perhaps one pace might represent the length of one or two squares on your map. If you are using plain paper, perhaps one pace might represent ¼ or ½ inch (1 or 2 centimeters). Write the scale in another corner of the paper.

MAKE YOUR OWN HIKING MAP
continued

3. Decide where north will be on your map. Pencil in an arrow showing north.

4. Decide on a route through woods, fields, or park. You may change the route as you make your map, but you ought to begin with a basic good idea of where to hike.

5. Choose a starting point for your hiking trail. At the bottom of your paper, make a pencil mark to show where the trail begins. Pick something clearly visible and distinctive for a landmark, such as a tree, a rock, or a sign to mark the beginning. That's your first landmark.

6. Orient your compass so that its arrow lines up with north. On your paper, draw a line from your first landmark toward north. Line up your bearing board so the north arrow points north. Use your bearing board to determine exactly how many degrees from north your first landmark is. At the pencil mark for the first landmark on your map, note the degrees rather than north, east, south, west directions. (North is at 0° on your bearing board, but the trail could begin at any of the 360 degrees.)

7. Stand at the first landmark, and select a second landmark. Again, look for a large landmark and something unusual that people can identify easily. Determine north with your compass. Then use your bearing board to determine the direction of the second landmark. State that angle in degrees on your map. If you wish, use a protractor and ruler to draw the angles and lines.

8. Pace off the distance from the first to the second landmark. Note the number of paces on your map.

MAKE YOUR OWN HIKING MAP
continued

9. Stand at the second landmark, and select a third landmark. Find north again. Then note the angle and paces on your map. Then you can go on to landmarks number four, five, six, and so on, all the way to the end of your route. As you go from one landmark to another, note any problems, such as steep places or water, that might change the route of your hike.

10. When you finish your map, connect your lines and dots along your trail. Sketch in the landmarks, and put in labels and names to make the map clear. You can erase extra lines if you wish.

11. If you wish, use colored markers to decorate and color your map, with all its landmarks and directions.

NOW YOU HAVE A USEFUL MAP—AND A GOOD-LOOKING ONE, TOO. LEARNING HOW TO FIND DIRECTIONS AND TO KEEP FROM GETTING LOST (AND PERHAPS FIND OTHER PEOPLE WHO ARE LOST) IS CALLED ORIENTEERING. LOTS OF PEOPLE LOVE ORIENTEERING. IT'S FUN, AND IT'S ALSO VERY USEFUL.

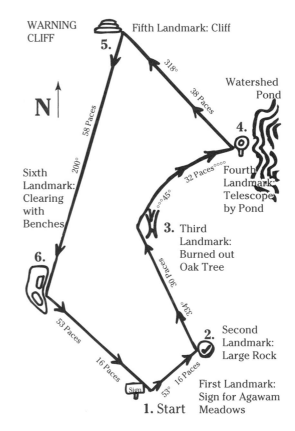

FIND YOUR OWN BURIED TREASURE

Here's a fun way to use your bearing board. Use it not to locate where landmarks are positioned, but where you are. There are times when that can be important, particularly when you need to return to some exact spot. Maybe you've been hiking, and you want to return to the car or your home. Or maybe that spot has some buried treasure waiting for you.

Here's what you need:

A few coins
Two pieces of paper
Trowel or small shovel
A handful of small stones
A pencil
Your bearing board

Here's what you do:

1. Take everything with you to the middle of a large yard or grassy park.
2. Wrap the coins in one piece of paper, and use a trowel or small shovel to bury them right where you are. Mark the spot with a small X of stones.

. . . .

FIND YOUR OWN BURIED TREASURE

continued

3. Look out at the edges of the yard or park for two landmarks a good distance apart. The landmarks could be a large tree trunk, a telephone pole, or the edge of a building.

4. Use the bearing board to note the exact locations for both landmarks. Use a pencil to draw your readings on the second piece of paper, so that they look something like this:

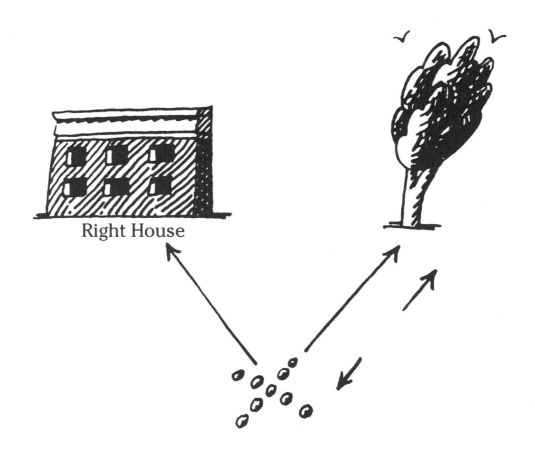

Right House

FIND YOUR OWN BURIED TREASURE

continued

Here's what you do a week later:

1. Return in a week or so to see if you can find the buried coins. Bring the board and the drawing with you.

2. Go back to the general area where you think the treasure is and face your two landmarks.

3. Put the drawing on top of your board so that your right-hand heading line points straight at its landmark.

4. Look at your left-hand heading line. If it doesn't point at its landmark, you could be seeing something like this:

5. To get the left-hand heading to line up, walk forward or backward along the right-hand line. Try forward first. If that makes your left-hand line get closer to its landmark, keep going until the line points correctly. If walking forward makes the line go farther away, walk backwards until both lines point straight where they should.

THEN LOOK DOWN ON THE GROUND FOR YOUR X OF STONES. THE BURIED COINS SHOULD BE WITHIN A STEP OR TWO OF WHERE YOU'RE STANDING.

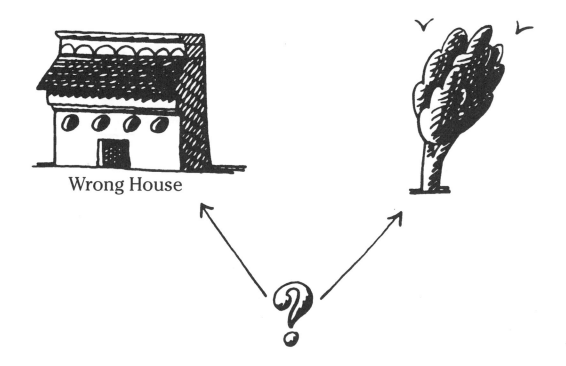

Wrong House

145

· · · · · · · · · · ·
PLAY A DIRECTIONS TRICK
· ·

You can't really use the face of your watch to get compass directions. But here's a trick you can do with it. Try it on your parents or friends.

Tell them, "I bet I can show you which way north, east, south, and west are. All I need is a watch." Don't say this inside at night, though. The trick works only outside in the daytime, when you can see where the sun is.

Here's what you need:

A watch that's running at the correct time and has an hour hand on it

Here's what you do:

1. Hold the watch flat in your hand. Angle it so that the hour hand points toward the sun.

2. Keep holding it that way. Look closely at the watchface.

3. If you're doing the trick in the morning, look in a clockwise direction between 6:00 and 12:00 for the halfway point between the hour hand and 12:00. That is south. Face south and tell the people, "There's south." North is behind you. West is on your right hand. East is to your left.

4. If you're doing the trick in the afternoon, look in a counter-clockwise direction between 6:00 and 12:00 for the halfway point between the hour hand and 12:00. That's also south.

> **IF YOUR PARENTS OR FRIENDS WANT TO KNOW HOW YOU DID IT, JUST TELL THEM THAT IT IS HARD TO EXPLAIN UNLESS THEY KNOW AS MUCH GEOGRAPHY AS YOU DO. ASK THEM TO CHECK YOUR DIRECTIONS WITH A COMPASS IF THEY WANT.**

ASK FOR DIRECTIONS AND GET UNLOST

When you ask for directions, many people will give you too few details, too many details, or put them in the wrong order. You stay confused despite the facts they give you.

When you ask for directions, you need to form a clear mental picture that you can use. That's a logical map, made up of the key facts—and only the key facts—that you need to reach your destination.

It's simple to see how a logical mental map works. The first step is how you ask for directions.

Here's all you need:

Two friends at school who have been to the same movie theater lately (or somewhere else within walking distance)

Here's what you do:

1. Ask the first friend, "Where's the movie theater?"

2. Listen to the answer. You'll probably hear something like this: "It's the one that's way far. It's by a bank, and you have to go over the bridge and up that big hill."

3. Try to visualize the route. You may find that difficult.

Here's what you do next:

1. Ask the second friend, "How do I get from right here to the movie theater?"

2. Listen to the answer. Because you asked this way, your friend is likely to start by pointing and then by giving step-by-step directions: "Go over there to Main Street and turn left. Turn right on Hill Street. Go up the hill and across the bridge. Walk along Hill Street until you see a bank sign."

3. Try to visualize the route. You'll probably form a good mental picture right away.

YOUR FRIEND HAS JUST GIVEN YOU THE BASICS FOR A LOGICAL MAP, ONE THAT IS BASED ON TURNS TO MAKE AND LANDMARKS THAT APPEAR ALONG THE WAY. FOR MOST TRIPS ALONG ROADS, THAT'S ALL YOU REALLY NEED TO KNOW. YOU CAN MAKE A MENTAL PICTURE OF WHICH WAY TO START GOING, WHERE TO CHANGE DIRECTIONS, AND WHAT LANDMARKS TO NOTICE. YOU DON'T HAVE A PERFECT MAP, BUT YOU DO HAVE A LOGICAL MENTAL MAP.

DESIGN YOUR OWN CREATIVE MAPS

*W*ould you like to make your own very creative maps? You can make colorful, interesting maps that no one else has even imagined. You can create a tee-shirt map or a map pillow you can hug. You can design a gift map specially for your own family, or make a fancy map of your neighborhood. This is your chance to be an artistic and creative mapmaker.

LOOK AT THE WORLD FROM THE TOP

Most often, a map shows the world in bird's eye view. Think about how ordinary things look to a bird flying over and looking down from up high. That makes everything look much different.

Try drawing these shapes as seen from up high. Your friends might have to guess what the shapes are.

- A person walking. Perhaps the bird sees only a head and shoulders, maybe feet and arms swinging.
- A rider on a bicycle. This could look funny. The bird sees a head and shoulders, wheels and handlebars.
- Your classroom with the children sitting at desks and around tables. Could you tell who's who if you saw mostly just tops of heads?
- A garden with rows of carrots, round fat cabbages, tall tomato plants, and different sorts of flowers. In the spring, you could use a map like this to help plan where to plant the seeds.
- A road with the cars and trucks moving along. What else would the bird see besides the tops of the cars and trucks?
- A lake with beaches all around and an island in the middle. You can see why a map sometimes makes a place look very interesting. The map makes you want to visit.

AS SOON AS YOU CAN IMAGINE THE WORLD FROM UP HIGH, YOU'RE READY TO DESIGN CREATIVE MAPS ALL YOUR OWN.

· · · · · · · · · ·
AN IMPOSSIBLE MAP STORY
· ·

This is a story that began in Argentina, but it's not a true story. It's an impossible story.

We'll call the king the Impossible King. When the Impossible King traveled around his kingdom, he saw a vast and wonderful land. He saw winding rivers, huge lakes, soaring mountains, and great cities. He was proud of what he saw, and he wanted the world to know the immense size and beauty of his kingdom.

So the Impossible King hired mapmakers to create a map of the kingdom. The mapmakers worked for years, and finally they presented the king with a wonderful map that showed all the mountain ranges, the big cities, and the large rivers and lakes.

The Impossible King was not happy. He really was impossible, and he hurt the mapmakers' feelings when he said the map was not good enough. The Impossible King wanted to see not only the mountain ranges but also every mountain peak. He wanted to see the streams that fed into the rivers. He wanted to see the towns as well as the cities.

The mapmakers went back to work and created another map, twice as big as the other. But now the king wanted to see the valleys between the mountain peaks, the puddles beside the streams, the little farmhouses at the edge of the towns.

The mapmakers made more and more maps. The Impossible King died, and new Impossible Kings and Impossible Queens came and went. They hired new mapmakers with each new generation. Each of the new mapmakers worked harder and harder and harder. Each left with hurt feelings.

Finally, the mapmakers created an Impossible Map. This map showed everything about the kingdom, and it was exactly the same size as the kingdom. No one could any longer tell the difference between the map and the kingdom.

WHERE WOULD THEY KEEP THEIR BEAUTIFUL MAP? NEXT, THE IMPOSSIBLE KINGS AND IMPOSSIBLE QUEENS HIRED CARPENTERS TO BUILD A FINE MAP CABINET.

. . . .

MAKE AN IMPOSSIBLE MAP

. . . .

You can see the Impossible King's problem by looking at real maps. Each map states its scale, how much 1 inch or 1 centimeter on the map represents in the miles or kilometers of the real places.

An atlas may picture shapes of continents and oceans across the whole world. So 1 inch or 1 centimeter on an atlas may represent 1,000 miles or 1,000 kilometers or even more. That means that 1 inch on the page of a world atlas may represent more than 63 million actual inches. Or 1 centimeter may represent 1 million actual centimeters.

Suppose you look at a city map where 1 inch represents only 2 miles. That's 1 inch to show you the look of 126,720 actual inches. Or a city map may use 1 centimeter to represent 200,000 actual centimeters.

Maps often state scales as a ratio like this: 1:1000. That might mean that 1 inch on the map represents 1,000 miles on real territory, or perhaps 1 centimeter represents 1,000 kilometers. The Impossible King began with a map on the scale of 1:1000. Then the mapmakers created a map with a scale of 1:500. Then the map was 1:250. Finally, the Impossible Map was 1:1. The map and the kingdom were just the same size.

Just for fun, you could make a 1:1 map of something small. You could make a map of something small but interesting. Choose your lunchbox, or a kitchen drawer, or your desktop at school. The map should be just the same size as the lunchbox, drawer, or desktop. Then you could make the same map at just half the size of the box, the drawer, or the desktop. That would be half of each measurement, half the length, half the height, and half the width.

LOOK FOR THE SCALE WHENEVER YOU LOOK AT A PRINTED MAP.
YOU'LL KNOW MORE ABOUT WHAT YOU ARE SEEING.

· · · · · · · · · · ·
DESIGN A MAP OF YOUR ROOM
· ·

Perhaps you are never lonely in your room because you share it with sisters or brothers. Or perhaps your room is a good quiet place to be alone. Your room may look a little dull. Perhaps you need to map it out, rearrange and redecorate it. Here's how.

Here's what you need:

A tape measure, measuring rod,
 or yardstick, if you wish
A directional compass
A ruler or straightedge
A pencil
Graph paper
Scissors

Here's what you do:

1. Use your tape measure, measuring rod, or yardstick to measure each side of your room. Or you can measure your room with your footsteps. If you want to measure your room with foot-

steps, walk from one side of your room to the other, but don't stride in the regular way. Instead, as you walk, carefully put the heel of one foot in front of the toes of the other foot, with no space in between. Write down the number of feet, meters, or footsteps that measure each side of your room.

2. Use a directional compass to find which side of your room faces the north. On the graph paper, write an arrow to indicate where you want north.

Ordinarily, mapmakers locate north at the top of their maps and south at the bottom. You can orient your map any way that fits your idea of your room, but be sure that you locate

· · · · · · · · · · ·
DESIGN A MAP OF YOUR ROOM
continued

north first, then put in east, south, and west at points clockwise from north.

3. Use a ruler or straightedge to draw the sides of your room onto graph paper. Draw the north side of your room so that it is also north on the graph paper. Let each foot, meter, or footstep you measured equal one, two, or three squares of graph paper. If you use a pencil, you can erase when you want.

4. Measure the distances along each wall to the windows and doors of your room. Mark them in the right place on the graph paper. You'll need to design lines or symbols to show windows and doors.

5. Measure the furniture in your room in feet, meters, or footsteps. On a separate piece of graph paper, draw the furniture outlines. Let each foot, meter, or footstep equal one, two, or three squares of graph paper, on the same scale you used for measuring your room. *Hint:* Like any good mapmaker, you need to decide what to leave in and what to leave out. Perhaps you want to show all your furniture but none of the small items that change like clothes or books.

6. Now use scissors to cut out the shapes of the furniture. You can place these shapes on the map of your room and move them around. You can see how the furniture is now and how you might like it arranged in the future.

7. Use your directional compass to see what directions the windows face. Maybe you want to arrange your bed toward an east-facing window so that the sun will shine on you and wake you up early in the morning. Maybe you want to arrange your bed to the north, south, or west, so you can sleep a little later sometimes.

> NOW YOU HAVE A USEFUL MAP OF YOUR ROOM. YOU COULD MAKE A MAP LIKE THIS OF YOUR WHOLE APARTMENT OR HOUSE. MEASURING WITH FOOTSTEPS IS NOT THAT UNUSUAL. THE MEASUREMENT CALLED A FOOT (12 INCHES OR ABOUT 30 CENTIMETERS LONG) IS A MEASUREMENT OF THE FOOT OF THE GREAT EMPEROR CHARLEMAGNE, WHO LIVED FROM THE YEAR 742 TO 814. MEASURE YOUR OWN FOOT WITH A RULER, AND YOU CAN SEE HOW UNUSUALLY LONG CHARLEMAGNE'S FOOT WAS.

DESIGN A MAP OF YOUR ROUTE TO SCHOOL

Don't look for exact scale and proportion on all maps. Some maps show just routes, roads, and lines. Maps of that sort can be especially useful when you travel. They're called schematic maps because they show you the scheme, or diagram, of a system, without putting in unnecessary details. When you travel around large cities, especially, you may see schematic maps that show train, subway, and bus routes.

Try drawing a schematic map of a route you take often, perhaps your route to school or to a friend's house. You can make the same sort of map whether you walk, take a bus, ride in a car or on a subway or train.

Remember that scale, proportions, and many details that are important on other maps are not important for this map. The only purpose of a map like this is to help people figure out how to get places.

Here's what you need:

A pencil
Ruler or straightedge
Graph paper

Here's what you do:

1. Pay close attention as you take your usual route. You may want to travel the route at a time when you're not in a hurry. If so, you may want to get someone to walk with you, drive you along the usual route, or take public transportation with you. Or else you can get a printed map of the school district or of your local community.

2. Use a pencil and ruler or straightedge to draw the lines of your route on graph paper. Show the roads you travel, and label the names. Label any bus or train stops a map reader would want to know. Show the corners you turn. Keep all the

· · · · · · · · · · ·
DESIGN A MAP OF YOUR ROUTE TO SCHOOL
continued

lines straight, even if you climb a hill or go around curves to get to school. Or if you have a printed map, trace the route on it with a marker or pen.

3. Decide what symbols to use on your map. Perhaps you walk to a bus stop, then take a bus, then walk on to school or a friend's house. You'll want to design a way to distinguish your walking from your bus route.

LOOK TO SEE IF YOU GO TO SCHOOL OR YOUR FRIEND'S HOUSE IN A STRAIGHT LINE. CHANCES ARE YOUR ROUTE IS NOT STRAIGHT AT ALL. A SHORTCUT MIGHT BE FUN. WHAT IF YOU COULD SAIL OR FLY DIRECTLY?

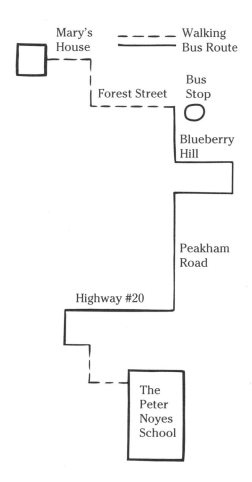

155
·

· · · · · · · · · · ·

DESIGN A FAMILY MAP

· ·

Create a picture map just for your own family, with their birthplaces and homelands. You may be surprised at how much you learn about the people you love.

You may wish to draw it onto a printed paper map, or you may want to use your own write-on placemat map. (Look on page 24 to see how to make your own.)

Here's what you need:

A map or your own placemat map of your country or the world

Paper

Pens, markers, or pens, in colors you choose

Small photographs of people in your family, if you wish

Regular household glue or paste, if you wish

Here's what you do:

1. Talk to people in your family, and look at the map. Find out where each of your parents, grandparents, sisters, and broth-ers were born. Look at the place where you were born and where your family has moved. Perhaps you can find where your ancestors lived and why they moved. You may discover that they emigrated from one country to another. You might want to collect extra information for your map, such as the origin of your family names.

2. Take paper and colored pens, markers, or pencils and draw all the important family locations onto your map. Be sure to note directions, with an arrow pointing north, and routes of family moves and trips.

3. Draw in pictures, perhaps of houses or people. Besides the pictures you draw, you may want to glue or paste on family photographs. You may find photos of yourself when you were a baby or of other people.

4. Put your map on display, or give it as a gift.

> **YOUR FAMILY WILL BE PROUD TO KNOW HOW CREATIVE YOU CAN BE.**

DESIGN A MAP YOU CAN WEAR

You can buy a tee-shirt with a decorated map on it. Or you can make your own.

You can copy a map that you particularly like—and then add your own creative decorations or pictures. You can begin with a map and pictures of a place where you like to go on vacation or of a place where you hope to travel some day. You can begin close to home with a school or hometown map. You can use your dream map or your family map.

If you're ambitious, you can even draw a picture of the world (or part of the world) as you would see it from outer space. This is a good project for a creative and artistic person.

Here's what you need:

A new plain white, blue, or black tee-shirt

A map or picture to copy, perhaps one you designed yourself

Scrap paper, pencil, pens, or markers, in colors you choose

A piece of cardboard

Sewing pins, if you wish

Squeezable tee-shirt or fabric paints, in colors you choose

A small wet sponge or cloth

Fluorescent, glitter, beaded, or puffy fabric paints, if you wish

Here's what you do:

1. Select a tee-shirt with the background color you like best. If you want to draw beautiful swirling white clouds as part of your picture, then you may wish

157
•

DESIGN A MAP YOU CAN WEAR

continued

to begin with a basic blue tee-shirt. If you want your map surrounded by a starry night, then select a black shirt. Or perhaps you want to begin with a white tee-shirt and add a variety of colors.

2. Wash the tee-shirt, but do not add fabric softener.

3. Select a map or picture you like. Perhaps you'll want to add decorations and pictures to the basic map. For example, if you outline a map of your town onto your tee-shirt, then you may want to add symbols and pictures to represent your home and your school.

4. Practice with scrap paper, pencil, and pens or markers of the colors you want for your tee-shirt. Carefully choose the sizes of the map and decorations you design. You don't want them too big or too little.

5. Stretch the tee-shirt out on a solid, flat surface. Put a piece of cardboard between the front and back of the shirt so the colors won't seep through. You may want to hold the shirt down with heavy books at each corner.

6. Follow your practice picture, and make pencil marks or put sewing pins in the places where you want the designs. Carefully mark the center and the edges. Before you begin, squeeze some of the paint onto a piece of scrap paper, so that you know the paint is going to flow freely.

7. When you're ready, draw the map and decorations on the shirt. As you work, hold the squeezable paint tubes very close to the surface of the tee-shirt. Keep a small wet sponge or cloth handy in case you want to wipe off a mistake. Then, if you wish, add fluorescent, glitter, beaded, or puffy fabric paints.

8. If you wish, write the name of your map in fancy lettering, and then finish the design with your own signature.

9. Let the shirt dry in place for at least 24 hours. Do not put it in an automatic dryer or out in the sun.

> NOW YOU'RE READY TO WEAR YOUR SHIRT. BUT WHAT DO YOU DO IF YOUR TEE-SHIRT IS JUST TOO NICE TO WEAR? GO ON TO SEE HOW TO MAKE IT INTO A PILLOW. THEN YOU'LL HAVE A MAP YOU CAN HUG.

. . . .

DESIGN A MAP YOU CAN HUG

. . . .

You can make your decorated tee-shirt—or any tee-shirt you like—into a pillow. Your pillow will look different from other pillows because of its peculiar tee-shirt shape.

Here's what you need:

A tee-shirt decorated with map and pictures

Sewing pins, needle and thread, and sewing scissors

Polyester fiber fill, pillow batting or foam, or clean, crumpled-up rag pieces

Here's what you do:

1. Make sure your tee-shirt is dry and clean. Then use sewing pins to pin together the ends of each sleeve and the edges of the collar. Use needle and thread to sew them shut. Get someone to show you how to use an over-hand stitch.

Caution: You need an adult to help you with sewing, especially if this is the first time you've tried it.

2. Stuff the shirt with polyester fiber fill, pillow batting or foam, or clean, crumpled-up rags. You can make the shirt just as fat as you want.

3. Pin together the bottom edges of the shirt, and sew them shut.

NOW YOU HAVE A FINE, FAT MAP PILLOW TO HUG—AND YOUR OWN FAVORITE PICTURE MAP TO DISPLAY ON YOUR BED.

MAP THE WHOLE WORLD

*Y*ou can make maps of the whole world, with all its curves and circles, its mountains and depths. This is not an easy job. You'll need to be creative. You can figure out how to make the world flat on a map, even though it's really a sphere. You can stack up your own mountain and figure out how to map it just as if it were real.

You can make an interesting map of one part of the world, a map you'll be proud to display.

Making a map is a good way to explore the world. You can even turn the world upside down or sideways—and get a whole different view of it.

. . . .

A FRIENDLY MAP STORY

. . . .

In the 1500s, the countries of Europe and Asia fell into one war after another. Sometimes two countries that were friends became enemies and went to war. Then countries that were enemies became friends and joined to fight yet other countries. It was difficult to keep track of what was happening where.

The merchants were particularly distressed. They wanted to bring in goods from foreign countries and then sell their own merchandise. They didn't want their import and export caravans to get caught in yet another outbreak of war.

The merchants needed up-to-date maps to tell them the safest, shortest, and most peaceful routes. They wanted maps that informed them of the latest military developments. Information on an outdated map could turn out to be fatally wrong. Plus, the merchants complained, the place-names on their old maps were hard to read, and the maps were always too big or too small.

A mapmaker of the time, Abraham Ortelius, knew he could provide just what the merchants needed. He got together about 30 maps. He had them printed in a convenient size, on only one side of the paper, and with the place-names sharply printed and readable. He sent scouts to find the latest information on wars and dangers on the import-export routes. Then Ortelius bound the maps together in a book.

That was the first atlas. The merchants were delighted. They wanted more and more of these books.

Ortelius went to his best friend for some help. Together, they went to work producing and printing these practical maps. People were eager to buy. The two friends could hardly print enough maps. The friends grew rich together.

· · · · · · · · · · ·

A FRIENDLY MAP STORY

continued

Who was this friend? He had two names. One name was his Flemish name, Gerhard Kremer. He had trouble in his Flemish homeland, though. Europe was plagued not only with wars, but with religious persecution. Kremer was a Christian Protestant, and at that time, the Christian Catholics were putting the Protestants in jail and even killing them. Kremer decided to leave for Germany, where he knew there were good people of his same religion. Soon, he was appointed as the royal mapmaker.

Now we know him by the Latin version of his name, Gerardus Mercator. Mercator lived from 1512 to 1594. After his business success with his friend Ortelius, he ran a fine map workshop. After he died, his son and grandson continued his workshop.

YOU HAVE PROBABLY SEEN A MAP OF THE SORT MERCATOR INVENTED. ON MERCATOR MAPS, SAILORS CAN FIND DIRECTIONS EASILY. THE WORLD LOOKS STRAIGHT AND EASY TO UNDERSTAND (EVEN THOUGH IT ISN'T). PEOPLE AROUND THE WORLD STILL LIKE MERCATOR MAPS. GO ON TO SEE THE PROBLEMS MERCATOR FACED AND THAT ALL OTHER MAPMAKERS FACE WHEN THEY ATTEMPT TO CREATE FLAT MAPS FROM A ROUND (BUT NOT PERFECTLY ROUND) EARTH. UNFORTUNATELY, YOU CAN ALWAYS FIND SOMETHING WRONG WITH A MAP, EVEN THE BEST AND MOST USEFUL.

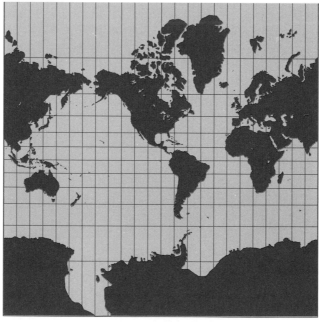

A Mercator World Map

. . . .
FIND OUT WHAT'S WRONG WITH YOUR MAP
. . . .

You can find something wrong with almost any map.

You can find ways the map is out of date because something about the world has changed. You can find distortions that no mapmaker can avoid entirely. You can find actual mistakes.

You may even find jokes. (Once in a while, you can catch a mapmaker writing something funny in very small print.)

Here's how to look for what's wrong with your map:

1. Look for distortions. Distortions are necessary. You can't make a flat map without distortions. But they do give the wrong impression. For example, look at your map and compare the size of Greenland with the size of South America. On a Mercator map, the island of Greenland looks almost as big as the whole continent of South America. Really, South America is about eight times larger than Greenland. (Look for Greenland at 74°N, 40°W.) Or look at Antartica. On a Mercator map, Antarctica looks like a huge land. Really, it's a small polar cap. On a globe of the world, you can see Antarctica in its real proportion.

2. Look at spellings. English-speaking mapmakers used to spell names the English way. Now mapmakers prefer to spell many names as the people in that place pronounce them. For example, look on your map for Beijing in China. An out-of-date map may spell it Peking. A good map may have both spellings. Look at Austria, and see if your map spells the main city as Vienna or Wien—or both. (Look for Beijing at 39°N, 120°E. Look for Wien at 48°N, 16°E.)

163
•

· · · · · · · · · · ·

FIND OUT WHAT'S WRONG WITH YOUR MAP
continued

3. Look for political changes. There are new countries in the world— and new names for old countries. These changes are a sign of political turmoil and sometimes war or civil war. As political changes go on over decades, you may even find an old name becoming new again. Through the years, the city of St. Petersburg in Russia became Petrograd and then Leningrad. Now it is once again St. Petersburg. (Look for St. Petersburg at 59°N, 30°E.)

4. Look for natural changes. Rivers and shorelines change constantly and sometimes over a fairly short amount of geological time. Look on your map at the city of Pisa in Italy. Once it was on the ocean. Now it is several miles inland. That change took hundreds of years. But only about 150 years ago (a short time as natural changes go), Henry David Thoreau wrote a book and drew maps of his walks around Cape Cod in Massachusetts. The coastline of Cape Cod changed so quickly that you couldn't walk along Thoreau's route now without going into deep ocean. (Look for Pisa at 43°N, 10°E. Look for Cape Cod at 41°N, 70°W.)

Here's how to rate whether your map is up to date:

These are old place names, with their latitude and longitude locations. See if you can find the new names on your map.

1. The Yangtze River, China (30°N, 117°E)

2. Canton, China (23°N, 113°E)

3. The Asian country of Tibet (32°N, 83°E)

4. The Asian country of Siam (16°N, 101°E)

5. The Asian country of Burma (21°N, 95°E)

6. North and South Vietnam (18°N, 107°E)

7. The country of the U.S.S.R. (particularly at 48°N, 59°E and at 49°N, 30°E.)

8. Kiev, Russia (50°N, 30°E)

9. Southern Rhodesia (17°S, 29°E)

10. A section of Ethiopia (16°N, 38°E)

11. The New Hebrides Islands, in the South Pacific (16°S, 169°E)

12. A part of the Gilbert Islands, in the South Pacific (5°S, 174°E)

13. British Honduras in Central America (17°N, 88°W)

14. West and East Germany in northern Europe (57°N, 8°E)

15. Czechoslovakia in Eastern Europe (49°N, 16°E)

16. Yugoslavia in Eastern Europe (44°N, 17°E)

· · · · · · · · · ·

FIND OUT WHAT'S WRONG WITH YOUR MAP

continued

You can find the new names on page 177.

- LOOK AT A DETAILED MAP OF YOUR OWN NEIGHBORHOOD, TOWN, OR SOME OTHER PLACE YOU KNOW WELL. SEE IF YOU CAN FIND A MISTAKE OR A PLACE WHERE THE MAP IS OUT OF DATE. FOR EXAMPLE, LOOK
- AT THE MAP WHERE YOU HAVE SEEN NEW HOUSES BUILT. YOUR MAP MAY NOT SHOW THE NEW STREETS. OR LOOK AT SCHOOLS. YOUR MAP MAY NOT SHOW RECENT SCHOOL CLOSINGS OR NEW SCHOOL BUILDINGS.

· · · · · · · · · · ·

MAKE A FLAT MAP OF A GLOBAL WORLD

· ·

Mapmakers around the world always face the same problem. How can they make a flat map of a round world? For centuries, mapmakers have pondered how to make the world flat without making much of it appear larger or smaller than it really is. Some mapmakers have come up with innovative ideas to get around the problem.

You could discover the problem for yourself just by peeling an orange. How do you get the orange segments to lie flat? Or try wrapping a globe with paper or foil, as if it were a fine present. Now what do you do to get the paper to lie in flat, regular shapes? You need to make a flat map that makes sense.

The most famous of mapmakers, Gerardus Mercator, created one way of flattening the world. He invented a rectangular map with latitude and longitude laid out in a grid. This method is called the cylindrical projection. Imagine the globe surrounded by a tube or cylinder. The mapmaker projects the shapes of land and ocean onto the cylinder. It's a good sort of map for navigation. You can use it to find clear directions. Unfortunately, no map is perfect, and the Mercator sort of map shows serious distortions. Near the poles, land masses appear much larger than they actually are.

So mapmakers tried other ways of mapping the round earth onto flat paper. For example, they tried placing a cone over the globe so that it contacts the globe on one line of latitude. These conic projection maps look at the world from either the North or the South Pole.

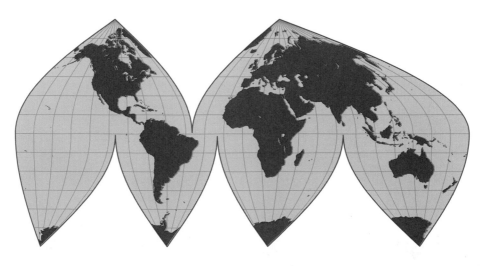

A Sinusoidal World Map

. . . .

MAKE A FLAT MAP OF A GLOBAL WORLD

continued

Then mapmakers tried another way. Imagine using a flat sheet to touch the globe at one point. That point becomes the center of the map. This is an azimuthal projection. This sort of map usually focuses on a specific land area.

Mapmakers also have tried dividing the world like the peelings of an orange. This is called sinusoidal projection. Then the mapmaker fills in the gaps between the sections. The map looks somewhat like a cylindrical projection. The advantage is that the sinusoidal projection cuts up the globe in a way that preserves the shapes and sizes of land and ocean.

You can make your own sinusoidal projection map from a globe. It will be a little like the orange peel method, except that you can use a modern material, clear flexible plastic.

Here's what you need:

A globe of the world

A measuring tape or a piece of flat ribbon

Scissors

A piece of clear, flexible plastic material long enough to go around the Equator plus 1 or 2 inches (3–5 centimeters) and wide enough to follow the curve to each pole. (You can find clear or slightly frosted plastic by the foot or meter at a hardware store. The best type is the sort used to protect things from rain or painting drips. For a small globe, use heavy-duty plastic food wrap.)

An indelible pen with a fine point

Removable tape

Here's what you do:

1. Measure the circumference of the globe at the Equator. Use a tape measure or a piece of flat ribbon.

2. Measure the distance on your globe from the North or South Pole to the Equator. Double that distance.

3. Use scissors to cut the plastic so that you have a rectangle the length of the Equator plus about 2 inches (about 5 centimeters) and the width of double the distance from the Equator to one of the poles.

4. Bring the two polar edges of the plastic sheet together. Use the fine-pointed indelible pen to draw a line along the fold. That line represents the Equator.

5. Remove the globe from its base.

  : ***Caution: Unless your globe is***
  : ***quite small, you will probably***
  : ***need adult help with this and***
  : ***the next few steps.***

167
•

. . . .

MAKE A FLAT MAP OF A GLOBAL WORLD
continued

6. Pull the plastic firmly around the globe so that the equatorial line on the plastic is over the Equator on the globe. Use the removable tape to tape the overlap at the Equator. *Hint:* Make your overlap in the middle of the Pacific Ocean so you won't split up a large land area.

7. As someone holds the plastic in place at the Equator, make overlapping pleats in the plastic at the poles. Make the surface as smooth as possible. Attach each pleat with removable tape.

8. Use the indelible pen to outline the continents and islands. Pay attention as you do. This is a good chance to observe where countries, islands, seas, and major rivers are located. You can outline individual countries and label them if you wish.

9. When you have finished, carefully remove your map from the globe. You can open all of the pleats by cutting through or removing the tape so these the map lies flat. *Hint:* If you have drawn across a piece of tape, cut through it rather than removing it.

10. If you wish, you can use scissors to cut out empty wedges from between the land masses of the South Pole and those in the Northern Hemisphere such as Asia and North America. You will begin to see how mapmakers make curved surfaces into flat maps.

11. If you wish, you can enlarge the land areas that are farther from the Equator to make the type of map created by a cylindrical projection. Where you see gaps, extend the boundaries until the lines meet.

> NOW YOU CAN SYMPATHIZE WITH THE PROBLEMS OF MAPMAKERS. YOU CAN SEE WHY THE FAR NORTHERN AND FAR SOUTHERN AREAS OF MOST FLAT MAPS APPEAR DISTORTED. PLACES LIKE GREENLAND, FOR INSTANCE, LOOK HUGE EVEN THOUGH YOU KNOW THEY ARE SMALL COMPARED TO THE REALLY LARGE LAND MASSES LIKE AFRICA AND ASIA.

. . . .

EXPLORE UPSIDE-DOWN AND ALL AROUND

. . . .

When you look at a map, you expect to see north at the top. When you travel south, you say you're going down, especially if you go to Australia, down under. None of that is real. The planet Earth is traveling through space with no ups or downs.

Mapmakers have not always made maps with north on top. The early Christian and Jewish maps show the holy city of Jerusalem on top. For many of them, that meant, essentially, that east was up. You won't be surprised to hear that the ancient Chinese drew maps with China in the middle. Any other land was off at the edge and hardly seemed to matter.

Try a map where up is down and down is up—and everything is sideways. You'll find the world looks odd. You can buy a map of the world where north is down and south is up, but it's more fun to create your own.

Here's what you need:

A placemat map of your country or of the world (Look on page 24 to see how to make your own.)

Markers or crayons, in colors you choose

Paper and pencil, if you wish

A damp sponge or paper towel

Here's how to color the world upside-down and sideways:

1. Turn your placemat map upside down. On a map of your country, mark your home place plus four major cities. On a map of the world, color in your own country plus three other countries. Look for cities or countries that you can locate easily when you're not looking at an upside-down map.

You may find their location a bit of a puzzle now that they're upside-down.

2. Turn your placemat map sideways. Make the Equator run up and down. Put east on top, and west on the bottom. Now try marking or coloring in four more cities and countries.

3. On a piece of paper, you may want to create a real puzzle for yourself. Try sketching the outline of your country, state, or province—upside-down or sideways. Sketch in pencil so you can erase and try again, if you wish.

4. When you're finished, use a damp sponge or paper towel to wipe off the marks on your placemat map. You'll want to use it again for other puzzles.

. . . .

EXPLORE UPSIDE-DOWN AND ALL AROUND

continued

YOU'LL GET A DIFFERENT VIEW OF THE WORLD AND A DIFFERENT IDEA OF SHAPES. YOU'LL GET A DIFFERENT IDEA OF HOW BIG THE LANDS ARE. YOU MAY EVEN GET A DIFFERENT IDEA OF WHAT'S IMPORTANT. IF YOU HAVE A GLOBE THAT YOU CAN REMOVE FROM ITS BASE, TRY TURNING IT UPSIDE-DOWN SOME DAY. THAT MAKES JUST AS MUCH SENSE, IF YOU THINK OF HOW THE WORLD LOOKS FROM OUTER SPACE.

. . . .
STACK UP A MAP
. . . .

Sometimes you need a map that shows you all about the mountains, hills, canyons, and slopes of the land. The term for that sort of map is topographic. After all, we don't live in a flat world.

Here's how to make your own mountain and your own mountain map. You'll need a good outside place, a yard, garden, or park where you can do some digging.

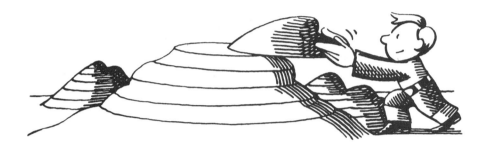

Here's what you need:

A flat place in the yard or garden, or else a heavy cardboard or plywood base, 16 × 20 inches (40 × 50 centimeters)

Enough dirt to build a hill on the base

A trowel or small shovel

A ruler

A small watering can or bottle full of water

16 slender twigs or sticks, each about ¾ inch (2 centimeters) long

4 pieces of string, each about 24 inches (60 centimeters) long

Pencil and paper

Markers or pens, in colors such as light yellow, light brown, brown, and dark brown

Here's what you do:

1. Choose a base for your hill. Use a trowel or small shovel to pile up dirt on the base. Do not shape or smooth your hill. You want it to look lumpy, like a real hill.

2. Stand your ruler on end, and keep piling on dirt until you have a pile about 9 inches (23 centimeters) above the base.

3. Use your watering can or bottle of water to moisten your hill. Pat down the sides until they're firm.

4. Stand your ruler on end again, and find the point at which your hill is 2 inches (5 centimeters) tall. Take four twigs and carefully stick a twig in halfway at each 2 inch (5 centimeter) point, all the way around the hill. Do the same with twigs at 4, 6, and 8 inches (10, 15, and 20 centimeters).

STACK UP A MAP

continued

5. Loop one piece of string around the hill at the 2 inch (or 5 centimeter) height. Lay it down over the twig ends for support. Then carefully pull it snug against the dirt at that level. Do exactly the same at each of the other levels.

6. Now look straight down on what you've got. You've begun a topographic sample shape with the strings. They follow the exact shape of the hill at regular, 2 inch (or 5 centimeter) increases in height above the base. If any two of them look far apart as you look at them from above, you'll find that they're showing a gentle slope on that part of the hill. If others look close together, they'll be on the steeper parts. The smallest one locates the top of the hill.

7. Use paper and pencil to draw a map of your hill. Outline the slopes as you look down on the hill. Then, color each contour level. You may want to begin with light yellow at the base of the hill, then go on to light brown, brown, and on to dark brown at the top of the hill. Be sure to put a legend in a corner of your map to tell what the colors mean.

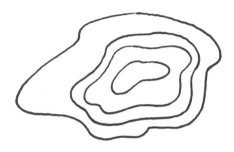

YOUR STRINGS TELL YOU JUST WHAT YOU NEED TO KNOW TO MAP THE HILL: HOW HIGH IT IS, HOW FAR AROUND, WHERE THE TOP IS, WHERE THE STEEPER PARTS ARE, AND HOW THE SLOPES ARE CONTOURED. THE COLORS HELP A PERSON TO SEE AT A GLANCE JUST HOW TO READ YOUR MAP.

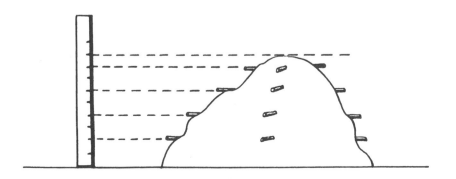

MAKE YOUR OWN THREE-DIMENSIONAL RELIEF MAP

You can build and paint a real, three-dimensional relief map. A relief map shows mountains and valleys, rivers and streams, roads and trails, and sometimes even buildings. It's as if you were seeing everything from an airplane.

You'll need access to a photocopy machine and a work table.

Here's what you need:

A detailed topographical map of the area you want to model. (You can buy a quadrangle map from a map store or bookstore, or you can order one from the United States Geological Survey, Denver, CO 80225 or Reston, VA 22092. If you're not sure what area you want to map, you can order a free brochure that describes the maps. Any area of the United States is available, and some other countries have quadrangle maps, too.)

A piece of cardboard or foam board to use as a base

Felt-tipped pens with fine points

Several wooden sticks such as chopsticks or tongue depressors

Ordinary household glue

A box of plaster of Paris

An old cup

Water

A spoon

A flat knife or small putty knife

A small damp rag

A metal tool you can use for shaping, such as a barbecue skewer, lobster pick, or a tool for modeling clay

Paints in green, blue, and brown, with brushes

Here's what you do:

1. Decide on the area of the quadrangle that you want to model. Choose one that has hills, but try to avoid too many confusing contours for your first map. Fold the map so that the area you plan to use is fully visible.

2. Here are some hints. A quadrangle map is marked off in $1\frac{5}{8} \times 1\frac{5}{8}$ inch squares (about 4×4 centimeters). Each square represents a land area about 0.6 miles (nearly 1 kilometer) across. For your first map, choose an area containing only four squares.

MAKE YOUR OWN
THREE-DIMENSIONAL RELIEF MAP

continued

3. Take the map to a copy store, and have the map photocopied and enlarged. Whatever type of contour map you use, enlarge it first. Have two copies made. Use one to build on and one to look at as you build and cover the contour lines.

4. Be sure to enlarge the map's scale at the same time that you enlarge the map. Then you will have no figuring to do.

5. Choose a piece of cardboard or foam board for the map's base. It should be a little larger than the map.

6. Look at the map carefully to see where the contours go and what level they are. Look at the map legend. The U.S. Geological Survey Maps have contours marked for every 20 feet (6 meters) rise. Each 100-foot (30-meters) contour line is dark tan and is specially marked. The 20-foot (6-meters) contours are light tan and lightly marked.

7. Make a guide to measure the heights as you build your hills or mountains. Carefully mark lines around a wooden stick at each of the 200-foot (60-meters) levels up to the highest level on your map.

8. Glue one map copy onto your base.

9. Start with about ½ cup of plaster of Paris in an old cup. Use a spoon to mix in enough water so that the mixture mounds when dropped from the spoon—just like a cooked pudding. Cover the cup with a damp rag whenever you are interrupted. Work quickly because plaster will set and become solid within a short time. You will need to mix more as you build.

• • • • • • • • • •

MAKE YOUR OWN
THREE-DIMENSIONAL RELIEF MAP

continued

10. Start heaping the plaster on the lowest contours of the highest mountains or hills first. Notice how the contours move up. Check with your wooden gauge to be sure you have the first layer at the right height. Use the metal shaping tool and another wooden stick to curve and form the contours. The contours usually move smoothly from one to another unless you see the contour lines very close together. That indicates a steep slope or even a cliff.

11. As you build, check the second map copy to be sure you are going along correctly. Use the wooden gauge to get the right height for each contour. The plaster will form natural-looking hills as you plop it on the map base. If you make a mistake, use the putty knife to level off the plaster and rebuild. Let the plaster harden when you are satisfied with a hill.

12. Continue to build the lowest contours first, adding to the tops of the hills as you go. Compare with the copy of the map. Wash your hands as you finish each section.

13. When you have finished all the hills, use the putty knife to put a thin coat of plaster on the flat areas.

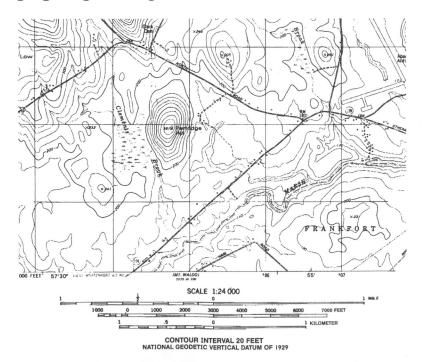

SCALE 1:24 000

CONTOUR INTERVAL 20 FEET
NATIONAL GEODETIC VERTICAL DATUM OF 1929

· · · · · · · · · · ·

MAKE YOUR OWN
THREE-DIMENSIONAL RELIEF MAP
continued

14. Clean up your plastering supplies and wash your hands.

15. Decide what kind of art you want to paint onto your model. Use paints and felt-tipped pens to color your relief map and draw in the streams, houses, woods, and fields. Use blue for the streams, brown for dry areas, green for fields, darker green dapples to show trees, black for highways, brown for dirt roads and trails, and marsh symbols for wetlands.

NOW YOU CAN SHOW OFF YOUR BEAUTIFUL RELIEF MAP. YOU CAN DISPLAY IT, OR USE IT AS A SCHOOL PROJECT. THERE'S ALSO ROOM IN THE FRAME FOR A TITLE AND YOUR SIGNATURE AS THE MAPMAKER.

. . . .

SOLUTIONS

. . . .

Find Out What's Wrong with Your Map; page 163.

1. The modern spelling for the Yangtze River is now Chang Jiang, which is closer to Chinese pronunciation.

2. The modern spelling for Canton is now Guangzhou.

3. The modern spelling for Tibet is now Xizang, although many people still call it Tibet. Tibet is now a province of China.

4. Siam is now Thailand.

5. Burma is now Myanmar, although many people with strong political views still call it Burma.

6. North and South Vietnam are now one country, Vietnam.

7. The U.S.S.R. is now Russia, plus 16 other countries, including Belarus and Kazakhstan.

8. The modern spelling for Kiev is Kyyiv.

9. Southern Rhodesia is now Zimbabwe.

10. Eritrea is a new country.

11. The New Hebrides are now Vanuatu, 80 islands joined as one nation.

12. A part of the Gilbert Islands is now Tuvalu.

13. British Honduras is now Belize.

14. West and East Germany are now one country, Germany.

15. Czechoslovakia is now two countries, the Czech Republic and Slovakia.

16. Yugoslavia is now six countries: Slovenia (45°N, 14°E), Macedonia (41°N, 22°E), Bosnia (44°N, 16°E), Croatia (45°N, 15°E), Kosovo (45°N, 16°E), and Serbia (44°N, 20°E).

Play Games with Strange and Funny Maps

Perhaps you can find some out-of-date maps, maps that you can cut apart however you want. You can use them to make a map cartoon or a Valentine card.

You can make a giant map of your town, or you can figure out how to gerrymander. Perhaps you can even hold a contest for the most artistic, strangest, and funniest maps of all.

CARTOON THE WORLD

Glance around at a globe or a flat map of the world, and you'll see several countries whose borders make strange shapes.

For instance, look at Spain and Portugal together. (Find them at 40°N, 4°W and 40°N, 8°W.) On a flat map, you could imagine the two countries as forming the head of a bearded man who's looking out into the Atlantic Ocean.

Or look at the United States. It could be a giant, running creature, with Maine for its head, Florida for a front paw, and Hawaii for a tail. (Look for Maine at 45°N, 70°W; Florida at 27°N, 81°W; Hawaii at 21°N, 158°W.)

You can create cartoons of shapes all over the world.

Here's what you need:

A globe and an atlas with maps of countries and continents (so you can get different views of the same lands)

Tracing paper or else an old map you can cut out

Pencil

Scissors

Household glue or paste

Construction paper

Markers or pens, in colors you choose

· · · · · · · · · · ·

CARTOON THE WORLD

continued

Here's what you do:

1. Decide on a country or continent that is good for a cartoon. Here are some you might want to try: Somalia (10°N, 50°E), Indonesia (2°S, 120°E), New Zealand (42°S, 174°E), Chile (34°S, 71°W), Great Britain (52°N, 0°). You can find good shapes all over your globe and maps. Look for countries with the irregular, natural borders that seacoasts and rivers make. Be sure to look at both the globe and the flat maps. The different projections and scales on various maps may show you a shape you didn't see at first.

2. If you have an old map, use scissors to cut out the shape. Or else use a pencil to trace the shape onto a piece of tracing paper and then cut that out.

3. Use household glue or school paste to mount the map shape onto construction paper. Carefully smooth out the map or tracing paper with your hands. Now you have a good basic shape.

4. Use colored markers or pens to make the shape into a cartoon. Add heads and tails. Add eyes, mouth, nose, and ears. Add weird animals, birds, or trees.

THIS IS YOUR CHANCE TO BE CREATIVE. YOU CAN TURN ORDINARY MAPS INTO STRANGE AND FUNNY SHAPES ALL OVER THE WORLD. THE EARLY MAPMAKERS DID THAT. THEY OFTEN HAD NO REAL INFORMATION ABOUT THE ACTUAL SHAPES OF LANDS SO THEY USED THEIR IMAGINATIONS TO MAKE INTERESTING AND ARTISTIC SHAPES.

GERRYMANDER YOUR CLASSROOM

Gerrymander is a strange word. It means changing the map of a voting area to increase the chances for one political party to win. The new map has twists and turns, zigs and zags, so that one political party gets an unfair advantage. The first gerrymander was in northeastern Massachusetts. It was 1812, and the governor in charge was Elbridge Gerry. People thought the new, unfair shape looked like a salamander, so they blended the word *Gerry* and the word *salamander* to make a new word, *gerrymander*.

Pretend that a weird but important election—for Official Wizard—is coming up in your classroom.

There are two candidates, you and one other person. Usually, in an election, each student has one vote. But this election is different. In this election, each district has one vote. Your classroom is divided into three districts. You want to win by a vote of two to one.

You decide to win the Official Wizard title by some gerrymandering.

· · · · · · · · · · ·

GERRYMANDER YOUR CLASSROOM

continued

Here's what you do:

1. Before you think about your own real classroom, try drawing a map of an imaginary classroom, with 21 students in it, seated something like this:

5	13	14	1	7	8
19	12	15	2	11	9
18	4	16	17	3	10
21	20	6			

2. Divide the imaginary classroom into three voting districts. These districts can be any size or shape, but they all must connect in some way. They can contain any number of students. You just want to make sure that two of the three districts will have enough votes for you to win.

Here's an imaginary poll of the 21 students. You can use it to see how to divide the three districts in the imaginary classroom:

- You are student #1, and you will vote for yourself.
- Students #2, #3, #4, #5, and #6 will vote for you because they're your best friends.
- Students #7, #8, #9, #10, and #11 will vote for the other candidate.
- Students #12 and #13 are very likely to vote for you, and they wouldn't mind being Assistant Wizard.
- Students #14, #15, #16, #17, #18, #19, #20, and #21 are all undecided. Three of them are interested in becoming Assistant Wizard. None of them really cares which candidate wins.

. . . .

GERRYMANDER YOUR CLASSROOM

continued

3. Try out some shapes and sizes for the three voting districts in the imaginary classroom to make sure you win. *Hints:* Use an pencil with an eraser, and try putting a special color or symbol beside each type of voter.

Here's a gerrymander strategy to help:

- Arrange the division of the voting district so that students #7, #8, #9, #10, and #11 (the ones who are not going to vote for you) are isolated. Make sure they're in districts where your supporters are in the majority.

- Also surround students #14 through #21 (the ones who are undecided) with your supporters. Make sure that however they decide, you'll still probably win.

  Perhaps you can think of several ways to gerrymander the classroom. Look on the diagrams for two possibilities.

MAYBE YOU STILL WON'T WIN THE ELECTION, BUT THE ODDS WILL BE STRONGLY IN YOUR FAVOR. YOU'LL AT LEAST BE THE OFFICIAL GERRYMANDERER. NOW THINK ABOUT WHAT WOULD HAPPEN IN YOUR REAL CLASSROOM OR YOUR REAL VOTING DISTRICT.

. . . .

CHALK A GIANT MAP

. . . .

What if you could make a map so big you'll never forget it? What if you and your friends could walk around on this map?

This is a good project for a school class or a group of friends.

Most people have just a general idea of the shape of their own town or city. They'll know which other towns or sections border it, but probably won't know the location of the border, the lengths, or directions. The easy way is to look at a detailed map. The fun way is to expand that map off the paper and onto a parking lot or playground.

You'll need permission to make a huge chalk drawing about 15 feet (4.5 meters) wide on a flat paved area, such as your school parking lot. The paved area for your map should be close enough that you can see it clearly from a second-floor window. You must be sure that the paved area is safe and away from traffic for the time you need to make the map.

Caution: Have an adult check on the safety.

If your school doesn't have a paved lot or high windows, you may be able to use the floor of a gym or activity room.

CHALK A GIANT MAP

continued

Here's what you need:

A pencil

A ruler

A photocopy of your town or city map, 8 ½ × 11 inches (about 22 × 28 centimeters). (Some maps are colored so that map details can't be photocopied, but you can still photocopy the basic outline, and that's all you need. Most copier machines allow you to adjust the size of the copy.)

A directional compass

Pavement chalk in white and other colors for an outdoor map or masking tape for an indoor map

Two rulers or yardsticks

Here's what you do:

1. Use a pencil and ruler to draw a grid on your map. Each square should be 1 inch (2.5 centimeters) on each side. Look at the diagram to see how to draw the lines. Now you're ready to begin work on the big map.

2. Go outside or to the floor surface you're going to use. Use a directional compass to find north. Use chalk or masking tape to mark an arrow pointing north.

3. From the same spot, use your directional compass to find east. Use chalk or masking tape to mark an arrow pointing east.

4. Still from the same spot, have your two friends pace off 10 feet (about 3 meters), one going north and one east. Use the compass to check that they're standing at exactly north and east from your spot.

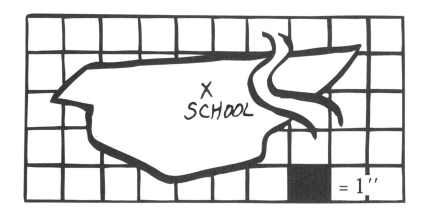

. . . .

CHALK A GIANT MAP

continued

5. Give your friends white chalk or masking tape and have them start marking lines back toward you. Use the compass to keep them on course.

6. Use rulers or yardsticks to mark off each foot (0.3 meter or 30 centimeters) along each line. Now you're ready to remake the grid on your paper map into a giant grid. The giant grid will have the same number of squares, but each square will be 1 foot (0.3 meter or 30 centimeters) instead of 1 inch (2.5 centimeters) square.

7. Pick a corner square on the paper map and locate the same square on the big grid. Draw the town border line from the small square onto the big square. Do

the same, one by one, with each square. Check the direction north with each square, so that you accidentally don't draw your map upside-down or sideways.

8. If the paper map has enough detail on it to show where your school and other landmarks are, you can chalk them down in color. If you're making an inside map, draw the landmarks on paper and tape them down.

> : NOW YOU HAVE A GIANT
> : VERSION OF THE TOWN MAP,
> : READY TO COLOR IN HOWEVER
> : YOU WANT. GO ON TO SEE
> : HOW YOU CAN MAKE A GIANT
> : MAP FOR YOUR SCHOOL ROOM.

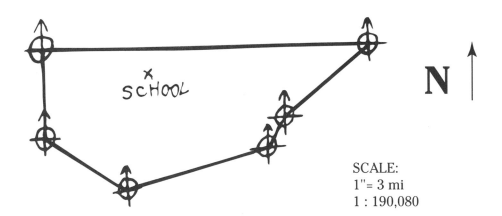

SCHOOL

N ↑

SCALE:
1"= 3 mi
1 : 190,080

TAKE YOUR TOWN TO SCHOOL

If you drew the grid for a giant map, you already have the basic guidelines you need to make a poster-size version of your town or city map. This is good for a school project or for a bulletin board at home.

Here's what you need:

A ruler

A pencil with an eraser

Posterboard, 14 × 22 inches (35 × 55 centimeters)

The town map with the grid drawn on it from Chalk a Giant Map, page 00

Coloring markers or pens

Here's what you do:

1. Use the ruler and pencil to cover your posterboard with very light lines to make boxes 2 inches (5 centimeters) square.

2. Use the grid on your original town map as the model. Locate all the corner points along the borders of your town in the correct 2-inch (5-centimeter) boxes. Do the same for any landmarks you want to show.

3. Erase the pencil lines. Use coloring markers or pens to color in the major features of your town.

ALONG THE BORDERS OF THE MAPS, YOU MAY WANT TO WRITE IN FACTS ABOUT YOUR TOWN: WHAT IS YOUR TOWN'S POPULATION? WHAT IS ITS EXACT LATITUDE AND LONGITUDE? WHAT IS ITS HEIGHT (OR ALTITUDE) ABOVE SEA LEVEL? HOW OLD IS THE TOWN? WHO WERE THE ORIGINAL SETTLERS? WHO ARE ITS FAMOUS CITIZENS?

. . . .

MAKE A MAP VALENTINE

. . . .

You can go back to a very old idea about maps. The idea is to use maps to do something creative for someone you love—and to show something about the world.

Back in the 1500s, a popular map showed the world as heart-shaped. You were supposed to give the map to show that someone you love means the world to you.

Another funny map from the 1500s showed the world shaped as a dunce or a fool. The idea was that the world is foolish—and also that the world is within one foolish human being.

Here's what you need:

A pencil

An old map that you can cut out

Scissors

Red construction paper

Household glue or school paste

A lace paper doily

A small hand stapler, if you want

A red or black marker or pen

Here's what you do:

1. Use a pencil to design a heart shape onto an old map. Then use scissors to cut the map into a heart shape.

2. On red construction paper, design a heart shape that is somewhat larger than the map heart.

3. Use glue or paste to attach the map heart to the red paper heart.

4. Glue or paste the two hearts onto a lace paper doily. (To make sure the doily is secure, you may want to use a small hand stapler to staple it on each side of the construction paper heart.)

5. Use a red or black marker or pen to write greetings to your Valentine right across the map heart.

PERHAPS YOU CAN THINK OF OTHER CUT-OUT SHAPES FOR MAPS. YOU COULD CUT OUT A RELIGIOUS SYMBOL SUCH AS A STAR OF DAVID. YOU COULD MAKE A HOLIDAY SHAPE SUCH AS A CHRISTMAS TREE. YOU'RE USING A MAP TO SHOW WHAT IS IMPORTANT TO YOU IN THE WORLD.

SOLVE OCEAN, SEA, AND ALL SORTS OF WATER MYSTERIES

*H*ere is your chance to try to count the oceans and seas and to find underground water. You can make a device that cleans water or that finds invisible water. You can figure out how to make an underwater map. You can make your own small Sargasso Sea. You can add a new map to your map collection, the ugliest map of all.

· · · · · · · · · · ·
TURN THE WHOLE WORLD AROUND
· ·

Here's how to create a surprising and maybe even an ugly map.

Use a placemat or layered map of the world, and turn everything around. (To see how to make your own, look on pages 24 and 26.) Look at the ocean instead of just the land. Then try coloring all the land a flat blue—and use brown and yellow to detail the ocean floors.

Sometimes, when you look at a globe or a world map, you see the vast expanse of ocean as flat blue. You don't see what's below the surface, and perhaps you don't get a good idea of how important and how really huge the oceans are.

But there is plenty to map down there. Huge volcanic formations form mid ocean ridges under the oceans. Deep trenches lie just off the coasts. Volcanoes create and destroy islands, constantly.

Here's what you need:

An atlas of the world and its oceans

A pencil

A layered map of the world or a placemat world map, with a plastic overlay sheet

Markers in yellow, light and dark brown, and blue

Here's what you do:

1. Look at the atlas to see the ocean ridges, mountains, volcanoes, and trenches.

2. Use a pencil to sketch the most interesting parts of the ocean on a plastic overlay for your lay-ered or placemat map of the world.

3. Color the oceans: yellow for deep trenches, light brown for lower slopes, dark brown for mountain peaks.

4. Then color all land a solid, flat blue.

> YOU'VE TURNED THE WHOLE WORLD AROUND, YET YOU'VE JUST CREATED A MAP THAT IS AS TRUE AND IMPORTANT AS ORDINARY MAPS. THIS MAP COULD BE THE MOST SURPRISING ONE IN YOUR COLLECTION.

. . . .

DRILL DOWN FOR A MAP

. . . .

How do mapmakers map something they can't see, like the bottom of a lake? Lakes, seas, and oceans are full of mountains, slopes, hills, and valleys, just as the land is. Knowing where they are is important. You know that if you've been swimming at a lake. You want to know where the steep slopes and dropoffs are.

Here's how to go about mapping your own lake.

Here's what you need:

Cellophane tape

Graph paper

A cardboard shoe box with a top

A ballpoint pen

Enough toy blocks or other small objects to fill about half the box

A ruler

A new, unsharpened pencil

Here's what you do:

1. Use a ballpoint pen to mark rows of points on the lid of the shoe box, each 1 inch (2.5 centimeters) apart, so it looks like this:

2. Use cellophane tape to tape the graph paper securely to the outside lid of the shoe box.

3. Use the pen to punch holes through each point on the lid. The holes need to be big enough to allow the pencil to slide through.

4. Wrap the whole pencil with a layer of tape running lengthwise. Use the pen to mark on the tape, and put a line across the pencil every ½ inch (1.3 centimeters). Mark the bottom line with an A, the next line up with a B, and so on all the way up the pencil.

5. Put layers of blocks down into the open box. Make some layers higher than others. You're making the lake bottom.

6. Tape the lid onto the box. Carefully slide the pencil down through each hole you've punched. Note how deep the pencil goes before it contacts one of the blocks. The A, B, C marks on the pencil side will show you that.

· · · · · · · · · · ·

DRILL DOWN FOR A MAP

continued

7. With the pen, write the letter down on the graph paper right next to its hole. Do this for every hole.

8. Remove the lid from your shoe-box lake, and separate it from the graph paper.

9. What you have is a set of depth points. Use your pen to circle the same depth points together, something like this:

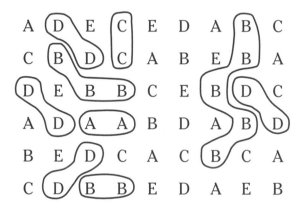

Don't let any of the contour lines cross one another. Remember that you have graphed a reverse hill, and only points at the same depth (the same letters on the graph paper) could make a possible contour under the lake. Your contour points also need to be close together, since just one depth point by itself could mean a rock sticking up or a hole in the lake.

: COMPARE THE LINES YOU DREW
: TO THE BLOCK SURFACES DOWN
: IN THE BOX. YOU CAN'T
: CAPTURE EVERY FEATURE BY
: USING DEPTH POINTS, BUT YOU
: DO GET MANY RIGHT. TO BE A
: REAL UNDERWATER MAPMAKER,
: YOU NEED A BOAT AND LONG
: ROPE. THEN YOU FIND DEPTH
: POINTS UNDERWATER BY
: LOWERING A LONG ROPE WITH
: MARKINGS ON IT EVERY 1 FOOT,
: 1 YARD, OR 1 METER.

· · · · · · · · · · ·
STIR THE SARGASSO PUDDLE

· ·

Wait for an afternoon when a heavy rain has left behind some deep puddles near your home. You need a puddle that's going to last at least 20 minutes, so that you can use it to experiment with currents.

The main experiment has you making your own personal version of the Sargasso Sea. That's a real section of the North Atlantic, located inside the North Atlantic Gyre. (That's another name for whirlpool, the giant circle of ocean currents. The North Atlantic Gyre rotates clockwise, and the South Atlantic counterclockwise.) The circling currents there create a calm surface. That calm part of the ocean tends to trap and hold floating vegetation, sometimes building it up into masses as big as islands.

It's called the Sargasso because the vegetation is sargassum, or gulfweed. Perhaps you can think of a good name for yours.

Here's what you need:

A deep puddle about 3 feet (1 meter) across. (Locate one that's formed in some dirt, not on top of pavement)

Some grass nearby that you can pull up to use as sargassum

A stick for stirring

Here's what you do:

1. Pull up two or three handfuls of grass blades. (Make sure that you have permission. You may want to get them from a woods or rough area rather than from a nice lawn.) Shake off the mud and dirt so that you have just grass blades.

193
·

STIR THE SARGASSO PUDDLE

continued

2. Scatter some of the grass blades gently near the middle of the puddle. Use the stick to stir the puddle very slowly, about 6 inches (15 centimeters) inside its edges and always in the same direction.

The grass will start to collect toward the center, and if you add more blades as you go, you can clearly see what happens to each of them as the currents work on them. It's the same process that works on a giant scale in the North Atlantic.

THE OTHER EXPERIMENT YOU MIGHT WANT TO TRY IS EVEN SIMPLER. GET SOME THIN, SHORT TWIGS THAT WILL FLOAT AND PILE THEM UP NEXT TO THE PUDDLE. THEN USE YOUR STICK TO CUT A SMALL OPENING AT THE DOWNHILL END OF THE PUDDLE. AS THE WATER STARTS TO DRAIN THROUGH THAT OPENING, A STEADY CURRENT WILL BUILD UP. TRY TO FLOAT A TWIG ACROSS THE DIRECTION OF THE CURRENT AND SEE WHAT HAPPENS.

· · · · · · · · · ·

MAP THE WATER UNDERGROUND

· ·

Aquifers are huge pools of underground water, mixed with gravel and rock, lying about ½ mile (0.8 kilometer) down. There is 30 times more water in them than in all the world's fresh water lakes and rivers. People often depend on aquifers for safe, clean drinking water.

Underground, here's how they look:

The water fills openings in rock and gravel—and spreads across underground areas so big that you may be surprised to see what happens if you draw them onto a surface map. Try it using the United States. What you'll get is a really unusual, *underground* map of the two biggest aquifers.

This is a good use for a layered or placemat map.

Here's what you need:

Cellophane tape, if you are using a placemat map

Tracing paper

A placemat map of the United States (To make your own, look on page 24.)

A printed map of the United States, with cities, states, and latitude and longitude marked on it

A pencil

A straightedge or ruler

. . . .
MAP THE WATER UNDERGROUND
continued

A clear plastic overlay or laminating sheet the same size as your placemat map

A blue marker

Here's what you do:

1. Use cellophane tape to tape tracing paper over your place-mat map. Or use the first layer of a layered map.

2. Use a printed map of the United States to find points for the first aquifer. Mark each location in pencil as small numbers on the tracing paper.

  (1) Newark, New Jersey (41°N, 74°W)

  (2) Washington, D.C. (39°N, 77°W)

  (3) Raleigh, North Carolina (36°N, 77°W)

  (4) Birmingham, Alabama (33°N, 87°W)

  (5) St. Louis, Missouri (38°N, 90°W)

  (6) Dallas, Texas (33°N, 97°W)

  (7) Corpus Christi, Texas (28°N, 97°W)

  (8) New Orleans, Louisiana (30°N, 90°W)

  (9) Charleston, South Carolina (33°N, 80°W)

  (10) Atlantic City, New Jersey (39°N, 74°W)

3. Use a straightedge or ruler to draw a pencil line connecting the numbers in order. Put in some curves where you want to show that the aquifer has natural, nonstraight edges. From Charleston to Atlantic City, use the Atlantic seacoast as the aquifer's border.

4. For the second aquifer, locate these points and mark them as small letters on the tracing paper:

  a. 42°N, 100°W

  b. 38°N, 105°W

  c. 35°N, 105°W

  d. 31°N, 103°W

  e. 36°N, 98°W

  f. 41°N, 96°W

5. Connect the letters in order, using a curvy line.

6. Tape a clear plastic overlay sheet on top of your tracing paper. Use the blue marker to trace the shapes of the aquifers. Color them in with a blue marker.

7. Remove the tracing paper and keep just the overlay on top of the map.

THERE'S YOUR UNDERGROUND MAP. APPROXIMATELY ANOTHER 100 AQUIFERS, ALL SMALLER, UNDERLIE OTHER PARTS OF THE UNITED STATES, AND THERE ARE HUNDREDS MORE AROUND THE WORLD. THAT'S WHY GEOLOGISTS SAY THAT THERE'S SO MUCH MORE FRESH WATER UNDERGROUND THAN ON THE EARTH'S SURFACE.

· · · · · · · · · · ·

MAKE A WATER-CLEANING DEVICE

· ·

Clean water is a constant problem around the world. Only about a third of the people of the earth have enough clean water—and even so they often have problems.

You may have seen water filters that help clean the water. Nature has its own ways of cleaning water. One natural cleaning process is by a filter of gravel and even dirt. As rain and other water seep under the ground, they pass through gravel and sand or dirt. Then they become one source of water for the underground aquifers. (Look at Map the Water Underground, on page 195, to see about underground aquifers.)

Here is one way of partly cleaning water. You'll need some muddy water, so that you can make it look clean.

Here's what you need:

A small glass bowl

A disposable plastic container (such as a 1-pound margarine or delicatessen container) big enough to sit on top of the bowl

Scissors or a hand-held bottle or can opener to make holes in the bottom of the plastic container

2 paper coffee filters

A handful of clean small gravel or stones

A cup of clean sand or cornstarch

A glass of muddy water

· · · · · · · · · · ·

MAKE A WATER-CLEANING DEVICE

continued

Here's what you do:

1. Fit the plastic container on top of the glass bowl.

2. Use the tips of scissors or the tip of a hand-held bottle or can opener to punch eight to ten very small holes in the bottom of the plastic container.

   : *Caution: You need an adult to*
   : *help you make the holes.*

3. Lay the two paper coffee filters into the bottom of the plastic container. Put a handful of clean small gravel or stones into the filters. Then pour sand or cornstarch on top. Now you're ready to clean the muddy water.

4. Pour a glass of muddy water onto the filters. Watch what happens as it slowly makes it way down into the bowl.

   : YOUR MUDDY WATER WILL
   : TURN MUCH CLEARER, BECAUSE
   : IT'S BEEN SCRUBBED ON THE
   : WAY DOWNWARD THROUGH THE
   : FILTERS. DON'T RUN THE RISK
   : OF DRINKING IT, THOUGH. THE
   : SAND, GRAVEL, AND PAPER
   : FILTERS CAN TRAP THE DIRT,
   : BUT THEY CAN'T KILL GERMS
   : OR BACTERIA.

· · · · · · · · · · ·

FIND WATER ANYWHERE

· ·

Our Earth is the water planet. You expect to find water everywhere. (After all, your own body is mostly water.) Here's how you can find water even in dry soil or sand.

Here's what you need:

2 drinking glasses
2 spoons of fresh soil or sand that you bring in from outside
2 small saucers or plates

Here's what you do:

1. Put two spoons of fresh soil in one of the glasses.

2. Put a small saucer or plate on top of each glass.

3. Leave them alone for a whole day. After 24 hours, carefully lift up the saucer on the glass with soil in it, and look at the bottom of the saucer. You'll find water droplets.

4. You won't find water droplets on the saucer over the empty glass. That's the control in your experiment. You know that the water droplets did not come from the air. They came from the soil because that's the only difference between the two glass-and-saucer setups. You can expect to find more water droplets in soil than in sand, but there is even a bit of water inside sand.

> **YOU COULD USE THIS EXPERIMENT TO PROVE THAT THERE IS WATER EVEN IN A DRY DESERT.**

SOLVE MYSTERIES OF THE PLANET EARTH

*Y*ou can make a wonderful gift—the inside of the Earth. You can measure how far it is around the Earth and predict an earthquake. You can melt a glacier or bake a first-time-ever earthquake cookie. The Earth is waiting for you.

MAKE A MODEL OF WHAT'S INSIDE THE EARTH

You can cut the world in half and show what's inside your own planet. This is a good project for a class or for a group of friends.

No one has ever been there. You can't dig through to the center of the Earth. The deepest hole ever drilled is in the Kola Peninsula in Russia. (You can find the Kola Peninsula at 67°N, 37°E.) That hole, the deepest one of all, is only 7½ miles (12 kilometers) deep. That's not much when you consider that the crust of the Earth is at least 2 miles (3 or 4 kilometers) thick under some oceans and up to 75 miles (121 kilometers) thick in mountain areas.

Although no one has ever been there in real life, scientists have developed theories about the center of the Earth. The study is important. What goes on in that unknown center of the Earth has a big effect on what happens at the surface where we live. Yet we still have only theories rather than definite facts about the center of the Earth.

We do know that the Earth is moving, and not just when volcanoes erupt. The continents may have separated more than 200 million years ago, and they may still be on the move. The oceans widen, and the shorelines change. Even solid rock is moving under our very feet, about as fast as a fingernail grows. (To see how the continents move, look at Discover the Lost Continent of Pangea page 225.)

You can create a model of your own planet. This model uses the latest scientific theories on how the Earth is formed.

Plan several days ahead on this project, because you will be working with plaster and paint. Your plaster mold will take a day or two to dry before you can finish it. Then you need to plan enough time for paint and surface plaster to dry, too.

. . . .

MAKE A MODEL OF WHAT'S INSIDE THE EARTH
continued

Here's what you need:

A craft knife

A hollow rubber ball

Plaster of Paris

Water

Shortening

A large spoon

A putty knife

A damp sponge or cloth

A pencil

A globe or world map

Acrylic paints, yellow, orange, brown, blue, and white

A drawing compass

A piece of white paper

A small knife and a thin wooden tool such as a toothpick, chopstick, or wooden barbecue skewer

An indelible marking pen, if you wish

Here's what you do:

1. Use the craft knife to carefully cut the hollow rubber ball in half along the seam.

   > *Caution: You need adult help with using a craft knife.*

2. Rub shortening over the interior half of the ball. This will be your mold.

3. Mix plaster of Paris with water according to directions on the bag. The amount you need will depend on the size of the ball.

> *Caution: You need adult help to use plaster of Paris. Follow all the directions and warnings on the package. Be careful not to get it on your skin.*

4. Use a large spoon to fill the mold with the plaster of Paris mixture. Be sure to push the plaster firmly into the ball to eliminate any air holes.

5. With the putty knife, level off the surface of the plaster of Paris so that it is even with the edges of the mold. Set the plaster of Paris aside to dry for a day or more, depending on the size of the mold and the humidity.

6. When the plaster of Paris no longer feels damp to the touch, remove it from the mold. If the rubber of the ball is flexible enough, you can just peel it back. If not, you may need to use the craft knife to cut the mold.

   > *Caution: You need adult help with using a craft knife. Be very careful not to cut into the surface of the form.*

7. Use a damp sponge or cloth to wipe the surface as clean of shortening as possible. If you wish, you can use a pencil to draw the outline of one hemisphere of the earth on the curved surface of the half ball. Use a globe or a world map as your guide. Don't worry about getting all the countries exactly

MAKE A MODEL OF WHAT'S INSIDE THE EARTH

continued

right. Remember that you can choose to draw the Eastern or Western Hemispheres, or you can choose the Northern or Southern Hemispheres as seen from the North or South Poles.

8. Use a drawing compass to draw circular layers on the flat surface of the plaster of Paris form. Look at the diagram to see how to draw them.

9. Paint the layers as they are in the diagram—or as you might like to imagine them.

10. Allow the paint to dry thoroughly.

11. After the paint is dry, carefully set the flat part of your half-world on a piece of white paper. Then look at a globe or world map, and see where to put in mountains. Sketch them in with a pencil.

12. Mix about one cup of plaster of Paris and water. With a knife, carefully cover the land areas of the hemisphere with plaster of Paris. Use extra plaster and

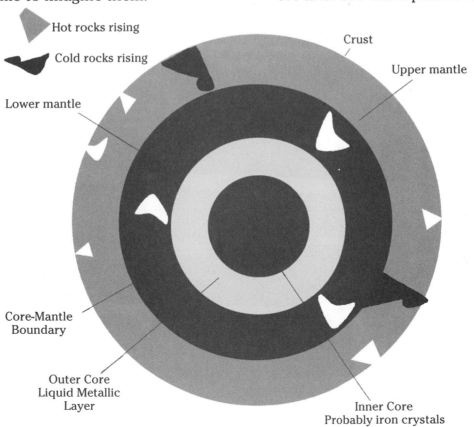

Hot rocks rising

Cold rocks rising

Crust

Upper mantle

Lower mantle

Core-Mantle Boundary

Outer Core Liquid Metallic Layer

Inner Core Probably iron crystals

. . . .

MAKE A MODEL OF WHAT'S INSIDE THE EARTH
continued

lift upward on the mountainous areas. Use a thin wooden tool, such as a toothpick or chopstick, to define the physical features. Let the plaster dry thoroughly.

13. Paint the hemisphere. Use green for forest and grasslands and yellow for deserts. Use brown and gray for mountains, with white on the tops of the tallest mountains. Use white for Arctic and Antarctic regions. Use blue, green, and a blue-green mix for the oceans. You may want to use green or blue-green for the seas and lakes, with a deeper blue for the oceans. Let the paint dry thoroughly.

14. If you wish, use an indelible marking pen to label the layers of the Earth. Or display your model with a sign to tell people about the layers.

NOW YOU HAVE A MODEL OF HALF YOUR PLANET, INSIDE AND OUT. IF YOU WANT TO MAKE A BASE TO DISPLAY YOUR EARTH, USE A GLOB OF COLORED CLAY. OR USE THE MODEL AS A PAPERWEIGHT. WHENEVER YOU FEEL LIKE SEEING THE INSIDE OF THE EARTH, YOU JUST LIFT UP YOUR PAPERWEIGHT. THIS PAPERWEIGHT MODEL MAKES AN INTERESTING AND BEAUTIFUL GIFT.

· · · · · · · · · ·

THE STORY OF A MAN WHO MEASURED THE EARTH FOR THE FIRST TIME

· ·

Eratosthenes (ER-a-TOS-tha-NEEZ) was one of the most learned people of the ancient world. He was born in Cyrene, a Greek city on the coast of Africa, about 284 B.C. His teacher was Plato, probably the most famous philosopher of ancient Greece. (Look for Cyrene at 32°N, 21°E.)

Eratosthenes was curious about everything. He became a mathematician, a poet, a philosopher, a historian, and the librarian for one of the first libraries at Alexandria in Egypt.

His books were not books as we know them but rather papyrus scrolls. The famous library contained over 700,000 scrolls covering all that people knew of the world at the time. With the help of his assistants, Eratosthenes was the first to sort the scrolls and bring facts together by subject.

Eratosthenes lived to be nearly 100 years old. He might have lived longer, but after he became blind in old age, he stopped eating and died of starvation. He did not want to live if he could not work with his beloved books. Go on to see how he measured the distance around the Earth.

ERATOSTHENES WANTED TO FIGURE OUT THE SIZE OF THE EARTH. NO ONE HAD EVER TRIED THAT BEFORE. HE SUCCEEDED EVEN WITHOUT THE ABILITY TO TRAVEL AROUND THE WORLD. GO ON TO SEE HOW HE DID IT—AND THEN TO TRY OUT HIS METHOD.

· · · · · · · · · ·

MEASURE THE EARTH FOR THE FIRST TIME

· ·

You can do a step-by-step math problem, the same one Eratosthenes did, to figure out the circumference (or distance) around the Earth. Use a calculator if you wish.

Here's what to do:

1. Eratosthenes knew of a well in the city of Syene. At noon on the summer solstice, June 20 or 21, he knew that the sun would shine directly down the well and cast no shadow. At that point, the sun was not at an angle. (Syene is now called Aswan. You may have heard of the huge Aswan dam that exists there now. Look for Aswan at 24°N, 32°E, and for the dam nearby.)

2. He knew that Alexandria was north of Syene and on nearly the same longitude. (Look for Alexandria at 31°N, 28°E.)

3. He observed shadows at noon of the solstice in Alexandria and found that the angle of the sun was 7.2°. There are 360° in a circle. He did some division like this: $360° ÷ 7.2° = 50$. He figured that the distance from Syene to Alexandria was one fiftieth of the circumference of the Earth.

4. Now Eratosthenes estimated the distance from Syene to Alexandria. Knowing distances then was not easy. In those days, people moved goods by camel train, and they used a unit of measure called a stadium (or stadia, in the plural). Camel trains ordinarily traveled 100 stadia per day. A journey from Syene to Alexandria took 50 days. You could figure the distance like this:
100 stadia $× 50$ days $= 5,000$ stadia, the distance between Syene and Alexandria.

MEASURE THE EARTH FOR THE FIRST TIME

continued

5. Since that distance seemed to be 1/50th of the way around the whole Earth, figure the distance around the Earth like this:
5,000 stadia × 50 = 250,000 stadia

6. Now you need to know how long stadia are. People today believe a stadium is equal to 157 meters. That's 47.85 feet. Find the circumference of the Earth like this:
250,000 stadia × 157 meters =

To find the distance around the Earth in kilometers, divide your answer by 1,000. To find the distance around the Earth in miles, divide the number of kilometers around the Earth by 1.609 kilometers per mile. If you want to know the answers, look on page 218.

MODERN GEOGRAPHERS ARE ABLE TO USE EXACT METHODS. THEY FIGURE THE DISTANCE AROUND THE EARTH, FROM POLE TO POLE, AT JUST ABOUT 24,859.73 MILES OR 39,999.31 KILOMETERS. YOU CAN IMAGINE THAT ERATOSTHENES WAS CLOSE TO THE RIGHT ANSWER. (HE WAS FIGURING THE CIRCUMFERENCE OF THE EARTH POLE TO POLE RATHER THAN AROUND THE EQUATOR. THERE IS A SMALL DIFFERENCE BECAUSE THE EARTH BULGES A BIT AT THE EQUATOR AND IS SOMEWHAT FLATTENED AT THE POLES.)

PREDICT AN EARTHQUAKE

How do you know when an earthquake is about to happen? Often, you have to watch animals and birds. They probably feel the beginning tremors of an earthquake before you do. And even though they can't know what an earthquake is, they seem to know trouble is coming.

Here are some signs:

- Your pets act nervous. They may run around as if they are looking for what's wrong. Your dog may howl in fear.
- Birds may fly away at great speed, or they may fly in circles. Birds that don't usually fly much, such as chickens, may suddenly head for the tops of trees.
- The mosquitoes and flies disappear all at once.

- Fish may jump out of the water. If you were at the beach just before an earthquake, you might see fish dying on shore.
- The water in a lake or pond might suddenly look different, too. You'd see an abrupt change in the level of the water, or the whole lake or pond would suddenly seem muddy.
- Seconds before an earthquake, you might hear mysterious roaring sounds or see lights in the sky.

WHAT DO YOU DO IF YOU THINK AN EARTHQUAKE IS ABOUT TO HAPPEN? YOU PROBABLY HAVE ONLY A FEW SECONDS TO TAKE ACTION. IF YOU'RE ON A STAIRCASE, RUN DOWN THE STAIRS. IF YOU'RE IN A BUILDING OR A CAR, STAY THERE. GET AWAY FROM WINDOWS OR OTHER GLASS AS QUICKLY AS POSSIBLE. IF YOU CAN, HIDE UNDER A STRONG TABLE OR A DESK. DO WHAT YOU CAN TO PROTECT YOUR HEAD FROM FALLING GLASS OR DEBRIS. AN EARTHQUAKE IS PART OF NATURE, BUT IT CAN BE A HORRIBLE EXPERIENCE FOR A HUMAN BEING.

WATCH AN EARTHQUAKE ON TELEVISION

When there's an earthquake in the television news, you'll hear about the Richter Scale. That's a way of measuring the strength of earthquakes. Here's how to figure out what the television news reporters are telling you.

The numbers sound something like 2.0, 4.6, 5.8, 6.3, or 7.1. Those are units on the Richter Scale.

When you hear numbers from the Richter Scale, what you need to remember is that the difference between each unit is very big. An earthquake that is 5 on the Richter Scale is 10 times stronger than an earthquake that is 4. And it releases about 32 times more energy.

The scale is named after Dr. Charles Richter, who invented it in 1935. It works like this. A scientist measures Earth tremors on a seismograph. If the tremors show an earthquake somewhere in the area, then the scientist must figure out the distance from the seismograph to the center of the earthquake—and then calculate how much stronger the tremors are at the center. (The center of an earthquake is the epicenter. An epicenter would be a bad place to be.) Then the scientist translates those figures into units on the Richter Scale.

· · · · · · · · · · ·

WATCH AN EARTHQUAKE ON TELEVISION
continued

Here are some sample numbers from the Richter Scale:

2.0 or less — A very small earthquake, not usually felt by people and recorded on just local seismographs.

4.5 — A moderately small earthquake, recorded on seismographs all over the world but usually not destructive. Several thousand of this sort occur every day.

6.0 — A major earthquake that could be destructive, depending on where it hits. Somewhere in the world, an earthquake of this magnitude occurs almost every day.

7.0 — A really major earthquake that does serious damage if it happens in a population center. Somewhere in the world, an earthquake of this magnitude occurs about every 2 weeks.

8.0 — A powerful earthquake, with a strong potential to cause damage and destruction. An earthquake of this magnitude occurs somewhere in the world about once a year.

8.8–8.9 — The greatest earthquakes ever recorded. They occur occasionally in human history and are always remembered.

THE RICHTER SCALE DOES NOT ALWAYS TELL YOU ABOUT HOW DEADLY AN EARTHQUAKE IS. FOR EXAMPLE, A STRONG EARTHQUAKE MAY NOT DO MUCH DAMAGE IF IT STRIKES UNDER THE OCEAN OR IN AN ARCTIC REGION. A WEAKER EARTHQUAKE MAY BE EXTREMELY DESTRUCTIVE IF IT HAPPENS IN THE MIDDLE OF A LARGE CITY. THE GREATEST DANGER TO PEOPLE AFTER AN EARTHQUAKE IS USUALLY THE FIRES THAT FOLLOW. FORTUNATELY, MOST EARTHQUAKES HAPPEN IN PARTS OF THE WORLD WHERE FEW PEOPLE LIVE. BUT EARTHQUAKES UNDER THE OCEAN ARE STILL DANGEROUS BECAUSE THEY CAN CAUSE HUGE AND DESTRUCTIVE WAVES.

COLOR THE RING OF FIRE

The Pacific Plate is a single, gigantic section of the Earth's crust. It lies beneath the ocean, and is constantly pushing against other plates that underlie the land areas of North America and eastern Asia.

Huge pressures build up along all its boundaries as it pushes, cracking the crust into a ring of fault lines that circles the whole Pacific. The pressures travel upward, too, sending earthquake tremors toward the surface and forcing hot lava flows up into volcanoes.

That's why the boundaries are called the Ring of Fire. They are the location for huge earthquakes. Plus 60% of the 1,200 active volcanoes of the world are right around the Ring of Fire.

Use a colored marker or pen to color the Ring of Fire on a placemat map or a layered map.

· · · · · · · · · ·

COLOR THE RING OF FIRE

continued

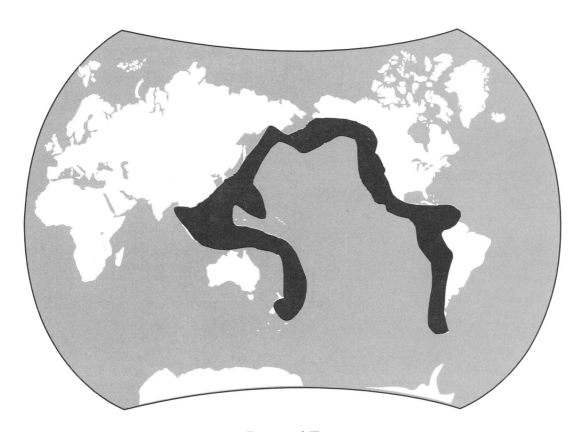

Ring of Fire

NOTICE THAT YOU ARE COLORING NOT JUST OVER OCEAN BUT ALSO OVER LAND. A HUGE NUMBER OF PEOPLE LIVE DIRECTLY ON THE LINE OF THE RING OF FIRE.

. . . .

CREATE AN EARTHQUAKE COOKIE

. . . .

Pacific Coast earthquakes and volcanic eruptions often occur directly on the Ring of Fire. To see how that happens, try this experiment. One of its good features is that you wind up with a giant cookie, ready to eat.

You need permission and help from an adult to do some baking. For the cookie recipe, look on page 215.

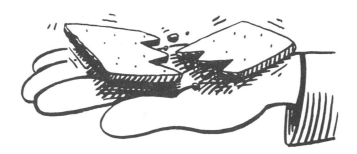

Here's what you need:

Scissors

Aluminum foil

A disposable foil baking pan, 9 × 13 inches (23 × 33 centimeters)

Cookie dough (see page 000)

A table knife

Chocolate sauce

A spray can of whipped cream

A supply of cookie decorating sprinkles

Here's what you do:

1. Use scissors to cut a piece of aluminum foil into a rectangle, 8 × 12 inches (20 × 30 centimeters). Roll it 12 inches (30 centimeters) wide. Crumple it, and fit it at one corner of the long side of the foil baking pan.

2. Spread cookie dough into the rest of the pan, and bake.

3. Cool your cookie. Then carefully pull out the foil and put it aside.

4. Use a table knife to cut carefully along a zig-zag fault line so that your cut goes only about halfway down through the cookie. Don't cut all the way down to the pan surface.

5. Cut carefully along several fracture lines that cross the zig-zag line.

6. Pour a stream of chocolate syrup into the fracture lines along their full lengths.

7. Spray enough whipped cream down into the fault line to cover it and stick up about ½ inch (about 1 centimeter).

8. Scatter the sprinkles onto the whipped cream and chocolate sauce.

· · · · · · · · · · ·

CREATE AN EARTHQUAKE COOKIE
continued

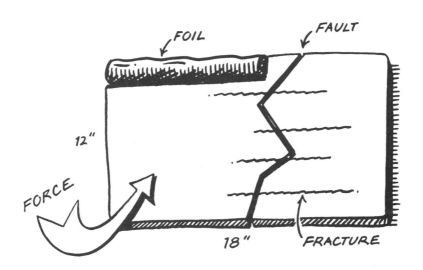

FOIL

FAULT

12"

FORCE

18"

FRACTURE

9. Now it's time for the earthquake. You may want to find someone to watch. Look at the drawing and position your cookie (still in the pan) so that the part where the foil was faces north. You need to make the earthquake happen by forcing the western part of the cookie toward the northeast. Do this by gently and steadily pushing down and northeast on it, until the fault breaks under the pressure.

LOOK AT WHAT HAPPENS TO EVERYTHING—THE COOKIE CRUST, THE CREAM, THE SAUCE, AND THE SPRINKLES. THE PRESSURE AT THE FAULT CRUMPLED AND MOVED THEM ALL, SHIFTING THE CRUST, LAVA, AND ROCK BENEATH THE EARTH'S SURFACE. IF ALL THIS WERE HAPPENING AT THE EARTH'S SURFACE, WITH CITIES AND TOWNS ALONG THE FAULT AND FRACTURE LINES, YOU CAN SEE HOW MUCH DAMAGE WOULD RESULT. THE GOOD NEWS IS THAT IT'S ONLY AN IMAGINARY EARTHQUAKE—AND A REAL COOKIE. ENJOY.

BAKE AN EARTHQUAKE COOKIE

Here's a recipe for your giant earthquake cookie. You can use the recipe for happy events, too, like birthdays and holidays.

Be sure you have adult permission and help with baking.

Here's what you need:

½ cup (1 stick or 125 milliliters) butter or margarine

½ cup (125 milliliters) light brown sugar

1 egg

1¼ cups (300 milliliters) unsifted flour

1 teaspoon (5 milliliters) baking soda

½ teaspoon (2 or 3 milliliters) salt

Here's what you do:

1. Preheat the oven to 350°F.

2. In the large bowl of an electric mixer, mix together butter or margarine, brown sugar, and egg, until light and fluffy.

3. Combine the flour, baking soda, and salt. Beat into the dough.

4. Grease a baking pan. Choose the size you want: 9 × 13 inches (23 × 33 centimeters) or a 12 inch (30-centimeter) round pizza pan.

5. Use a spatula to spread the dough to the edge of the pan. Bake 15 minutes until the cookie is golden brown. Cool on a wire rack.

6. When it's cool, frost and decorate your giant cookie.

. . . .
MELT YOUR OWN GLACIER
. . . .

Glaciers are big masses of ice, so it's natural to think of them as located only in the far northern and far southern latitudes, near the poles. But the fact is that more than 1,000 glaciers sit south of the United States-Canada border. Five of those are as far south as 38°N, 114°W, in eastern Nevada.

That's because glaciers can form in any area, including temperate zones, where more snow has fallen than has melted over the years. The unmelted snow packs down and solidifies as ice, only partly melting during the warmer months. Then the fresh water runs off, channeling its way toward streams and carrying silt, gravel, and rocks with it.

The run-off usually isn't sudden or dramatic, just steady. But seeing how it works to change the landscape around glaciers might surprise you.

Here's what you do:

1. Tear off foil, and crumple it to form a natural-looking mountainside that fills half the foil baking pan. Push down with your finger to create three channels that run down the mountainside like this:

Here's what you need:

Aluminum foil

A large disposable foil baking pan, in the range of 12 × 18 inches (30 × 45 centimeters)

A large shaker of table salt

A paper plate

Three pieces of chalk, in three colors

A styrofoam cup

Scissors or a craft knife

Three large ice cubes, when you're ready

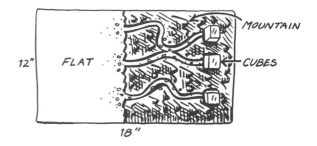

· · · · · · · · · · ·

MELT YOUR OWN GLACIER

continued

2. Spread a light layer of salt on the paper plate. Rub one piece of colored chalk back and forth over it until the salt is colored. Hold the chalk flat as you rub. Then pour it into the higher and lower parts of each channel, to represent gravel. Then do the same with your other two colors of chalk. Pour each different color of salt into each of the three channels, to represent silt and sand.

3. Use scissors or a craft knife to cut very small pieces from the styrofoam cup—so small that it takes about six of them to cover your thumbnail. Cut out about 25 total pieces and then scatter them along the three channels, on both the higher and lower slopes. They'll be the rocks.

   : *Caution: You need adult help*
   : *with using a craft knife.*

4. Spread a thin layer of white, uncolored salt on the flat surface where your channels reach the bottom of the pan.

5. Place the three ice cubes at the top of each channel. As the cubes melt, they will send an increasing flow of water down the channels and onto the flat surface. Watch closely to see how that keeps moving your deposits of silt and rocks down the mountainside. During run-off, the landscape around the glacier changes constantly. (At room temperature, your ice cubes should take 5 minutes or so to melt.)

After the cubes have melted completely, you'll also have much more water down on the flat surface than you might have expected. That's because seemingly small blocks of ice actually lock in large volumes of water.

: THE FIVE SMALL GLACIERS IN
: NEVADA COVER ONLY ABOUT
: 0.1 SQUARE MILE (0.3 SQUARE
: KILOMETER) ON THE SURFACE,
: BUT THEIR NORMAL RUNOFF
: DURING JULY AND AUGUST
: WOULD BE ENOUGH TO FILL
: A TRAIN OF TANK CARS 120
: MILES (NEARLY 200
: KILOMETERS) LONG.

· · · · · · · · · · ·

SOLUTIONS

· ·

Measure the Earth for the First Time, page 206.

6. 250,000 stadia × 157 meters = 39,250,000 meters
39,250,000 meters ÷ 1,000 meters in a kilometer = 39,250 kilometers around the earth
39,250 kilometers ÷ 1.609 kilometers in a mile = 24,394 miles around the earth, which is quite close to the actual measurement of 24,855.34 miles.

EXPLORE THE CONTINENTS END TO END

*C*ontinents are very large land masses. You would think they would be easy to count. People do agree on five of them: Africa, Antarctica, Asia, North America, and South America. Almost everybody also counts Europe as a continent, too, except for a few people who think that Europe is just a very large part of Asia. And it is true that no ocean or sea divides Europe from Asia. Australia is another problem. Some people say it's a small continent. Others count it as the world's largest island.

You can puzzle out continents for yourself.

You can make continent puzzles and continent coins. You can make a map from millions of years ago when the continents may have been all one big landmass—on the move to becoming separate lands. You can make a map of a part of the world as the dinosaurs might have seen it. You can construct a model of the frozen continent of Antarctica.

·········
PUZZLE OUT A CONTINENT
· ·

Designing and making a puzzle of your own can be much more fun than just playing with one out of a box. You get to choose what the pieces look like and what they form when they're all put together.

One good idea might be to think of the whole continent of South America as one puzzle. If you made each of its countries into a piece, some would be big and the others tiny. None of the 13 pieces would have regular edges, and neither would the continent when the puzzle was all put together. The players would really have to work at it.

But making a South America puzzle isn't hard.

Here's what you need:

A printed map of the continent that's about 9 × 12 inches (22.5 × 30 centimeters)

A piece of tracing paper the same size as the map

A pencil

Houshold glue, paste, or rubber cement

A piece of stiff cardboard or foam board the same size as the map

Large heavy books

A cutting board

A craft knife

Coloring markers or pens, in colors you choose

· · · · · · · · · · ·

PUZZLE OUT A CONTINENT

continued

Here's what you do:

1. Center the tracing paper onto the map. Use a pencil to trace all the way around the continent. Then carefully trace the borders for each country. Remember that the borders will have to fit together well as puzzle pieces.

2. Cover the back of your tracing paper with a light layer of glue, school paste, or rubber cement. Place it onto your cardboard or foam board and smooth it out with your fingers.

3. Put heavy books on top, and wait about 5 minutes until the glue is completely dry.

4. Put the map on a thick cutting board. Use the craft knife to cut out the continent and then the countries. Take your time. You may find it easiest to start at the south and cut out Chile and Argentina first.

Caution: You need adult help with using a craft knife.

5. With your coloring markers or pens, color the top surface of each cut-out piece however you want. Using lots of colors makes the puzzle slightly more difficult to put together.

WHEN YOU'RE ALL DONE, TRY THE PUZZLE YOURSELF. YOU MAY FIND IT A BIT HARDER THAN YOU THINK. THEN HAVE SOME FRIENDS TRY IT. BE READY TO GIVE THEM SOME HINTS ABOUT THE GEOGRAPHY OF SOUTH AMERICA. YOU MAY WANT TO GO ON TO MAKE PUZZLES OF OTHER CONTINENTS—OR OF STATES AND PROVINCES.

. . . .

MAKE CONTINENT COINS

. . . .

Your puzzle map of South America is one basic way to show the look of the continent. But how do you show the millions of people and where they live? That's another, important way to look at a continent.

Here's one way to picture the number of people for each country: Make paper coins for each of the countries of South America. Your coins will be different sizes according to how many people live in each country. You may be surprised by the differences in sizes. You'll be drawing your coins to scale and get everything from one extremely large coin to three small dots.

Here's what you need:

Three pieces of construction paper or posterboard, each 16 × 20 inches (40 × 50 centimeters), two of them white and the third in a color you choose

A drawing compass

Scissors

Coloring markers or pens, in colors you choose

Household glue or paste

Here's what you do:

1. Look at the chart of populations for each country in South America. They vary widely. For example, the population of Brazil is 50 times bigger than that of Uruguay and 1,736 times bigger than the population of Guyane. So you need a scale that will show them accurately,

· · · · · · · · · ·

MAKE CONTINENT COINS

continued

and that's why your coins will end up in different sizes. The scale is 1 inch (or 2.54 centimeters) the size across the coin (or the diameter) to represent every 10,000,000 people in a country. You can look at the chart, or you can figure it like this:

The population of a country ÷ 10,000,000 = the coin's diameter in inches

2. On two pieces of large white construction paper or posterboard, make a coin for each country. Use your drawing compass to make the circle a scaled size for each country. (The sizes

on the chart are close to right, but they are rounded off so that you can draw them.) For example, if you want to make a circle 2 inches (or about 5 centimeters) in diameter, set your drawing compass to 1 inch (or about 2.5 centimeters).

3. Look at the chart to see what size to draw ten coins, one for each country. Label each circle with the name of the country. Use coloring markers or pens to color each a different color.

4. Use scissors to cut out each coin.

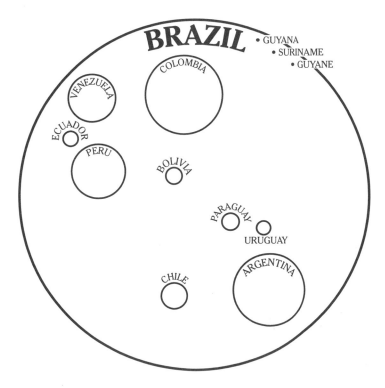

· · · · · · · · · · ·

MAKE CONTINENT COINS

continued

5. Arrange the coins on the third piece of construction paper or posterboard. Put Brazil down first, and then experiment with how to arrange the others on top of it. You may want to scatter them, or arrange their centers along a diagonal line.

6. Then use glue or paste to attach your new coins to the paper. Remember that you still have three countries left to go. These three are just too small for circles. Color and label dots for them to finish your map. (Look at the scale. Make one small dot and two slightly larger dots.)

BESIDES BEING AMAZED BY WHAT YOUR POPULATION COINS SHOW, PEOPLE WILL PROBABLY ASK YOU ABOUT GUYANE BECAUSE IT IS SO SMALL. ONE FACT YOU MIGHT WANT TO TELL THEM IS THAT DEVIL'S ISLAND, THE INFAMOUS OLD FRENCH PRISON, WAS LOCATED JUST OFF THE COAST OF GUYANE. UNTIL RECENTLY, GUYANE WAS FRENCH GUIANA.

HOW BIG TO MAKE
YOUR CONTINENT COINS

The Number of People as of 1995		How Big to Draw Your Coins (Rounded Off)
Argentina	32,650,000	3 inches or 8 centimeters
Brazil	154,500,000	15½ inches or 40 centimeters
Colombia	33,050,000	3⅓ inches or 8.5 centimeters
Guyane	89,000	A dot
Paraguay	4,156,000	½ inch or 1 centimeter
Suriname	420,000	A dot
Venezuela	21,169,000	2 inches or 5.5 centimeters
Bolivia	6,730,000	¾ inch or 2 centimeters
Chile	13,250,000	1¼ inches or 3.5 centimeters
Ecuador	9,923,000	1 inch or 2.5 centimeters
Guyana	840,000	A dot
Peru	22,355,000	2¼ inches or 5.5 centimeters
Uruguay	3,125,000	½ inch or 1 centimeter

· · · · · · · · · ·

DISCOVER THE LOST CONTINENT OF PANGEA

· ·

For millions of years, the crust of the Earth has been slowly spreading outward from midocean ridges. Forces in the Earth build up. They crack the crust of the Earth. They push whole continents apart and then push them back together.

The changes are so big, so slow, and so complicated that geologists and geographers can understand only parts of them. But one idea you might want to think about is Pangea. That's the name for a single, gigantic continent that could have existed between 200 and 500 million years ago. It may have been a supercontinent, existing long before human beings came into the world.

Then slowly, forces in the Earth may have pushed apart the supercontinent. One continent may have became three. Three continents eventually may have become six, plus Australia and all the islands of the world. You can use your placemat map to find evidence for the strange idea of Pangea. (Of course, no one really knows what happened millions and millions of years ago. But this is what geologists and geographers think happened.)

The word *pangea* means all and earth.

Here's what you need:

A placemat map of the world (see page 24 for instructions)
2 sheets of tracing paper
A pencil
Scissors

Here's what you do:

1. Set one piece of tracing paper on your placemat map of the world. Use a pencil to trace the outline of the African continent.

2. Then slide the tracing west on the placemat map, until you get it as close to the east coast of North America as possible.

3. Trace South America on a second piece of tracing paper. Slide and tilt it until it fits in with the northwest coast of Africa.

COASTLINES AND WHOLE CONTINENT SHAPES HAVE CHANGED OVER THE YEARS, BUT NOW YOU HAVE AN IDEA OF HOW THE CONTINENTS COULD ONCE HAVE FIT TOGETHER. THE CONTINENTS AND OCEANS ARE STILL CONSTANTLY CHANGING. THE CONTINENTS MAY EVEN BE SLOWLY COMING TOGETHER AGAIN. MILLIONS AND MILLIONS OF YEARS FROM NOW, THE CONTINENTS WILL BE ENTIRELY CHANGED AGAIN. THERE IS OTHER EVIDENCE FOR THE EXISTENCE OF OCEANS WHERE NOW THERE IS LAND. FOR EXAMPLE, SCIENTISTS HAVE FOUND BIG OCEAN SALT DEPOSITS FAR INLAND, IN THE STATES OF LOUISIANA AND MISSISSIPPI.

225

MAKE A DINOSAURS' MAP

Eighty million years ago, the probable outlines of the North American continent were so different from today's that you might find them hard to believe.

That was the Age of the Dinosaurs, when tremendous undersea and surface forces were still slowly forming pieces of the land mass that would be the continent of North America. Most of it was still underwater, and the Rocky Mountains had not yet been pushed above the surface.

Here's how to make a map of the world of the dinosaurs.

Here's what you need:

Removable tape

A map of the United States, with cities, states, and latitude and longitude lines marked on it, about 8½ × 11 inches (about 22 × 28 centimeters) or a little larger

A piece of tracing paper the same size as the map

A pencil

A clear plastic overlay sheet the same size as the map

Coloring markers or pens, in brown, green, red, and blue

Here's what you do:

1. Use removable tape to tape the tracing paper over the map.

2. To find one of the two land areas where the dinosaurs roamed, locate these points. Use a pencil to mark them as small numbers on the tracing paper:

    (1) Boston, Massachusetts (42°N, 71°W)

    (2) Washington D.C. (39°N, 77°W)

    (3) Raleigh, North Carolina (36°N, 77°W)

    (4) Birmingham, Alabama (33°N, 87°W)

    (5) Nashville, Tennessee (36°N, 87°W)

    (6) Dallas, Texas (33°N, 97°W)

    (7) Des Moines, Iowa (42°N, 94°W)

    (8) Duluth, Minnesota (47°N, 92°W)

3. Draw a pencil line connecting the numbers in order. Put in some curves where you want. We know only the general outline of this land mass.

4. For the second land mass where the dinosaurs roamed, locate these points. Mark them as lowercase letters on the tracing paper.

. . . .

MAKE A DINOSAURS' MAP

continued

(a) 49°N, 114°W
(b) 46°N, 112°W
(c) 42°N, 108°W
(d) 35°N, 109°W
(e) 30°N, 102°W
(f) 33°N, 117°W
(g) 39°N, 123°W
(h) 49°N, 123°W

5. Connect the letters in order, using a curvy line. Draw two extra, small shapes around points *c* and *d*.

6. Tape the clear overlay sheet on top of your tracing paper. Use a brown marker to trace the shapes of the two big areas onto it. Color them in as land.

7. Color the small areas at *c* and *d* green, to show that they were swamps.

8. Surround point *b* with red dots to show volcanoes there.

9. Color everything else as blue, because the rest was all water.

10. Remove the tracing paper, and keep just the overlay for your collection.

AS FAR AS ANYONE KNOWS, THAT WAS THE NORTH AMERICAN ENVIRONMENT OF THE DINOSAURS. THEY LIVED IN BIG, ISOLATED LAND AREAS, WITH MORE LAND RISING UP FROM BELOW AS SWAMPS AND VOLCANOES.

· · · · · · · · · · ·
BUILD A MODEL ANTARCTICA
· ·

With all its dangers, Antarctica remains the most mysterious continent on Earth.

Polar scientists keep base camps in Antarctica between the Ross Sea and the Weddell Sea. (Look for them at 75°S, 175°W and at 75°S, 40°W. Remember that the South Pole is at 90°S.) Otherwise, there are no human locations in Antarctica, just ice and rock about 2,800 miles (4,480 kilometers) wide.

You can make a cross-section model of Antarctica that shows how ice, ocean, and rock united to form the continent. You can show the layers of Antarctica, with the underwater rock, ice, and mountains that poke above the ice.

Here's what you need:

A heavy cardboard base, about 16 × 20 inches (40 × 50 centimeters)

Play dough that you make yourself, using:

> *A large mixing bowl*
>
> *Stirring spoon*
>
> *4 cups (1 liter) flour*
>
> *2 cups (500 milliliters) salt*
>
> *2 cups (500 milliliters) water*
>
> *2 teaspoons (10 millilters) vegetable oil*

A ruler

Art brushes

Tempera or water color paints in blue, white, and brown

A toothpick, small stick, or small flag to show the South Pole

Cardboard, if you wish

Scissors, if you wish

Household glue, if you wish

Here's what you do:

1. The model will stand up 5 inches (13 centimeters) tall on the cardboard base. Make it narrow from front to back. This is just a crosssection, not a full-scale model.

· · · · · · · · · · ·

BUILD A MODEL ANTARCTICA

continued

2. To make play dough, use a large mixing bowl and stirring spoon. Put flour, salt, water, and vegetable oil into the bowl and stir until the ingredients form a dough you can shape with your fingers. If the mixture stays too sticky to handle, add small amounts of flour, just one spoonful at a time.

3. Take handfuls of dough and build up the overall shape of the model on the cardboard base. Use a ruler to make it the right size. Keep working until you have the shape. Then let it harden for a few minutes.

4. Use art brushes to paint on details. Use blue for the sea water. Use white for the top surface of the rock, the ice, and ice shelves. Use brown for just a few of the rock areas. (Most will be covered with ice.) Paint all the surfaces of the model to match.

5. Push in a toothpick, small stick, or small flag to show where the South Pole is.

6. To make the model stand up by itself, mold extra dough on the back.

> WITH A MODEL THIS GOOD, YOU MAY WANT TO USE A CLEAN AREA ON THE CARDBOARD BASE FOR YOUR SIGNATURE. IF YOU LIKE, YOU CAN ALSO WRITE SOME LABELS AND ARROWS ON THE CARDBOARD TO SHOW THAT THE SOUTH POLE IS LOCATED AT 90°S, 0°, THE LONELIEST ADDRESS ON EARTH.

SOLVE MYSTERIES OF LOST PEOPLE, LOST ANIMALS, LOST COUNTRIES, AND LOST CONTINENTS

*H*ere is your chance to study mysteries all over the world. Perhaps you can find clues.

You can search for the lost city of Atlantis (which probably did exist). You can eat an ancient Native American food, all the way from the golden city of Norumbega (which may never have existed, at least not in the way people pictured it).

You can make a mystery map from outer space or search for the fossils of ancient plants and animals.

· · · · · · · · · ·

CHOOSE YOUR FAVORITE MYSTERY

· ·

Somewhere in the world, people say that a strange creature has suddenly appeared. Nobody agrees on exactly what it looks like. There are no clear photographs, and it's seen only once in a while. There's no evidence of where it came from or why it's moving around.

It's a mystery, maybe real and maybe not. As time goes by, only one thing is certain. More and more stories will be told about the creature, each tale stranger than the last.

If you don't already have your own favorite mystery, here are six from around the world. You could locate them on a placemat or bulletin board map. Or you can make a poster with drawings and some details about the mysteries of the world.

- *The Easter Island Statues.* On an isolated island in the Pacific Ocean stand dozens of giant statues looking out to sea. They stand as high as 70 feet (24.5 meters), and they weigh as much as 50 tons (45 metric tons). They have no bodies, just gigantic faces that seem to stare into the ocean. Nobody is certain when or how they were carved or how they were moved into formation. (Look for Easter Island at 28°S, 110°W.)

- *The Bermuda Triangle.* In the Atlantic Ocean, there is a place where dozens of boats and airplanes have sunk or disappeared for no obvious reason. The three points of land that outline the triangle are Melbourne, Florida (27°N, 81°W), Bermuda (32°N, 64°W), and Puerto Rico (18°N, 66°W). Some people believe that the skies and ocean there may be disturbed by powerful magnetic or ocean-current forces.

- *Nessie.* At Loch Ness in Scotland, a very deep mountain lake at 57°N, 5°W, rumors of a huge, snake-like creature have been around for centuries. Many people claim to have seen the creature rise up to ride on the surface and look around. They call her Nessie because they believe it's a mother snake, sometimes bringing up a smaller one with her. Photographs have been published, but so far all of them have been blurry—or outright fakes.

- *The Red Paint People.* The Red Paint People were some of the earliest people known in North America. They lived from about 10,000 years ago until about 3,000 years ago. But then they disappeared, leaving behind no traces except burial grounds and beautifully finished spear heads and sharpening stones—plus broken pieces of pottery, all of them decorated with a paint made from a kind of reddish brown earth called ocher. Today their lands lie in the northeastern United States and the Maritime Provinces of Canada, between 40°N and 48°N.

· · · · · · · · · · ·

CHOOSE YOUR FAVORITE MYSTERY
continued

- *Machu Picchu.* High in the mountains near Cuzco in Peru (at 13°N, 73°W), the ruins of an ancient and richly developed Inca city have been found. Elaborate stone temples, stairways, palaces, and house walls have been uncovered, all grouped together on a cliffside in mountains 20,000 feet (6,097 meters) above sea level. Most guesses about Machu Picchu say that the Incas may have started building it as a stronghold around the year 1200, keeping on until the 1530s, when the invading Spanish drove them away. But it's still a mystery. Nobody really knows what emptied the city.

- *Amelia Earhart.* Amelia Earhart was a famous American aviator during the 1920s and 1930s, and in 1928, the first woman to fly across the Atlantic. After many other daring, long-distance flights in the 1930s, she and her co-pilot Frederick Noonan decided to try an around-the-world flight in 1937. But something went wrong over the Pacific, in the huge area between New Guinea (10°S, 145°E) and Howland Island (1°N, 177°W), and their plane was never seen again. More than 50 years later, the wreckage of a possibly similar plane was found near Nikumaroa Island in Kiribati (1°N, 175°E), but there was no proof that it was hers.

WHILE SOME MYSTERIES NEVER DO GET SOLVED, MANY OTHERS HAVE BEEN—EVEN THOUGH IT CAN TAKE HUNDREDS OF YEARS FOR THE FACTS TO BE UNCOVERED. GO ON TO SEE ABOUT THREE WORLD MYSTERIES THAT CONFUSED AND FASCINATED PEOPLE FOR CENTURIES. KEEP YOUR WORLD MAP IN FRONT OF YOU, SO YOU CAN CHECK THEM OUT.

· · · · · · · · · · ·
DISCOVER THE UNDISCOVERED
· ·

Here are three ancient mysteries you can solve by looking at a modern map of the world.

A First Ancient Mystery:

For more than 2,000 years, European thinkers and mapmakers were fascinated by the idea of a mysterious, undiscovered continent lying far south.

At first, it was an ancient idea that the landmasses of Europe, Asia, and Africa had to be balanced by another heavy landmass, so that the Earth could have the balanced weight to rotate properly. (Actually, the pull of the sun and other heavenly bodies makes the Earth rotate. It doesn't need a balanced weight on each side.)

Then people's imaginations took over. Eventually, people were describing the unknown southern continent as longer and wider than any other continent, full of riches, with perfect weather and very beautiful people. One eighteenth-century Englishman even declared, as if he knew what he was talking about, that the continent was exactly 5,323 miles (or precisely 8,570 kilometers) wide, with a population of 50 million people.

The dreamers even began to call the continent by a nickname, the USC, for Unknown Southern Continent.

Solve the First Ancient Mystery:

Look as far south on your map as you can. Guess where the real Unknown Southern Continent turned out to be. *Hint:* Don't expect a land of jewels, perfect weather, or 50 million beautiful people. But do expect to find a very large, interesting, and still largely unknown Southern Continent. Get your map reading dividers to see if Antarctica is as wide as any of the other continents. See how it ranks in size among the other continents. (For the answer, look on page 242.)

A Second Ancient Mystery:

You could call North America the Inconvenient Continent. The first European explorers did everything they could to get around it, get through it, or ignore it. They really wanted a good sea route to Asia. They were dismayed to find a huge continent in between. Earlier, they had felt the same way about the large, inconvenient continent of South America.

The Europeans hoped—and then believed—that there must be a Northwest Passage, a large river, or even an ocean that divided the continent of North America.

· · · · · · · · · · ·

DISCOVER THE UNDISCOVERED

continued

Solve the Second Ancient Mystery:

Try finding a Northwest Passage yourself. Look as far north as 75°N, between 60°W and 172°W. It's there, but much of it is iced in for most or all of the year. You can see why it never made an easy, practical way for traders to get to Asia.

A Third Ancient Mystery:

Almost as much as they wanted gold, the early Spanish, Portuguese, Dutch, and other explorers wanted spices—and they wanted to find the Spice Islands. They imagined spices in abundance on these glamorous islands, along with gold, jewels, and (of course) very beautiful people. The early explorers kept maps of the Spice Islands highly secret. No one was supposed to know where they were.

Solve the Third Ancient Mystery:

Now you can find the Spice Islands on a map that anyone can see. Look for the Moluccan Islands at 2°S, 128°E, south of the Philippines and near Malaysia. There (and across the rest of Indonesia, between Borneo and New Guinea), the explorers from other parts of the world finally found the spices they wanted. Use your dividers to see which route was really shorter from the European trading countries like Portugal or Spain—to the west around South America or to the east around Africa.

WHEN CHRISTOPHER COLUMBUS LANDED ON ISLANDS IN THE CARIBBEAN, HE THOUGHT HE MIGHT HAVE FOUND THE SPICE ISLANDS. HE WORRIED, THOUGH, WHEN HE SAW THE CLOTHES THE PEOPLE WERE WEARING—AND NOT WEARING. COLUMBUS EXPECTED THAT THE PEOPLE OF A FINE PLACE LIKE THE SPICE ISLANDS WOULD BE WEARING ELEGANT CLOTHES WITH FANCY DECORATIONS AND ELABORATE EMBROIDERY. INSTEAD, THE PEOPLE OF THE TROPCAL CARIBBEAN ISLANDS WORE ALMOST NO CLOTHES.

. . . .

LOSE ATLANTIS ALL OVER AGAIN

. . . .

People often talk about the lost continent of Atlantis. Some legends say that it was a huge landmass that sank into the Atlantic Ocean thousands of years ago.

The more likely spot, though, is in the Aegean Sea somewhere north of Crete. Today there's a small island called Thira—and evidence that it might have been much larger about 1,600 years ago, or surrounded by other islands no longer there. (Look for Crete at 35°N, 25°E, and for Thira at 36°N, 25°E.)

Archeologists digging on Thira have found an ancient city buried under 900 feet (270 meters) of volcanic ash. Close to it is an extinct, blown-apart volcano. Whatever happened there, it was such a disaster that the ancient Greek writer Plato wrote about the Atlantis tragedy more than 1,000 years after it probably happened. He said:

> *Violent earthquakes and floods, and in a single day and night of misfortune...the island disappeared in the depths of the sea. The sea around Atlantis became an impassable barrier of mud....*

On a volcanic island, nothing could be more destructive than a sudden eruption and major earthquakes happening at the same time. To get a basic idea of how completely an island could collapse into the sea, you might want to try out this simple model.

Here's what you need:

4 styrofoam cups

A pencil

2 pieces of string about 8 inches (20 centimeters) long

Dirt, sand, and very small pebbles

A disposable rectangular foil pan, about 14 inches (35 centimeters) on its longest side

Modeling clay

Water

LOSE ATLANTIS ALL OVER AGAIN

continued

Here's what you do:

1. Fill three of the styrofoam cups with dirt, sand, and very small pebbles.

2. The empty cup will be your volcano. Use the pencil to draw cracks along its side and bottom surfaces, so that they look something like this:

3. Use the pencil point—very gently—to poke cracks into the cup along the lines you just drew. Also punch two holes opposite each other on the top rim of the cup.

4. Tie a knot on one end of each string. Thread your strings though the rim holes so the knotted ends stay inside the cup.

5. Turn the cup upside down and place it in the middle of the disposable foil pan.

6. Moisten your dirt with small amounts of water, and build it up around the cup in a volcano shape. Arrange the rest of your dirt and rocks around it in the pan to cover most of the surface. Cover the strings, too, but leave their ends showing.

7. Use the modeling clay to build a barrier about ½ inch (1 or 2 centimeters) high around the edges of the dirt.

8. Then, very slowly pour water into the pan between its walls and the barrier. That's your sea, surrounding a volcanic island.

9. When you're ready, tug up and outward on the strings. Your cup will crack open completely, the way a volcano would during an eruption. The strings will break the clay barrier, and the dirt and stones will collapse into the oncoming water. No more island.

IN ALL LIKELIHOOD, THAT'S HOW ATLANTIS COLLAPSED AND SLID INTO THE AEGEAN SO SUDDENLY. THE ERUPTION ALSO SENT SO MUCH VOLCANIC ASH INTO THE AIR AND SEA THAT, EVEN NOW, YOU COULD FIND LAYERS OF IT UNDER THE BLACK SEA AND THE NILE RIVER. ALL NATURAL SIGNS POINT TO THE COLLAPSE OF ATLANTIS AS ONE OF THE BIGGEST DISASTERS OF HUMAN HISTORY.

. . . .

MIX UP A NATIVE AMERICAN MYSTERY

. . . .

About 600 years ago, a mysterious city appeared on European maps of North America. The name of the city was Norumbega. It was a fabulous city with crystal columns, gold, and pearls. The people were clever, beautiful, and tall—and dressed in furs. They used words that sounded like Latin, and they worshipped the sun.

It was said there were beasts with tusks in the forest, bigger than horses.

The maps showed the city in various places up and down the east coast of North America, from what is now New Brunswick to what is now the state of Georgia. In a 1564 map, the famous mapmaker Mercator showed Norumbega as a European sort of city, with many towers and a moat around it.

Certainly, the mapmakers were using their vivid imaginations. Perhaps also, the French and English captains were luring sailors with tall tales of riches to be found in North America. Those who came looking for riches found mostly only hardships.

The French explorer Samuel de Champlain decided to solve the mystery of Norumbega once and for all. In 1604, he came to the Penobscot River, now in the state of Maine. (Look for Penobscot Bay at 44°N, 69°W.) All Champlain found was a mossy cross in the woods and a few wigwams on the shores of the river. On his maps after that, he applied the name Norumbega only to the river.

Yet there may be some truth to the tall tales of Norumbega. The Penobscot Indians (called the Wabinakis there) were known as tall and good-looking people, and no doubt they did dress in furs during the long winters. They did have a village along the Penobscot River where the city of Bangor is now located. (Look for Bangor at 45°N, 69°W.) The Indian people may have shown their visitors some quartz or worthless diamonds from the river bed. The pearls may have come from the multitude of clams along the seashore. The huge beasts with tusks were probably moose. Now Norumbega exists only around Bangor, where people enjoy using the fanciful name for malls and office buildings.

You can imagine the Penobscot people in their little river village—with no idea that the Europeans pictured it as a fabulous European-style city.

The Native American tribes of the northeast coast of North America tended to be peaceful people. They often gathered together for holidays and ceremonies (and still do), and sometimes they moved to islands for the summer so they could fish. When they traveled, they packed high-energy, long-lasting food. Here is a modern version of a real Native American trail mix.

. . . .

MIX UP A NATIVE AMERICAN MYSTERY

continued

Make this recipe in the fall when you get your Halloween pumpkin.

Here's what you need:

A pumpkin

2 tablespoons sunflower oil, peanut oil (30 milimeters), or other cooking oil

½ teaspoon (3 milimeters) salt

¼ teaspoon (1 milimeter) pepper

Choose the rest of your trail mix:

1 cup (250 milimeters) raisins

1 cup (250 milimeters) sunflower seeds

1 cup (250 milimeters) hazelnuts or cashews

1 cup (250 milimeters) peanuts

Here's what you do:

1. When you cut your Halloween pumpkin, use a knife to scrape out the pulpy material inside it. Separate the seeds until you have 1 ½ cups (360 milimeters) full. Let the seeds dry for a while.

> *Caution: You need adult help with cutting the pumpkin and scraping it.*

2. Preheat oven to 375° (190°C).

3. In a medium bowl, mix the pumpkin seeds, along with oil, salt, and pepper.

4. Spread onto a baking sheet or foil-covered pan. Roast for 15 minutes.

5. Mix with raisins, sunflower seeds, hazelnuts or cashews, and peanuts. (You can mix these as you wish, with more of your favorites.)

> OTHER NATIVE AMERICANS INVENTED A VALUABLE TRAIL FOOD, PEMMICAN. IN THE WEST, PEMMICAN WAS MADE OF DRIED BUFFALO MEAT AND FAT, MIXED WITH BERRIES AND SEEDS. IT KEPT PEOPLE ALIVE ON LONG TRIPS AND THROUGHOUT HARD WINTERS. THE ARCTIC AND ANTARCTIC EXPLORERS LEARNED ABOUT PEMMICAN AND CARRIED IT AS ONE OF THEIR MAIN FOODS. CAMPERS AND EXPLORERS STILL MIX A BATCH BEFORE THEY LEAVE.

MAKE A MYSTERY MAP FROM OUTER SPACE

Imagine our world under bombardment. Chunks of rock and ice from outer space keep hitting and crashing and exploding all over the world. These outer space rocks blast out huge craters. They flatten trees over a whole forest.

Long ago, they may have utterly destroyed the biggest creatures who ever walked the face of the Earth.

The military decides to take action. Then, suddenly, the President of the United States announces that life from outer space may have landed.

This is not a science fiction movie. This is really happening.

Make a map of mystery from outer space. This could be the most important map in your collection. Use a placemat, layered, or bulletin board map of the world.

Here's where to mark the biggest of the outer space mysteries:

1. Mark the Barrington Crater in Arizona. What made it? Probably a small asteroid, only about 150 feet (46 meters) across, blasted out this huge crater. (Look for Barrington Crater at 36°N, 112°W.)

2. Mark the Chicxulub Crater on the Yucatan Peninsula in Mexico. It's an ancient crater, but it may be a clue to the extinction of the dinosaurs. Perhaps a comet hit that was so big and exploded so intensely that it changed climate conditions around the world. That would have been 65 million years ago. The dinosaurs may all have died soon after the impact—along with most of the other animals of the world. Scientists figure that since the crater is more than 160 miles (257 kilometers) across, the comet or asteroid may have been as much as 6 miles (nearly 10 kilometers) wide. (Look for Chicxulub Crater at 21°N, 89°W.)

3. Mark the Tunguska site in Siberia, Russia. In 1908, a comet may have exploded as it entered the Earth's atmosphere. The blast flattened trees over 50 miles (80 kilometers) of Siberian forest on all sides. (Look for the Tunguska forest at 57°N, 97°E.)

4. You could make small marks across all the continents where small asteroids have hit. The Earth has a long history of attack.

5. You could mark a few locations of an advance warning system, too. The United States Air Force and others are setting up electronic detection systems to spot the hazards from outer space. Mark observatories and laboratories at Mt. Haleakala, Hawaii, and at Flagstaff, Arizona, and at

. . . .

MAKE A MYSTERY MAP FROM OUTER SPACE

continued

the Massachusetts Institute of Technology. (These are part of the Air Force GEODSS system. That's the Ground-Based Electro-Optical Deep Space Surveillance System. Look for Mt. Haleakala on the Big Island of Hawaii at 20°N, 156°W. Look for Flagstaff, Arizona at 35°N, 111°W. Look for the Massachusetts Institute of Technology at 42°N, 71°W.)

6. Now mark Antarctica. Several years ago, a chunk of rock the size of a potato hit there. Antarctica is a good place to find small meteorites, bits of rock from outer space, because the rocks lie on the snow, often in plain sight. In other places of the world, the rocks fall under the sea or are too little for anyone to notice easily. This particular rock may possibly be all the way

from the planet Mars. As scientists studied the Martian rock closely, they discovered fossil shapes that look like microbes. These shapes are similar to some forms of microscopic life on Earth. It's possible that one-celled life may have existed on Mars 3.6 billion years ago. (Life was just forming on Earth about that time. If this is evidence of life forms, it is truly ancient.)

WHAT COULD WE DO IF WE DISCOVERED A DANGEROUS ASTEROID OR A COMET ON A COLLISION COURSE WITH OUR EARTH? WE COULD USE BOMBS, ROCKETS, OR PERHAPS LASERS TO PUSH IT INTO ANOTHER ORBIT AND SEND IT SPEEDING AWAY.

LOOK FOR A LONG LOST ANIMAL OR PLANT

If you keep looking, you may find the imprint of an animal or plant that lived millions of years ago. When an animal or plant dies, sometimes it leaves an imprint in mud or clay. Over a very long time, the mud or clay hardens and becomes part of rock. For example, you may find a rock imprint of a leaf from long ago.

You might even find the fossil of an actual shell, plant, or animal that has hardened and become rock-like. Cell by cell, the plant or animal becomes chemically changed or petrified. Its shape is almost the same, but it looks like rock.

Fossils are everywhere. You can probably find one.

Here's where to look:

- When you're at the beach, look for shell fossils or the fossils of ancient sea creatures. Or notice rocks that wash up along streams and rivers. Some of these rocks may be limestone, natural chalk, or another soft sort of rock that takes imprints easily. (Get someone to help you identify types of rocks.)

- Look in places where you can see layers of rock, such as a place where you see construction or digging.

  Caution: Don't go anywhere that's not safe. You often need permission and an adult to go with you.

- Look around farms. A good place to find fossils is in old stone walls or in piles of stones left over from clearing a farm field or garden.

  Caution: Be sure you have the owner's permission to look, and get someone to go with you.

- You also may want to look for rocks that human hands may have shaped a long time ago. A sharpened or patterned stone may be a Native American arrowhead or part of an ancient tool.

  YOU MAY NEED A MAGNIFYING GLASS TO STUDY A ROCK. MANY FOSSIL IMPRINTS OR TOOL MARKINGS ARE TOO SMALL TO FIND EASILY.

. . . .

SOLUTIONS

. . . .

Discover the Undiscovered, page 233. Here are how the continents rank (including Antarctica and Australia), from the smallest in land mass to the largest:

1. Australia

2. Europe

3. Antarctica

4. South America

5. North America

6. Africa

7. Asia

FORECAST WEATHER AROUND THE WORLD

*Y*ou can design your own weather map, with your own special symbols. You can track the weather in your own neighborhood, and you can go on to track dangerous weather like hurricanes and tornadoes. You can track mysterious weather patterns that sweep over the world. This is your chance to become an around-the-world weather reporter.

· · · · · · · · · · ·

TRACK THE WEATHER ALL AROUND YOUR OWN NEIGHBORHOOD

· ·

Weather patterns around the world are so complex that even tracking them can be difficult. Predicting accurately is even harder.

That's because all weather develops and redevelops constantly. Wherever you live, the weather moving through is being pushed by a combination of global, regional, and local forces.

Over distances of just a mile or a kilometer or so, there are times when the behavior of the weather can be surprisingly different. You can see how that works with a simple experiment you can run with your friends. This experiment takes about 1 minute a day for 10 days.

Find three to five friends who live 1 or 2 miles or kilometers away from where you live.

Here's what each friend needs to conduct the experiment:

An outdoor thermometer

A rain gauge (To see how to make your own, look on page 246.)

A wind gauge (To see how to make your own, look on page 246.)

A ruler

A wristwatch that shows seconds

A notebook

A pen

Here's what you do:

1. Make sure that each person in the group has an outdoor thermometer set in a shady location. Then make or buy your own identical rain gauges and wind speed gauges.

2. Agree with your friends that each of you will check the weather—and record your findings in a notebook—at the same time each day for 10 days.

3. At the same convenient time, like 6:00 P.M. every day, each of you needs to go outside at home and do three things:

   One. Read the outdoor thermometer, and write down the exact temperature.

   Two. Use the ruler to measure rain in the rain gauge from the previous 24-hour period. Note the amount. Be sure to empty the rain gauge each time you take a reading.

   Three. To measure wind speed, stick the wind gauge into the ground in an open area, with the open ends of the cups facing into the wind you feel blowing. Start at zero seconds on your wristwatch, and count how many times the colored cup goes past the top of the yardstick during 1 minute. Take the wind gauge back inside each time you use it, so it will last the 10 days.

TRACK THE WEATHER ALL AROUND YOUR OWN NEIGHBORHOOD

continued

WHEN YOU START TO COMPARE WEATHER READINGS, IT WON'T TAKE LONG FOR DIFFERENCES TO START SHOWING UP. THEY WILL BE MINOR DIFFERENCES, JUST A DEGREE OR TWO, OR SLIGHTLY DIFFERENT CUPS-PER-MINUTE NUMBERS FOR THE WIND. BUT THE DIFFERENCES WILL GIVE YOU AN IDEA OF WHAT YOU COULD CALL MICROWEATHER, OR THE PATTERNS IN YOUR OWN SMALL NEIGHBORHOOD.

· · · · · · · · · ·

TRACK THE WEATHER WITH YOUR OWN RAIN AND WIND GAUGES

· ·

You can make your own wind and rain gauges so you can track the weather with your friends. Just make sure that each person has the same kind of gauge.

Here's what you need for each rain gauge:

An empty coffee can or a wide-mouthed glass jar

Here's what you need for each wind gauge:

A coloring marker, pen, or crayon

4 paper cups with handles

A wood screw

A large disposable plastic plate

A stapler

A yardstick or other long measuring stick

A screwdriver

Here's what you do:

1. To measure rainfall, set the coffee cup or jar on a level place outside. Choose a place where it won't tip over, where extra rain won't splash into it, and where bugs and leaves won't get into it. You can put it up high or pack sand around it so it won't tip.

2. To make a wind speed gauge, use a coloring marker, pen, or crayon to color one of the four paper cups so that it will stand out from the others.

TRACK THE WEATHER WITH YOUR OWN RAIN AND WIND GAUGES

continued

3. Use the wood screw to punch a hole in the center of the plate.

4. Use a stapler to staple the four cups to the plate edge. Make sure that their open ends all face the same way.

5. Pick a point about 6 inches (15 centimeters) in from one end of the yardstick. Use the screwdriver to drive the screw all the way through the yardstick. Then carefully unscrew it so you have the hole left.

   Caution: You need adult help with the screwdriver.

6. Attach the plate to the yardstick by inserting the screw through the plate and back into its hole. Don't tighten it all the way.

NOW YOU'RE READY TO USE YOUR GAUGES AND TO KEEP TRACK OF THE WEATHER WITH YOUR FRIENDS. YOU MAY BE SURPRISED TO SEE DIFFERENCES SO CLOSE TO HOME. PLUS YOU MAY SEE WHAT IS NOT AVERAGE ABOUT YOUR WEATHER FOR THAT 10 DAYS. PERHAPS IT'S USUALLY COOL AT THAT SEASON OF THE YEAR, BUT YOUR NOTES SHOW IT HAS BEEN VERY WARM. MAYBE YOUR NEIGHBORHOOD IS GETTING MORE RAIN OR SNOW THAN USUAL. MAYBE YOU'VE SEEN SOMETHING REALLY UNUSUAL, LIKE HAIL OR EVEN THE INFLUENCE OF A HURRICANE. GO ON TO SEE HOW SOMETHING HAPPENING IN ONE PART OF THE WORLD CAN HAVE A DRAMATIC INFLUENCE ON WEATHER ACROSS THE REST OF THE WORLD.

. . . .

SEE WHAT THE CHILD IS DOING THIS YEAR

. . . .

This is your chance to see the workings of a powerful worldwide weather force. This is a problem apparently related to a changing ocean current. The current has a very strange name for something so powerful. It's called El Niño. In Spanish, that means the child.

El Niño is a strong and unstable Pacific Ocean current near the Equator. It arrives every 3 to 7 years, and if it is a child, the people it hits believe it is a problem child.

Fishermen of Peru in South America named it long ago. Around Christmas every few years, when the fishermen were celebrating the birth of the Christ Child, they were also experiencing a disaster. A warm and mysterious ocean current swept along the western coast of South America. The fish died. The seabirds that fed on the fish died. Floods roared inland, and disease spread among the people.

During El Niño, the trade winds that usually blow east to west (and drag the surface water of the ocean in that direction, too) are weak and hardly noticeable. Instead, strong El Niño winds blow west to east across the Pacific. Those strange winds bring warm water from tropical regions near the Equator. Nothing seems to be right.

Strangely, El Niño may bring too much rain and snow to some parts of the world and too little water to other parts of the world. Scientists believe it may have contributed to flooding, heavy rains, and blizzards in North America and South America. At the same time, it may have brought severe drought that has dried up farmland and killed animals and people on four continents: Africa, Australia, North America, and South America. (On a world map, look especially at Africa between 30°N and 10°N and at Queensland in Australia, 20°S, 148°E.)

El Niño may even encourage the birth of hurricanes.

You can see what's going on for yourself.

Here's what you need:

Removable tape

A clear plastic overlay sheet

A placemat or layered map of the world

Coloring markers or pens in black, red, and blue

Here's what you do:

1. Use removable tape to attach the clear plastic overlay sheet onto a placemat or layered map of the world. Use a black marker or pen to label the overlay El Niño.

2. Use a red marker to draw in ocean currents of El Niño. Look at an ocean current map to see

SEE WHAT THE CHILD IS DOING THIS YEAR
continued

how different they are. Use a blue marker to draw the wind arrows. To see how, look at the diagram.

3. Use the black marker to draw lines or symbols for climate problems in North America, South America, Africa, and Australia.

NOW YOU HAVE A SIMPLIFIED PICTURE OF THE MYSTERY OF EL NIÑO AND THE TROUBLE IT CAUSES. USUALLY, AFTER A FEW WEEKS OF HAVOC, EL NIÑO SWEEPS AWAY FROM THE COASTLINES OF PERU AND ECUADOR AS MYSTERIOUSLY AS IT ARRIVED. HOWEVER, SOME SCIENTISTS THINK THE EFFECTS CAN GO ON FOR YEARS. AND NO ONE KNOWS HOW TO FORECAST THE CHILD OR WHAT CAUSES IT. WATCH YOUR NEWSPAPER TO SEE WHAT EL NIÑO MAY BE DOING NEXT YEAR.

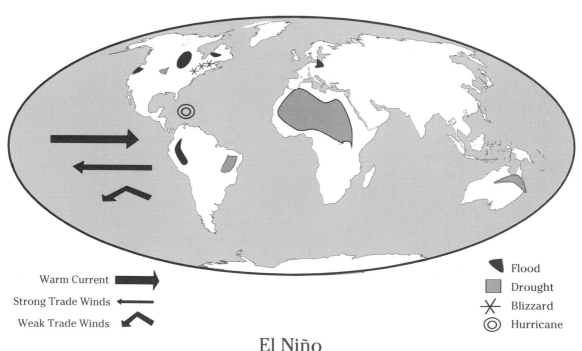

Warm Current
Strong Trade Winds
Weak Trade Winds

Flood
Drought
Blizzard
Hurricane

El Niño

TRACK A HURRICANE

You can be all ready to track a hurricane as soon as one appears. And you can keep records of tornadoes, even though they pass by too quickly to keep track of over days.

Here's what you need:

Removable tape
2 clear plastic overlay sheets for your map
A placemat map of the world
Coloring markers or pens
Paper or self-sticking paper, if you wish

Here's what you do:

1. Use removable tape to fix one clear plastic overlay sheet onto your placemat map of the world or of your country.

2. Use a coloring marker or pen to color or stripe in the areas where you might expect hurricanes. Use a marker of a second color to color or stripe in the areas where you might expect tornadoes. Notice that in some areas you need to alternate stripes to show that these places are at risk for both hurricanes and tornadoes.

3. Keep your map until you hear news of a hurricane coming. Then tape on a second clear plastic overlay sheet, and get ready to track its route. You can expect that hurricanes begin as several thunderstorms over tropical ocean waters. These storms may be small and far away, so that you don't hear about them in the news. Then the storms may develop into a tropical depression. At that point, the winds have begun a circular motion, and they are spinning at less than 39 miles per hour (62 kilometers per hour). You may not hear news of a tropical depression unless it develops into a tropical storm and moves closer.

4. Design a symbol for your map to show a tropical storm that may develop into a hurricane. Draw the symbol on your second overlay. Or you can design the symbol on paper, and stick it on with removable tape. Or use self-sticking paper for your symbol. A tropical storm may slow down and fade away, or it may develop into a hurricane. It becomes a hurricane when the winds reach 74 miles per hour (118 kilometers per hour).

· · · · · · · · · · ·

TRACK A HURRICANE

continued

5. Design a symbol for your map to show a full hurricane. You can draw it on the plastic overlay or on paper. Then you're ready to track the route of the hurricane. A hurricane is usually between 200 and 300 miles across (320 to 480 kilometers), with rain storms far beyond that distance. It's a huge system of weather. In the Northern Hemisphere, you can expect to track a hurricane from southeast toward the northwest. But it may also move toward the north or northeast. The hurricanes in any hemisphere are blowing along with the trade winds and curving toward the poles. Since the trade winds run east to west across the tropical part of the Atlantic Ocean, you can expect the Atlantic hurricanes (and many other kinds of ocean storms) to do the same.

6. Keep tracking the hurricane every day when you see a newspaper or hear the news on radio or television. Usually, after a hurricane hits land, it begins to break up and lose its force. The routes of hurricanes are difficult to predict, though, so you may be in for some surprises.

7. Keep a record of tornadoes in the news, too. Design a symbol for tornadoes. Colliding air masses cause tornadoes. The United States has the most tornadoes of any country in the world, with perhaps 1,000 a year.

8. See how hurricanes and tornadoes fit in with the shaded areas on your map. Perhaps they hit in areas where they are expected.

· · · · · · · · · · ·

TRACK A HURRICANE

continued

Look for news of the destruction they cause when they hit. Sometimes you may hear news of typhoons and cyclones. Those are the same sort of storm as hurricanes, except that typhoons originate in the Pacific Ocean and cyclones originate in the Indian Ocean.

HOW DO HURRICANES GET THEIR NAMES? DURING WORLD WAR II, PILOTS BEGAN A TRADITION OF NAMING STORMS AFTER THEIR WIVES AND GIRL FRIENDS. THEY NAMED ONE BESS, AFTER MRS. TRUMAN, THE WIFE OF PRESIDENT HARRY TRUMAN. WHEN PRESIDENT TRUMAN OBJECTED, THEY NAMED ONE HARRY. IN THE 1950S, THE UNITED STATES WEATHER BUREAU BEGAN DRAWING UP AN ALPHABETICAL LIST OF WOMEN'S NAMES JUST BEFORE HURRICANE SEASON. THEN IN THE 1970S, THE WEATHER BUREAU BEGAN DRAWING UP A LIST WITH A MAN'S NAME, THEN A WOMAN'S, THEN A MAN'S, RIGHT DOWN THE ALPHABET. WOULD YOU WANT A HURRICANE TO HAVE YOUR NAME?

Hurricanes and Tornadoes

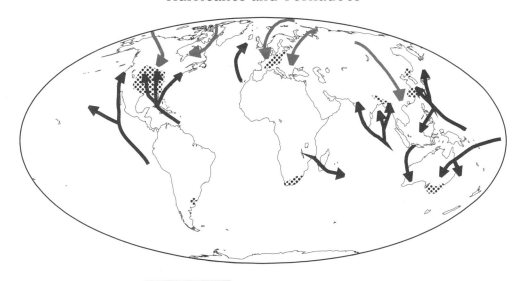

Tornado Areas

Hurricane, Typhoon and Cyclone Paths to Sea & Land Areas

Blizzard Paths

FIND OUT ABOUT ANIMALS AROUND THE WORLD

*Y*ou can predict when birds will migrate and see something about the mystery of their flight. You can make masks for a ceremony that celebrates a divine antelope. You can choose new favorites among the animals.

. . . .

CHOOSE YOUR FAVORITE ANIMAL

. . . .

Everybody has a favorite kind of animal. Maybe yours is a monkey or a horse, a dolphin or a tiger—or maybe a dinousaur from long ago. Your choice of a favorite animal is supposed to say something about your personality and how you picture yourself.

There's certainly no shortage of choices. About 25,000 different kinds of fish, 8,500 kinds of birds, and 5,000 kinds of mammals now live in the world—plus 5,000,000 varieties of insects.

The oceans, land areas, and climates of the Earth make natural habitats for them all, some habitats as tiny as wrinkles in tree bark (or even smaller if you count one-celled animals like bacteria) and others as big as the 12,000-mile (19,200-kilometer) flyways used by Arctic terns when they migrate from pole to pole.

Each animal species is naturally adapted to suit the geography around it and the complicated set of challenges it presents.

- Hummingbirds need to dart from one flowering plant to another and hover, so they have wing joints that allow 200 beats a second, speeds up to 55 miles per hour (88 kilometers per hour), and even the ability to fly upside down.

- Whales need to feed on cold-water plankton but breed their young in warmer waters, so they migrate thousands of miles each season.

- Polar bears need size, sharp hunting instincts, and heavy white coats to survive and blend into the harsh Arctic geography around them. They have all three.

The animals of the world—and the power and mystery they have—have fascinated humans since early times. Ancient cave paintings show animals as prey and also something more, as symbols of power and wealth, and even as gods. Sometimes, ancient people prayed to the animals they hunted and asked the animals to forgive them for taking their lives.

PERHAPS AS YOU FIND OUT MORE ABOUT ANIMALS, YOU'LL FIND NEW FAVORITES. GO ON TO SEE THE LEGEND OF A DIVINE ANTELOPE WHO BROUGHT PEOPLE THE GIFT OF AGRICULTURE.

THE LEGEND OF THE GIFT OF AN ANTELOPE

The legend is that long ago, the Bamana people of West Africa did not know how to till the soil. They could not grow the food they needed. At the dawn of time, a great antelope spirit called Chi Wara appeared to teach them.

Now the Bamana people are expert farmers.

The Bamana people live mostly on savanna or grasslands, near the upper Niger River of West Africa. (Look for the river at 15° to 20°N, 3° to 5°E.) A savanna presents problems for farmers to solve because it has rain in only one season rather than rain all year round.

The people there grow mostly crops of millet and sorghum—or rice in places where the Niger River overflows its banks every year. Millet and sorghum are good crops for savanna growing because these grains can stay alive even when the land is dry. But millet and sorghum stay dormant during the dry seasons. They grow again only when the rains come.

For centuries, the people have begun the planting season with songs and prayers in hope of a good harvest. They dance in honor of the great antelope and in honor of their work of tilling the soil and planting the crops.

Before the rains come, dancers and drummers play out the legend of the Chi Wara.

Men and women dress as male and female antelope. The woman's headdress stands for the Earth. The man's headdress represents the sun. On the back of the woman's costume is a fawn, to represent the human beings. Grasses or rushes flow from the man's headdress to show the water.

The dancers dance together just as the sun, earth, and water combine to grow the plants—and just as men and women work together to till the soil. As part of the dance, the dancers enter the fields with sticks to till the soil.

YOU MIGHT SEE THE DANCE OF THE GREAT ANTELOPE AT AN AFRICAN BALLET. AND YOU CAN MAKE YOUR OWN ANTELOPE DRUMS FOR A GOOD HARVEST. GO ON TO SEE HOW.

MAKE CHI WARA DRUMS

You may wish to make drums for a planting ceremony. These are drums you tie around your waist. You can use just one. Or you can tie several drums around your waist, with one upside down so you can hit the metal bottom for bell-like sounds.

Here's what you need:

Acrylic paints, in burnt sienna, black, yellow, or other colors you choose

Paint brushes

2-pound (1-kilogram) or 1-pound (550-grams) coffee cans with plastic tops

Cord or twine

Wooden chopsticks to use as drumsticks and digging sticks

Here's what you do:

1. Use acrylic paints and brushes to paint the outside of the coffee cans. Paint a base of burnt sienna. Then paint black and yellow designs. Or paint the cans in other colors you choose. Let the paint dry completely.

2. Cover the cans with the plastic tops. Tie a long piece of cord or twine below the top of each can. Leave enough to tie around your waist.

3. Use the chopsticks to beat the drums.

YOU CAN DISPLAY YOUR ANTELOPE DRUMS, OR YOU CAN HOLD A REAL CEREMONY. FOR THE CEREMONY, THE PEOPLE DANCE AND LEAP IN A CIRCLE. THE ANTELOPES LEAD. THEN THE DUMMERS FOLLOW. THEN OTHER DANCERS COME INTO THE CIRCLE, PERHAPS PAUSING TO WATCH THE ANTELOPES AND THEN JOINING IN THE DANCE. AS THE ANTELOPES DANCE, THEY PRETEND TO DIG FURROWS IN THE GROUND TO PREPARE FOR PLANTINGS. THEN THE OTHER DANCERS FOLLOW AS IF PLANTING THE SEEDS.

WATCH BIRDS MIGRATE

If you're lucky, you can see what happens in the skies every fall as North American birds begin their flight to warmer climates. Even if you live in a city and don't see animals around you very often, you may still be able to watch a bird migration.

Here's when to watch:

- Watch the fall weather for cool, clear days. The day is particularly good for migrating birds if the winds are blowing from the west or northwest.

- Early in the morning and at twilight, you have a good chance of seeing smaller birds like robins and orioles in the air. Because they can't glide for long, they fly by almost constantly flapping their wings. The generally calmer air at the beginning and end of fall days makes flying easier for them.

- Also, look for formations of ducks and geese early and later in the day. Like robins and orioles, ducks and geese also fly by constant flapping. If you watch carefully, you'll see that their flight looks smoother and straighter than the flights of smaller birds.

- During the middle of the day, look for larger birds with long wingspans, like crows, hawks, and big woodpeckers. They cover distance by gliding. Often, warmer, rising air currents during the day provide lift and help them along.

- Before a migration begins or during the migration, you may see flocks of birds, many more than usual on the ground or in the air. Watch when they leave, and see if they're headed south.

257

. . . .

WATCH BIRDS MIGRATE

continued

HOW DO BIRDS KNOW WHEN TO FLY SOUTH? THEY MAY FEEL THE COLDER TEMPERATURES. THEIR INSTINCTS MAY BE TRIGGERED WHEN THEIR SOURCES OF FOOD, SUCH AS INSECTS, BEGIN TO DISAPPEAR. AND HOW DO BIRDS KNOW THEIR DIRECTIONS? NO ONE KNOWS FOR SURE. BIRDS THAT FLY AT NIGHT MAY PREFER CLEAR SKIES PARTLY BECAUSE THEY ARE GUIDED BY THE MOON AND STARS. OR THE BIRDS THAT FLY BY DAY MAY SOMEHOW GUIDE THEMSELVES BY THE SUN OR BY HOW THE EARTH LOOKS AS THEY FLY. SOME SCIENTISTS BELIEVE THAT THE EARTH'S MAGNETISM MAY HELP BIRDS KNOW HOW TO FLY. BIRDS MAY SOMEHOW BE BORN WITH THE KNOWLEDGE. MIGRATION SEEMS TO BE ONE OF THE GREAT MYSTERIES OF THE EARTH. GO ON TO SEE ONE MYSTERY MIGRATION.

. . . .

FLY NORTH AND SOUTH WITH THE RED KNOTS

. . . .

Imagine traveling from northern Canada to the southern tip of South America and back every year.

That's what a small shore bird called the red knot does, migrating between Tierra del Fuego in Argentina and the islands north of Hudson Bay in Canada.

The distance is about 9,000 miles (14,500 kilometers) each way. The young birds make their first trips all on their own, without any help from their parents. The trip is one of the most amazing combinations of long-distance migration and navigation in nature. Tracking it will certainly make an unusual addition to your collection of map overlays.

Here's what you need:

At atlas with detailed maps of North America and South America

Removable tape

One clear plastic overlay sheet

A placemat or layered map of the world

Coloring markers or pens, in red, blue, and black

Here's what you do:

1. Use the atlas to locate these points:

Tierra del Fuego, Argentina	55°S, 65°W
São Paulo, Brazil	24°S, 46°W
Suriname	5°N, 55°W
Delaware Bay, United States	38°N, 75°W
Hudson Bay, Canada	63°N, 85°W

FLY NORTH AND SOUTH WITH THE RED KNOTS
continued

2. Use removable tape to attach the clear plastic overlay sheet to your placemat map. Use a red marker to draw a continuous, curving red line that connects the points. Follow the coast of South America toward São Paulo, then go overland to Suriname, overwater to Delaware Bay, and directly to Hudson Bay.

3. To the west of the red line, over South America, draw a black box and an arrow pointing to the red line. Write in these facts:

```
FEBRUARY TO JUNE:
ADULT BIRDS MIGRATE NORTH           ➤
```

4. Near Delaware Bay, make a second black box and arrow. It reads:

```
MAY IN DELAWARE BAY:
FEEDING ON CRAB EGGS                 ➤
```

This is where the red knots stop on their way north, just when horseshoe crabs eggs are being laid. A single bird can eat over 100,000 eggs before moving on.

5. Go to Hudson Bay, where the red knots arrive to hatch their young. Start a new blue line—and head back south. This line should run parallel to the red line all the way south to Tierra del Fuego, but keep it separate by drawing it a bit to the east of the red line.

6. In a space off to the east of the blue line, make two more black boxes with arrows that go back to the line:

```
◄           JULY:
            ADULT BIRDS RETURN SOUTH
```

7. At the top of the overlay, label it "Red Knot Migration."

8. Draw a third black box. Make a drawing for it that looks like this:

```
◄           LATE AUGUST:
            YOUNG BIRDS START FIRST TRIP
```

The drawing shows the red knots' powerful, inborn sense of navigation. When taking off as flocks, both the young and the adult birds are often seen scattering in several directions before homing in on the exact course they need for their route. Then they fly together—and in the overwater section between the southeast coast of the United States and Suriname, they keep going 24 hours a day for a whole week, without stopping.

FLY NORTH AND SOUTH WITH THE RED KNOTS

continued

OTHER CREATURES TRAVEL ON LONG AND MYSTERIOUS MIGRATIONS. IMAGINE FRAGILE-SEEMING BUTTERFLIES MAKING THEIR WAY FROM CANADA AND THE EASTERN UNITED STATES ALL THE WAY TO MEXICO AND CALIFORNIA. THAT'S WHAT MONARCH BUTTERFLIES DO. PICTURE THE FLIGHT OF THE TINY RUBY-THROATED HUMMINGBIRDS. THEY FLY NON STOP ACROSS THE CARIBBEAN SEA TO THEIR WINTER QUARTERS IN SOUTH AMERICA. SOMETIME YOU ALSO MIGHT LIKE TO TRACK WHALES AS THEY TRAVEL UP AND DOWN THE OCEANS SO THAT THEY CAN BE IN THE RIGHT PLACE AT THE RIGHT TIME.

FIND OUT ABOUT PEOPLE AROUND THE WORLD

*T*his is your chance to find out about people around the world, about people who are a lot like you and people who are very different. You can play a game of chance to find out who in the world has enough to eat and enough clean water. You can find out about the world's languages and religions. You can find out where the world is living, what sports the world is playing after school today, and what the world is having for dinner tonight. This is your chance to keep up with what the people of the world are doing.

SPIN THE WHEELS OF LIFE

About 6 billion people now live in the world, not too many of them with backgrounds, ideas, or daily lives even remotely like yours.

As just one person in the 6 billion, how unusual is it that you happen to be a student growing up in North America? What are the chances that one person would be your age, live where you do, eat what you do, speak your language, or even play the same games?

There's a real chance, of course, because your neighborhood and school are full of people much like you. But what about the whole rest of the world?

One way to understand how you fit into the world is to spin a wheel of fortune. You'll find out how usual or unusual you are.

These are the three Wheels of Life:

National Origins
World Religions
World Languages

You'll find out where your nation, your religion, and your language fit in the world.

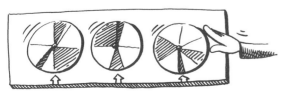

· · · · · · · · · · ·

SPIN THE WHEELS OF LIFE

continued

Here's what you need:

3 paper plates, each 6 inches (9 centimeters) across

A calculator, if you wish

A protractor

A ruler

Pencil and paper

Posterboard, 14 × 22 inches (35 × 55 centimeters)

3 two-pronged paper fasteners

Coloring markers or pens, in colors you choose

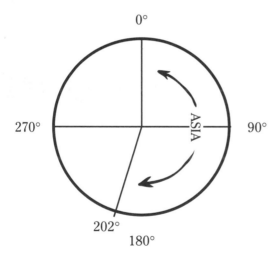

Here's what you do:

1. Think of each plate as representing the whole world—and also as a compass, 360° around. You can look at the chart on page 271 to see how it works. Suppose you want to show on one plate that 56.2% of the world's people live in Asia. (Of every 100 people

in the world, about 56 live in Asia.) Here's how to convert that fact into a compass heading that you could draw on the plate. Use a calculator if you wish:

First, convert the percentage to a decimal, like this:
56.2% ÷ 100 = 0.562

Second, multiply that number by 360° around the circle:
0.562 × 360° = 202.3°

Round off the number:
202.3° is about the same as 202°

Now you have a way to divide your plate.

2. Use a ruler and pencil to draw a straight line from the center of the plate to the top. That point at the top is 0°. Use your protractor to find the distance between 0° and 202°. Pencil in a dot for 202°. Then draw a straight line from the center to the edge of the plate at 202°. Label that section Asia.

3. Begin again with Africa at 16.2% of the world's population. Figure how to mark that percentage on the plate. If you need help, look for the answers on page 266. Set your protractor at the edge of the section for Asia. Consider that as 0°, and find the number of degrees you need for Africa. Label that section Africa.

4. Keep drawing in sections for other national origins. Look at

. . . .

SPIN THE WHEELS OF LIFE

continued

the chart to see how. Always use your protractor to find the right size for each section. Soon the sections will fill the entire circle of the plate. Label each section as you go.

5. Follow just the same steps to draw a plate on World Religions and the third plate on World Languages. Label each section.

6. Arrange the three plates on the posterboard. Mark where you want them, and use scissors to punch three holes through the posterboard right where the center of each plate should go. Use a pencil to punch a hole through the center of each plate. Attach each plate with a two-pronged paper fastener.

7. Use the coloring markers or pens to decorate the plates and put labels on the posterboard so that people know what each wheel means.

8. Mark big red arrows on the posterboard just at the top of

each wheel and pointing toward each wheel.

> NOW SPIN EACH PLATE. SEE WHERE THE RED ARROW IS POINTING WHEN THE PLATE STOPS SPINNING. YOU PROBABLY WON'T LAND ON YOUR PART OF THE WORLD, YOUR RELIGION, AND YOUR LANGUAGE. YOU'RE PLAYING THE WORLD GAME OF LIFE. THE MORE TURNS THE PLATES NEED TO FIND YOU, THE MORE UNUSUAL YOU ARE AMONG THE WORLD'S 6 BILLION PEOPLE.

HOW TO DRAW THE WHEEL FOR NATIONAL ORIGINS

National Origin	Percentage of the World's People	Degrees to Mark on the Wheel
Asia	56.2%	202°
Africa	16.2%	58°
Europe and the countries of the former U.S.S.R.	13.6%	49°
Latin American and the Caribbean	8.6%	31°
North America	4.9%	18°
Oceania, including Australia	0.5%	2°
Totals	100%	360°

HOW TO DRAW THE WHEEL FOR WORLD LANGUAGES

Language	Percentage of Native Speakers	Degrees to Mark on the Wheel
Mandarin Chinese	16.5%	59°
English	8.6%	31°
Hindi and Urdu	8.3%	30°
Spanish	6.4%	23°
Russian	5.8%	21°
Arabic	3.7%	13°
All 200+ others	50.7%	183°
Totals	100%	360°

HOW TO DRAW THE WHEEL FOR WORLD RELIGIONS

World Religion	Percentage of People	Degrees to Mark on the Wheel
Christianity	32.9%	118°
"No Religion" and Atheist	21.2%	76°
Islam	17.8%	64°
Hinduism	13.2%	47°
Buddhism	6.0%	22°
Judaism	0.3%	2°
All others	8.6%	31°
Totals	100%	360°

. . . .

SPIN THE WHEELS OF SURVIVAL

. . . .

Look at any map that shows the deserts, mountains, polar areas, and deep jungles of the world. Even at a glance, you can see large areas of difficult terrain and harsh climate.

In huge areas of the world, climate, water, and food problems make everday life a basic struggle for survival. In fact, only about one third of the Earth's total population lives near clean, safe drinking water. In most of the world, population is rising faster than food production.

Here are three direct ways to understand how difficult daily survival is for most of the world's people.

Make three Wheels of Survival:

Wealth
Food Supply
Water Supply

Here's what you do:

1. Make three paper plates into wheels just as for Spin the Wheels of Life, on page 263. Then look at the charts on page 269 to see how to divide two of your wheels into sections to show how much wealth people around the world have and how much food they have.

2. Use your third paper plate to represent the world water supply. Divide it into just two sections. Label one section Clean,

Safe Water. That's one third of the wheel. Use your protractor to mark off 120°. Label the other section Not Safe. That's two thirds of the wheel. Use your protractor to mark off 240° (or all the rest of the wheel).

3. Arrange the three finished plates on the posterboard with the Water Supply wheel on the left, the Food Supply wheel in the center, and the Wealth wheel on the right. Punch a hole through the center of each plate, and use two-pronged paper fasteners to attach each of them to the posterboard. Draw labels on the posterboard and plates so that people will know what each plate represents.

4. Draw big red arrows on the posterboard just at the top of each wheel and pointing toward each wheel.

This is a good project for a class or a group of friends. If you have nine people, you can do a classroom demonstration.

SPIN THE WHEELS OF SURVIVAL

continued

Here's how to do a classroom demonstration of the Wheels of Survival:

1. Now you're ready for a demonstration if you wish. You're going to show how likely it is that any given group of people in the world will have good living conditions, with clean water, adequate food, and enough money for other needs. You need a group of nine students to assist in the demonstration.

2. Ask three students to spin the Water Supply wheel. If the arrow points at "Not Safe" for any of them, ask those people to stand aside for a moment.

3. Ask three more students to spin the Food Supply wheel, along with anybody who got "Clean, Safe" after spinning the Water Supply wheel. If the arrow points at "Less Than 2,000 Calories" for any of them, ask them to stand aside.

4. Ask the last three students to spin the Wealth wheel, along with anybody who made it through the first two spins. If the arrow points at poverty for any of them—"Less Than $400" or "$400–$1,600" —ask them to stand aside.

5. See if anyone is still at the board. That's anybody who spun the three wheels and got clean water, adequate food, and enough money. You will probably end with five or six students standing aside while three or four are still at the board.

> AS NEW PEOPLE COME INTO THE WORLD, MANY OF THEM WILL LIVE EACH DAY WITH THE PROBLEMS OF WATER, FOOD, AND POVERTY. THE AVERAGE INCOME AROUND THE WORLD IS $3,600 PER YEAR PER PERSON. THAT'S $3,600 TO COVER THE NEEDS OF ALL THE MEMBERS OF A FAMILY, INCLUDING CHILDREN.

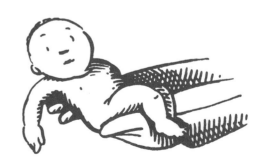

HOW TO DRAW THE
WEALTH WHEEL

Wealth Per Person	Percentage of the World's People	Degrees to Mark on the Wheel
$8,000 or more	14%	50°
$4,000–$8,000	9%	32°
$1,600–$4,000	12%	43°
$400–$1,600	14%	51°
Less than $400	51%	184°
Totals	100%	360°

HOW TO DRAW THE
FOOD WHEEL

Daily Calories Per Person	Percentage of the World's People	Degrees to Mark on the Wheel
3,000 or more	12.2%	44°
2,500–3,000	15.4%	55°
2,000–2,500	33.1%	119°
Less than 2000	39.3%	142°
Totals	100%	360°

. . . .

HAVE DINNER WITH THE WORLD

. . . .

Everyone ought to eat a variety of different foods. Around the world, though, there is frequently one basic food that people eat often. They may eat it with many other foods, and they may cook it any number of ways. But that one food is a main crop and a major way that people make a living. They may import and export that food. They may teach others to love it.

Here's another chance to spin a wheel. This time you get to see the major foods people are eating all around the world.

Here's what you do:

1. Make a plate just as for Spin the Wheels of Life, on page 263.

2. Look at the chart on page 271 to see how to use your protractor to divide your plate into sections.

3. Attach your plate to a poster-board with a two-pronged paper fastener. You may want to decorate the board with pictures of the basic foods of the world. Draw a red arrow at the top of the plate.

4. Try a spin. See how many of these basic foods you have tasted. Maybe you'll want to join the people of the world for dinner tonight—and try something new.

SOMEDAY MAYBE YOU COULD TRY THE FAVORITE SNACK FOODS OF THE WORLD, TOO. IN CHINA, FOR EXAMPLE, PEOPLE LOVE TO EAT CRUNCHY, CRISPY CHICKEN FEET. THE UNITED STATES EXPORTS 100 MILLION POUNDS A YEAR FOR THESE SNACKS CALLED PAWS.

HOW TO DRAW THE DINNER WHEEL

Basic Food	Percentage of the World's People Who Depend on It	Degrees to Mark on the Wheel
Rice	55%	198°
Potato	7%	25°
Wheat/Pasta /Bread	7%	25°
Cassava	7%	25°
Fish, Meat, Poultry	6⅔%	24°
Beans	5%	18°
Couscous	4%	14°
Corn	4%	14°
Okra	3%	11°
Taro Root	1%	4°
Breadfruit	⅓%	2°
Totals	100%	360°

 Rice

 Potatoes

 Fish

 Beans

 Corn

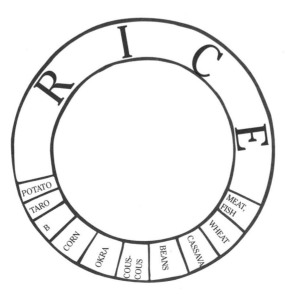

B=BREADFRUIT

TRY THE SPORTS WHEELS

All over the world, students your age are just as interested in sports and games as you are. Some of their favorite sports, however, are different from the ones you're likely to play or watch.

The sports you like depend mostly on where you live in the world—but not entirely. Think about your own friends and classmates. Does everyone like exactly the same sports? They don't, and that's because any group of people, large or small, will have its own likes and dislikes.

This is a way to see what your class really thinks about sports—and how the class compares to the whole rest of the world. When you're done, you'll have two more wheels to spin:

Our Favorite Sports
The World's Favorite Sports

Here's what you need:

Graph paper
A pencil and paper
A calculator, if you wish
A ruler
2 paper plates, each 6 inches (9 centimeters) across
A protractor
Coloring markers or pens
2 two-pronged paper fasteners
Posterboard, 14 × 22 inches (35 × 55 centimeters)

Here's what you do:

1. Survey your class to see what sports each person likes best, second best, and third best. Keep track of the results on graph paper so it looks something like this:

	BEST	SECOND	THIRD
BASEBALL			✓
HOCKEY		✓	
SOCCER	✓✓		
AMERICAN FOOTBALL		✓	
?			✓
?			

· · · · · · · · · · ·

TRY THE SPORTS WHEELS

continued

2. Make a pencil check mark for each vote a sport gets. Add new sports along the side of the graph as people mention them.

3. When you're done, give each sport 10 points for every first place it got, 5 points for every second place, and 3 points for every third place. Then pick the 5 sports that receive the highest totals.

4. Figure the percentage for each sport. Divide its points by the total of all points. Then multiply that number by 100. (Use a calculator if you wish.) For example: 122 total points for baseball ÷ 297 total points for all sports = 0.41

   $0.41 \times 100 = 41\%$

5. Now use graph paper and a ruler to make a chart of the favorite sports for your class. Rank them, something like this. (This is just an example.)

Sport	Total Points	Percent of Total
Baseball	122	41%
Hockey	88	30%
American Football	37	12%
Soccer	30	10%
Canadian Football	20	7%
Totals	297	100%

6. Make one paper plate divided to show the favorite sports for your class. To see how to change the percentages into degrees to mark on your wheel, look back at Spin the Wheels of Life, on page 263. Use your protractor to draw the sections on the paper plate. Draw and label the name of each favorite sport on the Our Sports wheel. Use coloring markers or pens to make the differences clear.

7. Now mark the second plate with favorite sports around the world. These cover the whole world and show you only the top 5 most popular sports. Look at the chart on page 274 to see how to mark the degrees on your wheel. Draw and label each sport on the World Sports wheel.

8. Arrange the two finished plates on the posterboard so they'll fit. Punch a hole through the center of each, and use two-pronged fasteners to attach each plate.

9. Draw big red arrows at the top of each wheel, pointing toward each wheel.

10. Decorate the posterboard with sports drawings or cut-out pictures.

· · · · · · · · · · ·

TRY THE SPORTS WHEELS

continued

Here's how to use your Sports Wheels:

1. Get people to try spinning the wheels. With the first one, they'll see how likely it is that their own favorite sport is also a class favorite, and how popular it is.

2. Spinning the second wheel will show something else—the likely favorite sport for any one person in the whole world. Maybe it will match up with your favorites, and maybe it won't.

> TRY IT. YOU'LL HAVE FUN SEEING WHAT SPORTS MOST PEOPLE IN THE WORLD LIKE. YOU MAY WANT TO LEARN ONE OR TWO OF THEM AS NEW ONES FOR YOURSELF.

HOW TO DRAW THE WORLD SPORTS WHEEL

Best Sport	Percentage of World's People Who Like It	Degrees to Mark on the Wheel
Soccer	35%	126°
Martial Arts	23%	83°
Cricket	18%	65°
Field Hockey	17%	61°
Basketball	7%	25°
Totals	100%	360°

· · · · · · · · · ·

SCRAPE THE SKY

· ·

Throughout the world, everywhere from Asia to North America, the biggest cities are growing much faster than the country areas around them. The world population is increasingly urban, with more than 70% of its growth happening in cities already larger than one million people.

One Canadian in three now lives in either Toronto (43°N, 80°W), Montreal (45°N, 74°W), or Vancouver (49°N, 124°W). More than half the people in the United States live in the 40 largest urban areas.

It's a trend that calls for its own kind of map.

Here's what you need:

Your world placemat map or a flat map of the world with the basic latitude and longitude lines on it. (A big map is best if you can get it.)

A large collection of pennies or very small toy blocks

Here's what you do:

1. Look at the chart of the most heavily populated urban areas in the world. You will represent each city by building a tower of pennies or blocks on the map.

· · · · · · · · · · ·

SCRAPE THE SKY

continued

THE WORLD'S TWELVE MOST
POPULATED URBAN AREAS

City	Country	Latitude, Longitude	Population in Millions as of 1995
Tokyo-Yokohama	Japan	35°N, 140°E	28.5
Mexico City	Mexico	19°N, 100°W	24.4
São Paulo	Brazil	24°S, 47°W	22.0
Seoul	South Korea	37°N, 127°E	19.4
New York	U.S.A.	41°N, 74°W	14.6
Osaka-Kobe	Japan	35°N, 135°E	14.0
Bombay	India	19°N, 73°E	13.7
Calcutta	India	23°N, 88°E	13.0
Rio de Janeiro	Brazil	23°S, 43°W	12.9
Buenos Aires	Argentina	35°S, 58°W	12.3
Manila	Philippines	14°N, 121°E	11.4
Moscow	Russia	56°N, 37°E	10.7
		Total	196.9

SCRAPE THE SKY

continued

2. Count how many pennies or blocks you have and decide how many people each penny or block will represent. Because your towers will have to show a total of 197 million people, you could decide that each penny or block will represent 1 million people. But you probably don't have 197 pennies or blocks on hand. Perhaps you have enough so that each can stand for 2 million or 3 million people. Or you can shorten the list of cities a bit, removing Manila and Moscow so that you have only 10 cities to represent.

3. Use the latitude and longitude directions to locate the cities on your map.

4. Stack up the right number of pennies or blocks, on top of those locations.

5. When you're done, you'll have a display that you could call the Urban Map of the World. It doesn't show all the large cities, but enough to show where one person out of every 30 in the world lives.

ASK PEOPLE WHO SEE THE DISPLAY ABOUT THEIR OWN URBAN HISTORY. ASK IF ANYONE HAS A FAMILY MEMBER WHO LIVES—OR HAS LIVED—IN ONE OF THE BIG URBAN AREAS YOUR TOWERS SHOW. NO MATTER WHERE YOU LIVE, YOU WON'T HAVE TO ASK MANY PEOPLE BEFORE YOU START FINDING PERSONAL CONNECTIONS TO THESE CITIES. THAT'S TRUE EVEN IF YOU DON'T LIVE NEAR ANY OF THESE CITIES.

. . . .

MOVE SIX BILLION PEOPLE—SLIGHTLY

. . . .

If you've ever studied Japan, you may know that its population is 125 million. That's half the size of the United States' population, and five times as big as Canada.

You may not know that 85% of Japan's people live on only 15% of its land area. On a map of Japan, look at the main island of Honshu (36°N, 140°E). You'll see the range of mountains running up the middle of the island, southwest to northeast. Not many people live (or can live) in the mountains. But on the eastern coast, you'll also see Tokyo-Yokohama, where about 30 million people live in one of the densest urban areas in the world.

You'll see big areas of difficult or uninhabitable land in other countries, too. That's partly why you hear so much about the problem of urban crowding and overpopulation.

One piece of graph paper is enough to show you how real it is. You can use the graph paper to represent one square mile of the Earth's land area.

Here's what you need:

A pencil

A ruler, if you wish

Graph paper

A calculator, if you wish

Here's what you do:

1. Use a pencil and a ruler to draw a square on the graph paper.

Make the square ten graph units on each side. (Now your square contains 100 smaller squares.)

2. Then do a math problem. There are about 6 billion people in the world, and about 58 million square miles (93 million square kilometers) of land area. How many people does that put on your one square mile? Use a

. . . .

MOVE SIX BILLION PEOPLE—SLIGHTLY

continued

calculator if you wish, and figure it like this:

6,000,000,000 ÷ 58,000,000 = about 103 people per square mile

3. Represent those 103 people with ten little circles, scattered evenly on your square like this:

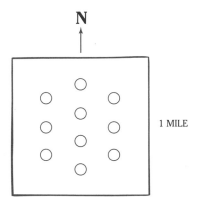

4. Now do a drawing problem. The fact is that 36% of the Earth's land area is almost completely uninhabitable Arctic and desert areas. To represent that on your square, go to its northeast corner and use a pencil to shade over 36 of its squares, like this:

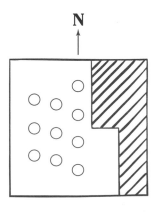

5. Because three of the people circles are shaded over, you must move them to open areas toward the west, spacing them around the seven circles already there.

6. Much of the Earth is also mountainous, jungle, swampy, or barren. Some people can live in those areas, but not many. So you'll have to shade over a block of 16 more squares. After you do that, you will have to move two or three more people circles.

> YOU CAN SEE WHAT'S HAPPENING. MORE AND MORE PEOPLE MUST OCCUPY THE LIVABLE PLACES OF THE WORLD—AND EVEN WITHIN THAT SPACE, NOT ALL LOCATIONS HAVE ENOUGH WATER AND GOOD SOIL FOR GROWING CROPS. AS THE WORLD'S TOTAL POPULATION CONTINUES TO GROW STEADILY, SO DOES THE DIFFICULTY OF SUPPORTING IT.

. . . .

KEEP YOUR TOOLS HANDY

. . . .

To get along in the world, you ought to know at least two ways of measuring. Those are the metric system (meters, grams, etc.) and the English or standard system (inches, pounds, miles, etc.). But you may also want to choose a time-honored measuring method favored by people all over the world. Use your own hands, arms, and feet.

The human body was the first ancient way of measuring. (Maybe you know that the height of a horse is still measured by hands. A foot is about the length of a large human foot. And from early times, a mile was measured as 1,000 paces of a Roman soldier.)

Try it. Your own body is very convenient. You always have your tools handy.

Here's what you need:

Your own hand, thumb, index finger, arm, foot, and memory

A pencil and ruler to use just this once

Here's what you do:

1. Use your ruler to measure some parts of your body. Notice that some of the measurements come out very conveniently. Pencil them down on this list:

Width of your thumbnail _____

Length of your index finger _____

Width of the palm of your hand _____

Length of your thumb from knuckle to tip _____

Distance from the end of your thumb to the end of your little finger, with your fingers spread out _____

Length from elbow to fingertips _____

Length of your foot _____

· · · · · · · · · · ·

KEEP YOUR TOOLS HANDY

continued

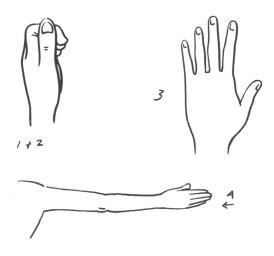

2. Find a part of your thumb or thumbnail that will show you ½ or 1 inch (5 or 10 centimeters.)

3. For measuring larger things, look at your hand and index finger. Depending on your age and size, you can use them to help you find the length of 12 inches, 1 foot, or 30 centimeters.

4. Your own foot may not be 12 inches (or about 30 centimeters) long, but look at the length from your elbow to your fingertips. Some easy-to-remember part of that will be 12 inches or part of a meter. It works—and as a bonus, you even get a 2-inch (or 5 centimeter) circle.

CONSIDER THE CASE OF OLIVER SMOOT AND HIS FRIENDS. THEY WERE ALL COLLEGE STUDENTS ABOUT 40 YEARS AGO, WHEN THEY DECIDED TO MEASURE THE LENGTH OF A BRIDGE WITHOUT ANY TOOLS AT ALL. SO THEY MADE SMOOT THE TOOL. THEY LAID HIM DOWN ON THE BRIDGE AND KEPT FLIPPING HIM OVER, END TO END. THE BRIDGE TURNED OUT TO BE 364.4 SMOOTS LONG.

· · · · · · · · · · ·

TRADE MONEY AROUND THE WORLD

· ·

If you have a pen pal from another country, consider taping a dime into one of your letters. Then ask for a small coin in trade. You'll have the beginning of a small collection.

Don't worry about getting a dime's worth back. The point is just trading. But if you do want to understand the foreign coin that comes back, ask your friend how many of these coins it takes to make up a unit in that country's money. For example, there are 100 pence in a British pound and 100 centimes in a French franc. Then find out what your friend might be able to buy with that coin, and see if you can compare the coin to your own money. (For example, a South African rand is worth about 25 United States cents.)

Your daily newspaper can tell you what the money of some other countries is worth on a particular day. Most newspapers have a table called Foreign Exchange or Dollar Exchange, in the same section with the stock market numbers.

WHEN YOU FIND THE MONEY EXCHANGE SECTION, PICK OUT A COUPLE OF COUNTRIES THAT INTEREST YOU. SEE HOW MANY OF THEIR UNITS IT TAKES TO MAKE A DOLLAR. IF YOU CHECK BACK EVERY FEW DAYS, YOU'LL SEE THAT THOSE NUMBERS GO UP AND DOWN BY SMALL AMOUNTS. THOSE CHANGES ARE CAUSED BY THE CONSTANT CHANGES IN BUSINESS AROUND THE WORLD.

If you go to:	You can trade one U.S. dollar for about:	
Japan	110	Yen
Mexico	8	Pesos
South Africa	4	Rand
South Korea	800	Won
England	65	Pence
France	5	Francs
Italy	1600	Lira
India	35	Rupees
Thailand	25	Baht

CREATE HOUSES FOR THE WORLD

*T*his is your chance to figure out how people build their houses. You can be a designer who figures the ins and outs of modern houses. You can build a model of a Native American house and an igloo. You can try out a bamboo house, the sort of house that shelters millions of people across Africa.

. . . .

BE A LOCATION DESIGNER

. . . .

Location is the science of where. Where is the best place to build a house? Where is the best place to lay out a new town, a shopping center, or a farm? Where can you go to create a wildlife preservation area? Where could a city fit in new community gardens? Where would a marina or new boat docks fit best around the edges of a lake?

If you choose location wisely, you avoid trouble. Picture designing a city park location, for instance, so as to avoid crime. Or picture planning out farm fields to avoid soil damage and to encourage the best conditions for crops.

You can create your own personal location design project. Suppose you acquire a beautiful piece of land right at the edge of your favorite lake. You decide to build a summer cottage and then some other nice additions.

You can draw your own plot plan, or you can look at the drawing below. Then decide where you want everything. Think about factors that ought to influence your decision.

Here's what to decide about your building plans:

- Where do you want to build your cottage? You may want your cottage near the road because that's convenient. Or you may want it on the lake shore, so that you can see the beautiful water views.

- In what direction do you want your cottage to face? If your cottage faces south, you will have maximum light and warmth in the winter, but if your cottage faces east, you will see the water better. Usually, the front part of a house faces the road, but in this case, the best views are away from the road. What rooms do you want facing the water? Where do you want to locate a porch for your cottage?

- Where do you want to put a well to bring water to your cottage? You may want the well near wetlands where the water will be near the surface, but not right in wetlands or swamps. You may need an expert to help you find a place far away from a septic system or farm land. You might need help to find a good underground source.

BE A LOCATION DESIGNER

continued

- What utilities do you want for your cottage? You may want to plan for the wires that bring electricity, gas, telephone, or television. Do you want them on overhead wires from the road, or do you want the wires buried in pipes under the ground? (Assume they all come from the direction of the road.)

- Where do you want to build a dog house? Your dog probably wants to be near the cottage, and you want to provide the dog with protection from bad weather.

- Where do you want to put up a bird house, bird feeder, and bird bath? Birds like a location at the edge of woods so they're not out in the open and exposed to predators. On the other hand, the people probably want the bird feeder and bath in plain view, so they can enjoy watching the birds.

- Where do you put in your garden? You may want different locations for flowers, for special trees, and for a vegetable garden. You would need to consider how much sun and shade your plants would get. Trees make a difference near a house, too. Deciduous trees (the kind that lose their leaves in the fall) give shade in the summer but allow the sun to come in during the winter. Evergreens would keep sun out in both summer and winter.

- Where do you want a boat dock? Make sure the water is deep enough for boats.

- Where do you want a picnic table and children's swing set? You want these in safe places, away from water danger and from wetlands that breed mosquitoes.

- Where do you want your driveway and mailbox?

- Do you want a playhouse, a workshop, a garage, or a storage shed? You can probably think of many good additions to your own fabulous summer cottage.

· · · · · · · · · · ·

BE A LOCATION DESIGNER

continued

THE NEXT TIME YOU WALK AROUND A SCHOOL, A CAMP, A HOSPITAL, AN ANIMAL SHELTER, OR EVEN A CITY, THINK HOW YOU COULD REDESIGN THE LOCATION TO MAKE IT BETTER. A LOCATION DESIGNER CAN MAKE TRAFFIC FLOW MORE SMOOTHLY, WITH FEWER TRAFFIC JAMS, FEWER ACCIDENTS, AND LESS DANGER TO PEOPLE. A LOCATION DESIGNER CAN HELP MAKE A SCHOOL, A CAMP, OR A SWIMMING POOL INTO A SAFE, HAPPY PLACE.

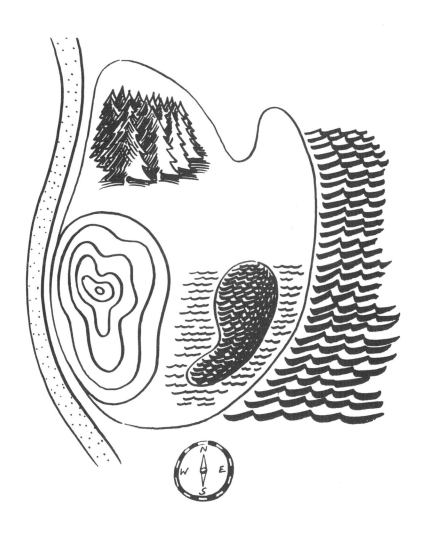

BUILD A MODEL TEPEE FROM WESTERN AMERICA

Western Native Americans were hunters and warriors. They had to keep on the move constantly in order to hunt, and they often had to move because of warfare with competing tribes.

Their houses fit their lives. They used tents that they could take apart easily and that they could carry with them. They made these tepees out of skins from the buffalo and other animals they hunted. You can still see real tepees on some Indian reservations or in American history museums.

You can build one model tepee or a whole Indian village.

Here's what you need:

Parchment-type paper, 8½ × 14 inches (22 × 36 centimeters)

A pencil

2 rulers

Scissors

A drawing compass

Cellophane tape

Poster paints or crayons

Straight thin sticks about 10 inches (25 centimeters) long. (You can use natural sticks from bushes or trees, or buy thin wooden sticks at a hobby or craft shop.)

A sewing needle and button thread

Here's what you do:

1. Follow the diagram to mark out your tepee model on parchment paper. Use a ruler and pencil to measure in 7 inches (about 18 centimeters) on the 14-inch (36-centimeter) side of the paper. Mark that midway point *A*. On the other long side of the paper, measure 7 inches (about 18 centimeters). Mark that midway point *B*.

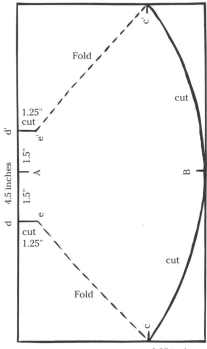

2. From each end of one long side (*B*), measure 2¼ inches (6 centimeters) up from the corner on the 8½-inch (22-centimeter) side. Mark *c* and *c′*.

3. From the long side opposite, find the midpoint mark *A* and make marks on each side, 1½ inches (4 centimeters) to the left and to the right. Mark *d* and *d′*.

BUILD A MODEL TEPEE FROM WESTERN AMERICA
continued

At right angles to the *d* and *d'* marks, measure 1½ inches (three centimeters). Mark those points *e* and *e'*. Use scissors to cut from *d* to *e* and from *d'* to *e'*.

4. Use a ruler to draw lines from point *e* to point *c* and then from point *e'* to point *c'*. Those are the fold lines.

5. Draw a curve from *B* to *c* and from *B* to *c'*. (You can use a

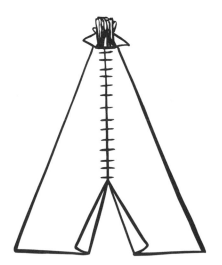

drawing compass to make the curve, if you wish. To do so, place rulers along the fold lines. Where the rulers meet is where you will need to place the point of the compass. Be sure you have it on a surface that will not be marred by the pointed end of the compass. Open the compass to point *B,* and draw the curve on the paper from *B* to *c* and then to *c'*.)

6. Use scissors to cut along the curve.

7. With cellophane tape, reinforce the underside of the *cd* and *c'd'* lines. Fold the paper along the fold lines between *c* and *d* and between *c'* and *d'*.

8. Use poster paints or crayons to decorate the outside of the tepee. Use the colors of real tepees. The animal skins provided earthy browns for the background, and the Indians would have decorated the tepees with red and blue from berries and greens from leaves and grasses. Here are a few design ideas.

9. Fold back the bottom flaps about 3½ inches (9 centimeters) up from the bottom. Fold back flaps at the top of either side of the 1¼-inch (3-centimeter) cuts.

BUILD A MODEL TEPEE FROM WESTERN AMERICA
continued

10. Carefully place about six of the sticks on the inside of the tepee. Hold one end of the sticks even with the bottom curve. The tops should stick out. Tape them in place with cellophane tape.

11. Use the needle and button thread to sew the tepee together. Begin at the top below the cut, and sew over and under until you are about 3½ inches (9 centimeters) from the bottom. Hold the edges together as you sew.

> *Caution: You may need adult help with sewing.*

WESTERN MOVIES SHOW SO MANY TEPEES THAT YOU MIGHT THINK ALL NATIVE AMERICANS LIVED IN THEM. BUT LIKE ALL PEOPLES, THE NATIVE AMERICANS CREATED DIFFERENT SORTS OF SHELTER TO SUIT THEIR OWN CLIMATE AND GEOGRAPHY—AND EVEN THEIR RELIGIONS. FOR EXAMPLE, THE NAVAJO PEOPLE IN WHAT IS NOW THE SOUTHWESTERN UNITED STATES BUILT HOGANS FROM LOGS AND MUD. BY TRADITION, THE DOOR FACED EAST. IN A PLACE WHERE THE WINDS USUALLY BLOW OUT OF THE WEST, AN EAST-FACING DOOR PROVIDES BETTER SHELTER. BUT THE DOOR ALSO MAY HAVE HAD RELIGIOUS SIGNIFICANCE SINCE IT FACED THE RISING SUN AND HERALDED THE BEGINNING OF DAY. OTHER NATIVE AMERICANS OF THE SOUTHWEST BUILT A SORT OF APARTMENT BUILDING, THE PUEBLOS. SOMETIMES SEVERAL STORIES HIGH, THE PUEBLOS WERE MADE OF STONE OR ADOBE AND WERE PRACTICAL FOR A HOT, HARSH CLIMATE. THE APACHES AND OTHER NOMADIC PEOPLE OF THE PLAINS BUILT WICKIUPS. THOSE WERE FRAME HUTS COVERED WITH BRUSH OR BARK.

BUILD A MODEL IGLOO FOR THE WINTER HOLIDAYS

In the harsh Arctic winter, the Inuits often lived snugly in snow houses. Inuit is another name for the Eskimos. The snow houses actually kept them warm and comfortable. They could even do their cooking inside.

Make this model snow house, and use it as a Christmas or winter decoration.

You need a work space that will not be in anyone's way. Plan some time to finish your house. You can move the house and put away your materials between work sessions.

Here's what you need:

A large piece of rigid cardboard

A drawing compass

2 or more boxes of sugar cubes

Non-toxic white glue in a squeeze bottle, the type used to glue wood

A #1 triangular file

Card-weight paper 8 ½ × 11 inches (22 × 28 centimeters), the same weight as index cards

A ruler

Scissors

Here's how to draw a floor plan of your snow house:

1. Draw the floor plan directly onto the cardboard. Open your drawing compass to 3 inches (about 8 centimeters), and draw a circle in one corner. That will be the living area.

2. Open the compass to 2 inches (about 5 centimeters), and draw an overlapping circle across about 2 inches (5 centimeters) of the first circle. This will be the storage area.

3. Open the compass to about 1⅛ inches (3 centimeters), and draw a circle overlapping the smaller circle by about 1½ inches (about 4 centimeters). This is the entry way.

4. Draw two curved lines about 1 inch (2.5 centimeters) apart off the smallest circle. This will be the wind shelter. The dogs sleep in this area to get out of the wind.

Here's how to make the model igloo:

1. Place the first layer of sugar cubes onto the circles on your floor plan. As you put the sugar cubes around the curves, use the file to bevel one end of each

BUILD A MODEL IGLOO FOR
THE WINTER HOLIDAYS

continued

cube on a slant. When you file each cube at a slant, you make the cubes fit together well. Make two layers this way. Apply the white glue quite thickly to the base and the edges of the pieces. Then fit them together.

2. Let the first two layers dry for half an hour or longer. Check the last cube you set to be sure it is stuck tightly before you go on to add the next layer.

3. At this point, you will need to start curving the wall of the house toward a dome. You will need to bevel cubes for a third layer along the base of each cube. Let each beveled layer dry before you add the next layer. (Look at the diagrams of the slanted cubes. The Inuits built their igloos in a spiral of elaborate, shaped blocks.)

4. The storage area will have fewer layers than the main area. Continue filing the side and bottom edges of each layer at a greater angle than for the main area. You'll have to cut and shape the sugar cubes to fit.

5. The wind shelter should be even smaller. When you build upward, you will need to bevel and slant all the inside corners.

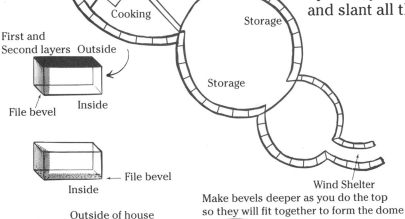

Sleeping Space

Cooking

Sitting Space

Cooking

Storage

Storage

First and Second layers   Outside

File bevel   Inside

Inside   File bevel

Outside of house

Inside of house

Wind Shelter
Make bevels deeper as you do the top so they will fit together to form the dome

· · · · · · · · · · ·

BUILD A MODEL IGLOO FOR
THE WINTER HOLIDAYS

continued

6. To keep the curved sections in place, cut a piece of card paper stock the size of the layer. To get the measurement, put a ruler across the width of the circle. Open the drawing compass to half that distance and make a circle on the card paper stock. Use scissors to cut out the circle. Glue the paper in place over the layer you just placed. Glue the next layer to the paper. Continue doing this until you have completed the igloo.

   Note: The diagram is for guidance only. You may use a different number of sugar cubes to make up each layer. The base for the large section may take about 17 cubes—more or less. The actual number will depend on how deeply you cut the bevels and how closely your cubes fit together.

IF YOU WANT TO FINISH YOUR IGLOO FOR A CHRISTMAS CENTERPIECE, PUT SOME COTTON BATTING AROUND IT, AND SPRINKLE IT WITH GLITTER. YOU CAN ADD SOME SMALL PLASTIC OR CERAMIC ESKIMO FIGURES AND DOGS, REINDEER, SANTA CLAUS, AND ELVES.

· · · · · · · · · ·

BUILD A MODEL AFRICAN BAMBOO HOUSE

· ·

People build with what they have, and they build houses to shelter them in their own climate. If you live in the Arctic, you build with snow. If you live in the American West, you have buffalo hides. If you live in regions of Africa, you have bamboo, mud, and dung.

You may have seen pictures of villages in Africa. The people make houses using a frame of poles or bamboo tied together. They build walls with a sort of plaster made of red clay or a mixture of mud and dung. Then they use colored clay or ashes to create the decorations, colorful designs of geometric figures.

There are several types of African bamboo houses. People may build a roof from rushes or from the bark of a banana tree. Sometimes, they hold the bamboo together with vines or hemp (the same sort used to make ropes). They may mold the clay into bricks to build the house.

These houses are ideal for the climate and use natural materials. Here's how you can make your own model of a round bamboo house.

Here's what you need to make the bamboo frame:

Old newspapers, if you want

Lightweight cardboard, such as a file folder

A ruler

Scissors

A craft knife

1 bundle of bamboo. (You can buy bamboo by the bundle at a garden center or hardware store. People use it as stakes to hold up plants. Often, it's painted green, but you may find it in its natural tan color.)

White household glue

Here's what you need to finish the walls, if you wish:

Modeling clay, play dough, or plaster of Paris

Putty knife

Poster paints and brushes

Here's what else you need to make the roof:

Drawing compass

Dried corn husks, corn stalks, or reeds

Cellophane or reinforced tape (the kind used to tape packages)

Here's how to make the bamboo house frame:

1. Find a work surface you can get a little messy. You may want to put down old newspapers.

2. Use a piece of lightweight cardboard, such as a file folder, for

293
·

BUILD A MODEL AFRICAN BAMBOO HOUSE

continued

the frame of your house. Use a ruler to measure two strips, each 4 × 11¾ inches (about 10 × 30 centimeters). Use scissors to cut out the strips, and save the rest of the file folder for the roof of the house.

3. Use the craft knife to split the bamboo pieces. Start splitting at one end. The piece should split quite easily at least part of the way. Split again for the rest of the way. You might get three or four lengths from one piece of bamboo.

Caution: You need adult help with using a craft knife.

4. Cut the bamboo pieces into lengths of 4 inches (10 centimeters). You'll need about 50 pieces for one house.

5. Spread one of the cardboard pieces with white glue. Glue the second piece directly onto it. The second layer will make your house stronger, but it will be flexible enough to form the circular shape of the house.

6. Use the ruler to measure a door opening onto the cardboard frame. Position the door at the center of the frame, and make it

1 × 2½ inches (1.5 × 6.5 centimeters). Cut the door on the top and one side, so it can open and close.

7. Glue the strips of bamboo to the cardboard frame. Begin at one edge. Glue strips as close together as you can. Continue until you come to the door. Cut small pieces to glue to the area over the door. Keep going along the frame until you come near the other edge. Then stop. Leave about ¾ inch (about 2 centimeters) clear at that edge, without bamboo.

8. Glue small bamboo pieces to the door itself.

9. Glue slivers of bamboo to any bare spots. Allow the glue to dry completely.

10. Now apply glue to the edge not covered by bamboo. Form a circle, with the bamboo facing outward. Stick the glue-covered edge under the bamboo-covered edge. Hold the pieces together for a minute or more while the glue sets. Set the circular house on end to dry. Leave the door open outward.

Here's how to finish the walls:

1. If you wish, you can cover the bamboo frame with modeling clay, play dough, or plaster of Paris. Use a putty knife to apply the clay or plaster. Let it dry thoroughly.

· · · · · · · · · ·

BUILD A MODEL AFRICAN BAMBOO HOUSE

continued

2. If you wish, use poster paints and brushes to paint shapes and designs on the side of the house. Use red, green, brown, and black.

Here's how to make the roof:

1. Use the other piece of the file folder to make a base for the roof. Open your drawing compass to 5 inches (about 13 centimeters). Make a circle on the cardboard. Make a mark on the edge of the circle. Next use your ruler. Place the ruler across the circle so that the 8-inch (20-centimeter) spot on the ruler is at the mark. Move the 0 point of the ruler so that it intersects the rim of the circle. Draw a line.

2. Draw a line from those two points to the center of the circle. Use scissors to cut out the wedge.

3. Make a cone out of the remainder of the circle. Overlap the two edges about 2½ inches (about 6 centimeters). Mark the spot where they overlap.

4. Glue the overlapping edge to form the cone. Apply tape to help hold the cone together. Let the glue dry completely.

5. Use tape to attach the roof to the house walls. Tape from underneath so the tape shows as little as possible. To hold it

securely, you may want to use reinforced tape. The roof will overhang somewhat, just as it would on a real house.

6. Use the dried husks, corn stalks, or reeds to cover the roof of the house. If you need to dry them, put a layer between paper towels, and place in the microwave. Microwave on low power until they have dried. Cut them to lengths of about 1 inch (2 or 3 centimeters). You'll need to split and flatten reeds or stalks.

> *Caution: You need adult help with cutting these.*

7. Glue them in layers. Start at the edge of the roof, and work up. Put the glue on only the top ½ inch (or 1 centimeter) of each layer. Make each layer overlap the layer before it, just like shingles. As you come to the point of the roof, you'll need to shape the layers more and make them more pointed. Use scissors to cut them.

> NOTICE THAT A ROUND HOUSE MAKES THE BEST USE OF SPACE WITH THE SMALLEST AMOUNT OF BUILDING MATERIAL. AFRICANS USUALLY HAVE A SEPARATE HOUSE FOR THEIR KITCHEN, SO THEY DON'T FILL THE MAIN HOUSE WITH SMOKE OR RUN THE RISK OF A FIRE.

MAKE FRIENDS AROUND THE WORLD

*T*his is a chance to make friends around the world. You can write to a pen pal in another country. You can collect stamps, coins, or cards from around the world.

If you're feeling creative, you can make designs for people around the world. You can design—and wear—a special round-the-world friendship pin. You can design a logo for your favorite foreign country, an international symbol that anyone can use, or a national costume.

Now you can find out how students are different from you— or the same. You can even find out how they make excuses for being late to school.

TRADE A DAY IN YOUR LIFE

What if you could go to another country, live there, and go to school for a day?

Basic, everyday things would suddenly be different—the language you'd speak, the food you'd eat, the clothes you'd wear. But many other things would be at least somewhat familiar, and you would probably have a really good time seeing what an ordinary day is like for students in a different part of the world.

Try it out. Depending on where you live, Tokyo (36°N, 140°E), Sydney (35°S, 151°E), and Paris (49°N, 2°E) are all either far away or really far away.

Just read over the following table and fill in the blanks to describe your own regular day. Imagine a Tokyo, Sydney, or Paris day. For you, what things would be most different? Most fun? Or pretty much the same?

WHEN YOU HAVE A MOMENT, SHOW THE TABLE TO SOMEONE WHO HAS LIVED OUTSIDE YOUR COUNTRY, SOMEONE WHO CAN FILL IN THE ? COLUMN WITH DETAILS ABOUT ANOTHER COUNTRY. THAT COULD GET EVEN MORE INTERESTING.

. . . .

TRADE A DAY IN YOUR LIFE

continued

A TYPICAL DAY

	You	Tokyo	Sydney	Paris	?
Breakfast		Noodles	Toast Vegemite*	Roll	
School Clothes		Student Uniforms	Slacks or Skirts, Hats	Slacks or Skirts	
School Bag		Briefcase	Book Sack	Briefcase	
To School On		Subway or Bus	Train or Walk	Subway or Walk	
Lunch		Obento**	Egg Sandwich	Ham Sandwich	
Sport		Judo	Rugby	Soccer	
Snack		Cola and Milk Mix	Ice Cream	Pastry	
Special Activity		Pachinko***	Surf Training	Cycling	
Dinner		Fish, Rice	Lamb	Soup, Beef	
Homework		4 hrs.	2 hrs.	3 hrs.	
TV		NTV	ATV	France 2	

*= A vegetable spread, with horseradish
**= A boxed lunch of rice and soup, delivered to school
***= A small pinball machine

DESIGN A COUNTRY LOGO

Every day, you see logos—the symbols that companies and teams use to identify themselves. There's the eyeball shape for CBS (the Columbia Broadcasting System), the bluejay on Toronto baseball caps, the markings on sneakers, among thousands of others.

For countries, flags have always served that purpose. Their colors and unique designs symbolize countries. But maybe you'd like to invent something special for a country that interests you—a logo that would capture its special features and be recognizable at a glance. It wouldn't be a substitute for a flag, just something extra.

Here's what you need:

Books and other information about a country that interests you
Plenty of paper and a pencil
Coloring markers or pens

Here's what you do:

1. Look over the books and other information you have and think about the basic art elements for your logo. Is there an animal, a natural feature like a mountain, a food, a business, a dance, a monument, a sport, or some history that is unique to that country? Should you use just one, or combine several of those into a single symbol? What colors would be right for it?

2. Sketch out some of your ideas in pencil, and then with coloring markers or pens. Try out shapes and color combinations until you like one or two sketches best.

3. Do a final, careful version of the one or two.

> TO SEE HOW OTHER PEOPLE MIGHT REACT, SHOW YOUR FINISHED WORK TO A PARENT OR FRIEND. TELL THEM THAT IT'S A LOGO FOR A COUNTRY AND SEE IF THEY CAN NAME THE COUNTRY.

(CANADA)

(JAMAICA)

· · · · · · · · · · · · · · · · · · · ·

DESIGN AN AROUND-THE-WORLD FRIENDSHIP PIN

· ·

The Olympic flag shows five interlocking rings in blue, yellow, black, green, and red. They symbolize friendly competition, and so does the athletes' custom of trading souvenir pins. Here's how to make your own beaded friendship pin in the Olympic colors.

Here's what you need:

10 silver or brass safety pins, each ³⁄₄ or ⁷⁄₈ inch (19 or 22 millimeters) long

A package of 4 or 6 millimeter seed beads in different colors

A sharp fingernail file or small paring knife

A silver or brass safety pin, 2 inches (5 centimeters) long

Here's what to do:

1. On each of the ten small safety pins, string beads onto the front (or sharp) shank of the safety pin. String the beads like this:

   Pins # 1 and # 2, all blue beads

   Pins # 3 and # 4, all yellow beads

   Pins # 5 and # 6, all black or brown beads

   Pins # 7 and # 8, all green beads

   Pins # 9 and # 10, all red beads

   Close each pin when you are done putting on the beads.

2. Use the point of a sharp fingernail file or small paring knife to pry open the loop at the base of the large safety pin.

*: **Caution: You need adult help with this step.***

3. Open the large safety pin. Hold it in one hand with the front (or sharp) shank facing away from you. With your other hand, put on the ten small safety pins. String on the base of each closed pin, with the beads facing away from you. Then thread each small pin around the loop of the big pin and onto the back shank.

*: **Caution: You may need adult help with this step, too.***

4. Close the large safety pin.

: WHEN YOU WEAR YOUR PIN,
: THE BEADS WILL HANG FREELY
: FROM THE LARGER BASE PIN.
: ANY MOTION WILL MAKE THEM
: LOOK JUST A BIT LIKE A
: PROUDLY WAVING FLAG. YOU
: HAVE AN INTERNATIONAL
: FRIENDSHIP PIN THAT
: EVERYONE WILL NOTICE.

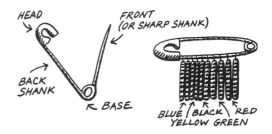

HEAD
FRONT (OR SHARP SHANK)
BACK SHANK
← BASE
BLUE | BLACK | RED
YELLOW GREEN

WRITE TO A PEN PAL IN ANOTHER PART OF THE WORLD

People learn English as a second language almost everywhere in the world. A student your age who is learning English might like to write to you. And you may be learning another language that you want to practice. Besides, it's fun to make a friend from far away.

One way to find a good pen pal is to write directly to a school in a place that interests you. For example, if you live in a town named after a town in Germany or Scotland, you could write to a school in that sister town. Or your school may already have a pen pal program.

Here are organizations that can find a pen pal for you. If you want a pen pal from one of these organizations, send a letter asking for information and an application. Include a long self-addressed, stamped envelope.

Each of these organizations charges a fee, almost always quite small. Several of them offer newsletters and magazines for international pen pals.

• Gifted Children's Pen Pals International (GCPPI)
  3076 Silver Maple Drive
  Virginia Beach, VA 23452-6772

For people ages 4 to 18. Associated with MENSA. Small fee required. In operation since 1976.

• International Pen Friends
  1308 68th Lane North
  Brooklyn Center, MN 55430

For people ages 8 to adult, with school, youth group, and stamp collector's programs. Small fee required. *People and Places* magazine available. In operation since 1967 and regarded as the largest and most widespread of these organizations.

· · · · · · · · · · ·

WRITE TO A PEN PAL IN ANOTHER PART OF THE WORLD

continued

• Kids Meeting Kids
  380 Riverside Drive, Apt. 8H
  New York, NY 10025

For people ages 5 to 20, with school and youth group programs available. Small fee required. *Kids Meeting Kids Can Make a Difference* newsletter available. In operation since 1982.

• Student Letter Exchange
  630 3rd Avenue
  New York, NY 10017
  FAX 212-286-8240

For students ages 9 through college. Small fee required. In operation over 50 years.

• World Pen Pals
  1694 Como Avenue
  St. Paul, MN 55108
  FAX 612-647-9268

For students ages 12 to 20. Associated with the International Institute of Minnesota. Small fee required.

IF YOU HAVE ACCESS TO A COMPUTER, YOU ALSO MAY BE ABLE TO FIND A PEN PAL ON THE INTERNET AND EXCHANGE E-MAIL. ONE SITE TO TRY IS http://www.worldkids.net/eac/age1.html. IT WAS REACHABLE, SAFE AND RELIABLE, AND DID NOT CHARGE EXTRA FEES AS OF 1996. FOR OTHER PEN PAL SITES ON THE INTERNET, GET A PARENT, TEACHER, OR LIBRARIAN TO HELP YOU. YOU MAY FIND THE RIGHT INTERNATIONAL FRIEND.

· · · · · · · · · ·
START AN AROUND-THE-WORLD STAMP, COIN, OR CARD COLLECTION
· ·

You may already collect sports cards, postage stamps, coins, or post-cards—or maybe something really unusual. A collection is a good way to look into other cultures and other ways of living, and stamps, coins, and cards are often small works of art. If you think they're beautiful and inter-esting, you'll like to have them.

Here are ideas on how to start and create a worldwide collection:

- Choose your collection. You can't collect everything, so select some-thing that particularly interests you. You can buy packets of stamps on one country, theme, or subject. Or you can plan to get a postcard from every country in Europe—whether from pen pals or from people you know who travel. You may want to select trading cards on a theme: only one sport, only one team, or only players born in your state or province.

- Decide if you want a collection that you find or a collection you buy. For example, you may want to collect only stamps or postcards that arrive in the mail. Or you may want to save money just for special stamps, coins, or sports cards.

- You may want to subscribe to a magazine or newsletter for collectors. Some post offices offer magazines particularly for children who like to collect stamps—and sometimes without charge. So many people have collections that you have a good chance of finding specialized books, magazines, newsletters, or sites on the Internet.

- Don't collect in the hope of making money. Someone may tell you that a certain coin or sports card set is sure to go up in value. You don't know whether that's true or not. But you do know that there are many professional collectors who are already trying to make money on collections. Some of them may be trying hard to make money from you. You should start a collec-tion because your collection is interesting and fun, not because you might make a profit.

. . . .

START AN AROUND-THE-WORLD STAMP, COIN, OR CARD COLLECTION
continued

- If you shop to buy something for your collection (or order by mail), make a list of what you want most. Don't let yourself be tempted to spend too much money for something you may not really like. Stick to your wish list. Many full sets are nearly duplicates of other full sets, especially with sports cards and stamps.

- As you shop for your collection, consider buying a less expensive type, such as sports cards that are not in perfect condition or stamps that have postmarks. You'll still enjoy your collection, and you can save money.

- You'll have a huge choice if you collect postage stamps. Some countries even issue postage stamps as a major export. One way to buy stamps is by the kiloware, stamps cut from envelopes and sold all together by weight. Then you can go through them and see if any of them interest you. Another interesting way to collect stamps is to buy first-day covers. That's an envelope with a new stamp postmarked on the first day that stamp can be used. You find out about the first-day stamp issue ahead of time, and then address the mail to yourself.

- Store your collection carefully. You can store stamps in a special stamp album. One good kind has blank loose-leaf pages like a notebook. You can also keep sports or other cards in plastic sheets inside a loose-leaf binder. Slide them in slowly so you don't damage them. Store valuable coins in a container so they won't bump into others and so that they won't get scratched. Pick up a valuable coin by the rim. Don't rub it or even breathe on it. (You may rub pennies with a pencil eraser to make them bright and shiny, but don't do that to a valuable coin.) Don't expose stamps or cards to direct sun or bright lights. Don't keep a collection in a basement, garage, or attic.

- Label your collection. Leave space in an album to write something interesting about each stamp, coin, or card. You'll want the important information about the item, plus when and where you got it.

START AN AROUND-THE-WORLD
STAMP, COIN, OR CARD COLLECTION
continued

WHEN YOU COLLECT STAMPS, NOTICE HOW COUNTRIES WORD THEIR NAMES, AND LOOK FOR THE SYMBOLS THEY USE. YOU MAY SEE ONLY THE INITIALS OF THE COUNTRY: U.S.A. FOR THE UNITED STATES OF AMERICA, R.S.A. FOR THE REPUBLIC OF SOUTH AFRICA, K.S.A. FOR THE KINGDOM OF SAUDI ARABIA. YOU MAY SEE ONLY EMBLEMS FOR THE COUNTRY. ON BRITISH STAMPS, YOU'LL SEE THE HEAD OF THE QUEEN OUTLINED. ON STAMPS FROM SAUDI ARABIA, LOOK FOR A PALM TREE AND CROSSED SWORDS. LOOK FOR STAMPS THAT USE INTERESTING, HISTORIC NAMES FOR THEIR COUNTRIES: EIRE FOR IRELAND, HELVETIA FOR SWITZERLAND, HELLAS FOR GREECE, NIPPON FOR JAPAN.

PLAN AN AROUND-THE-WORLD PARTY

*Y*ou can throw an around-the-world party. You'll have your choice of food from around the world, including a special world birthday cake and ice cream volcanoes.

You can play inside and outside around-the-world games.

It will be the best party yet.

. . . .

MAKE WORLD PARTY INVITATIONS

. . . .

Now that you're a Geography Wizard, one way to celebrate might be with a birthday, classroom, club, or a school-vacation party that has games and food from all over the world.

To start your friends off with some hints about what will happen at the party, you can even make up a special invitation.

Here's what you need:

*A photocopy of the world map, 8½ ×
11 inches (22 × 28 centimeters)*

A black marker or pen

Some spare magazines

Scissors

Regular household glue

Here's what you do:

1. Mark the map with a big dot at the approximate location of the party.
2. Look through the magazines to get small photos and pictures you can use. Good subjects would be planes, trains, buses, kids on bikes, and kids running.
3. Use scissors to cut out the best magazine pictures. Arrange the cutouts on the map so they all seem to be zooming toward your dot.
4. When everything fits and looks good, glue down the cutouts with regular household glue.
5. Use a black marker to print a headline at the top: "People Are Coming from Everywhere to the Party." At the bottom, print another headline: "So Should You." On the back, print the date, time, and address of the party.

WHEN YOU'RE DONE WITH BOTH SIDES OF THE INVITATION, GET PHOTOCOPIES MADE TO HAND OUT. IF YOU CAN'T GET TO A MACHINE THAT DOES TWO-SIDED COPYING, RUN THE SIDES SEPARATELY AND THEN STAPLE THEM TOGETHER.

CREATE PARTY FOOD FROM AROUND THE WORLD

Here's a menu for your around-the-world party. Are you ready to try something new? You can create food from far away across the world, perhaps including foods you've never eaten before. You can even bake a world birthday cake and make an ice cream volcano.

Caution: You may need adult help with cutting, chopping, peeling, and baking. Make sure you have permission and help to use a machine such as a food processor, an electric mixer, or a microwave oven.

Tropical Tutti-Frutti Punch

*

Crackers, Pita Bread, Party Bread
Carrot Sticks, Celery Sticks, Cucumber Rounds,
and Other Raw Vegetables

with

French Orange-Herbal Spread
Mexican Avocado Dip

*

Around-the-World Pizza

*

A World Birthday Cake

*

Ice Cream Volcanoes

GO ON TO SEE RECIPES FOR THE AROUND-THE-WORLD PARTY MENU.

STIR UP TROPICAL TUTTI-FRUTTI PUNCH

Here's a party drink from the tropics, good in hot weather. Begin it the day before the party.

Here's what you need:

2 or 4 ice cube trays

A bottle of maraschino cherries

¼ cup (60 milliliters) maraschino cherry juice

1 or 2 small oranges

½ cup (125 milliliters) lemon juice

1 quart (1 liter) pineapple juice

A 12-ounce (about 355 milliliters) can frozen orange juice concentrate

2 quarts (2 liters) cold ginger ale

Here's what you do on the day before the party:

1. Place one maraschino cherry in each section of half the ice cube trays. Save the maraschino cherry juice and keep it in the refrigerator until tomorrow.

2. Peel each orange and separate it into segments.

3. Place one orange segment into each section of the remaining ice cube trays.

4. Fill the trays with water and place in the freezer.

5. Refrigerate the ginger ale.

Here's how to mix the punch just before the party starts:

1. Combine lemon juice, pineapple juice, frozen orange juice concentrate, and maraschino cherry juice. Stir to melt the orange juice concentrate.

2. Add the fancy ice cubes from the freezer.

3. Pour the cold ginger ale over all and stir.

> THIS MAKES 16 TO 20 SERVINGS OF PUNCH. TUTTI-FRUTTI IS AN ITALIAN WORD FOR THE FLAVOR OF MIXED FRUITS. THIS PUNCH IS GOOD IN ITALY—OR ANYWHERE ELSE THAT PEOPLE ARE THIRSTY.

· · · · · · · · · · ·
MAKE A FRENCH ORANGE-HERBAL SPREAD
· ·

For your next food, move from the tropics to a country famous the world over for its fabulous food.

Here's what you need:

8 ounces (464 grams) of cream cheese or other soft, mild cheese

½ cup (125 milliliters) sour cream or whole-milk yogurt

1 teaspoon (5 milliliters) grated orange rind

⅓ cup (80 milliliters) stuffed olives

2 scallions

Here's what you do:

1. Mash the cheese and sour cream or yogurt together in a medium bowl.
2. Stir in grated orange rind.
3. Chop the olives and stir them in.
4. Cut the scallions into thin slices and stir them in.
5. Keep in the refrigerator until ready to serve.

This makes about 2 cups (500 milliliters). Serve as a spread with crackers, pita, or party bread.

MAKE AN AVOCADO DIP FROM MEXICO

Move on to a party dip from another country famous for its good cooking.

Here's what you need:

3 ripe avocados

2 tablespoons (30 milliliters) lime juice

¼ cup (60 milliliters) sour cream or whole milk yogurt

¼ teaspoon (1 milliliter) ground cumin

3 plum tomatoes

2 slices of red onion

¼ cup (60 milliliters) chopped cilantro leaves

Salt and pepper, as you wish

Here's what you do:

1. Peel the avocados and remove the pits. Put them in a medium bowl and add lime juice. Mash with a fork. Or else use a food processor or blender, and blend at low speed until smooth.

2. Stir or blend in the sour cream or yogurt and the ground cumin.

3. Remove seeds from the tomatoes and dice the tomatoes.

4. Dice the onion slices.

5. Stir in tomato pieces, onion pieces, and cilantro.

6. Sprinkle in a little salt and pepper, if you wish. Mix thoroughly.

7. Refrigerate until ready to serve.

THIS MAKES ABOUT 3 CUPS (ABOUT .7 LITER). SERVE AS A DIP FOR CRACKERS, CHIPS, AND YOUR FAVORITE RAW VEGETABLES.

. . . .

BAKE AROUND-THE-WORLD PIZZAS

. . . .

Each party guest can make a special pizza, just big enough for one. Before the party, buy English muffins or else 4-inch (10-centimeters) pizza shells, enough for each guest.

Then let your guests choose an around-the-world topping: Italian, Greek, or Spanish. Put out bowls with the ingredients for each topping. (You may need to label them. The idea is to try something new and different.) Ask the party guests to spread on the topping they want to try.

Here's what you need for the Italian topping:

Tomato sauce

Mozzarella cheese, sliced or shredded

Mushroom slices

Onion slices

Sausage or pepperoni, precooked and
  thinly sliced

Garlic powder

Oregano and basil

Here's what you need for the Greek topping:

Spinach pieces

Feta cheese

Graviera cheese, grated

Tomatoes, sliced

Greek olives

Dill weed, rosemary, and thyme

Here's what you need for the Spanish topping:

Eggplant, diced

Manchego cheese

Green pepper, sliced

Ham, precooked and cut in pieces

Spanish onion, sliced thin

Pimento, sliced

Here are three ways to finish the pizzas:

• Toast in a toaster oven on medium-high setting for 2 or 3 minutes.
• Bake in a regular oven at 350°F (175°C) for 5 or 6 minutes.
• Heat in microwave oven on medium-high power for 2 or 3 minutes.

WHICHEVER WAY YOU CHOOSE, HEAT UNTIL HOT AND BUBBLY. THEN ENJOY YOUR OWN ITALIAN, GREEK, OR SPANISH PIZZA.

. . . .

DECORATE A WORLD BIRTHDAY CAKE

. . . .

When is the world's birthday? No one knows, of course, but you may know the birthday of an important citizen of the world.

You can bake and decorate a really beautiful world birthday cake. You may want to frost on a world as seen from outer space, with mostly blue oceans and swirly clouds. Or you might get ambitious and frost on a world of continents and oceans.

This is a good project for an artistic and creative person. Besides cake-making things, you'll need a world map, tracing paper, and a pencil.

Here's how to bake your cake:

1. Prepare your favorite three-layer cake recipe. Use a cake mix if you wish.

2. Bake the three layers in pans like this: two 9-inch (23-centimeter) round cake pans and one 9-inch (23-centimeter) round-bottomed steel bowl.

3. Cool the cake thoroughly on wire racks.

Here's what you need to finsh your cake layers:

A 3.4 ounce (9.6 grams) package instant pudding mix, in a flavor you choose

1½ cups (375 milliliters) milk

2 cans prepared or a double recipe of white frosting

Food coloring in blue, green, and brown

Here's how to finish your cake:

1. Stir up the instant pudding mix according to the directions on the package, but use only 1½ cups (375 milliliters) milk.

2. Put one round pan layer upside down on a cake plate. Use a spatula to spread about half the pudding onto it.

3. Put the second round pan layer on top of the first one. Spread the rest of the pudding on it.

4. Position the layer from the rounded bowl on top. Now you have a flat-bottomed earth. The top of the cake is the North Pole or the South Pole, whichever you decide.

5. Apply a smooth thin layer of frosting to the whole cake.

6. Put a piece of tracing paper on a world map, and use a pencil to trace the hemispheres, with continents and islands as you want. This is to give you a model to help frost the cake. Cut out your tracings, and arrange them on the cake.

7. With a barbecue skewer or toothpick, outline your tracings onto the light frosting. Then carefully remove the tracing paper, and discard.

· · · · · · · · · · ·

DECORATE A WORLD BIRTHDAY CAKE

continued

8. Now divide the remaining icing into four small bowls. Place two-thirds in one bowl. Carefully stir in drops of blue food coloring. Divide the rest of the frosting into the other three bowls.

9. Stir in drops of food coloring to make the frosting green in one of those bowls.

10. Stir in drops of food coloring to make the frosting tan or brown in another bowl.

11. Leave the rest white.

12. Cover each bowl with a damp cloth or paper towel to keep the frosting from drying out while you work.

13. Ice the ocean areas blue first. Start at the edge of the continents you have outlined, and work toward the center.

14. Ice the desert areas with tan or brown frosting. Check your map as necessary.

15. Ice the rest of the world green, with white for the far north and far south.

: **FINISH WITH BLUE BIRTHDAY**
: **CANDLES FOR THE WHOLE**
: **WORLD OR FOR A SPECIAL**
: **PERSON IN THE WORLD.**

· · · · · · · · · ·

SCOOP UP ICE CREAM VOLCANOES

· ·

Who else ever made and ate a volcano? Don't worry. This volcano is ice cream, and the lava is fudge sauce.

Here's what you need for the fudge sauce:

2 squares (2 ounces or about 125 milliliters) of unsweetened chocolate
½ cup (120 milliliters) water
1½ cups (360 milliliters) corn syrup
Pinch of salt

Here's how to make the fudge sauce:

1. In a small saucepan, combine the chocolate and water. Cook over low heat on the stove until the chocolate is melted and the mixture is thickened.
   : *Caution: You need adult help in*
   : *using the stove.*
2. Remove from heat. Slowly add the corn syrup and salt.
3. Put mixture back on the burner. Bring to a simmer and stir frequently for 10 minutes.
4. Allow the sauce to cool until the pan feels just warm to the touch.
5. You can make the sauce a day or so ahead of the party. Then, when it's time for the party, warm the sauce slightly on the stove or in a microwave oven. *Remember:* If the sauce is too hot, it will melt the ice cream too quickly, and it won't run down the sides like lava.

Here's what else you need for the ice cream volcanoes:

Ice cream in a tan or brown color, such as chocolate, coffee, caramel, or maple walnut
Lightweight cardboard, if you wish
Removable tape, if you wish

Here's how to fix the ice cream volcanoes:

1. If you wish, make a cone-shaped mold for each guest. Form lightweight cardboard into a cone. Hold together with removable tape. Pack the ice cream into the molds and freeze hard.
2. Or when it's time for the party, you can use a regular scoop and pile up the ice cream in dishes to look like rugged volcanoes.

· · · · · · · · · · ·

SCOOP UP ICE CREAM VOLCANOES

continued

Here's how to serve the ice cream volcanoes:

1. Refrigerate the dishes you plan to use for the ice cream volcanoes.

2. Wait until just before serving to take the ice cream from the freezer.

3. Work quickly. Remove the molds or scoop the ice cream and put it in the dishes.

4. Let the party guests spoon chocolate lava over their volcanoes.

EXPLAIN THAT THIS IS NOT JUST AN ORDINARY ICE CREAM SUNDAE. TELL THE PARTY GUESTS TO WATCH HOW THE CHOCOLATE LAVA FLOWS DOWN THE SIDES AND THICKENS AS IT FLOWS OVER THE COLD ICE CREAM.

. . . .

PLAY THE WEIRD CLUES GAME
(AN INSIDE PARTY GAME)

. . . .

This is a game that everyone can win—eventually. It's a good game for two teams of players. Besides the teams, you'll need a person to direct the game and read the clues.

All you need is a world map and some pins or stickers to put on it.

The game director reads one weird clue at a time. Each team takes turns guessing the country or place. (You can guess what the clue means, too, if you want, but all you really need to do is guess the final place.) Whichever team guesses first can put a pin or sticker on the map. If neither team guesses right within 5 minutes, the game director goes on to read the next clue.

You'll hope that before the game director reads too many weird clues, one team will guess right.

Weird Clues #1:

- There's no D.C. in this country, but there is a D.F.
- Instead of hot, it gets *caliente* (kal-ee-YEN-tay) here.
- If you had a dog from this country, it might be a Chihuahua.
- No cowboys here, just *vaqueros* (vah-KARE-ohs).
- This country has a sauce and a state both called Tabasco.
- You can get here quickly from San Diego or El Paso.

Weird Clues #2

- I went so far from my home
  On my long trip to Rome.
- That I trekked through Quebec
  And ballooned to Cancun (kan-KOON).
- But then I got lost in downtown Caracas (kah-RAHK-us)
  And missed my flight to Ougadougou (oo-ga-DOO-goo).
- So I rented a raft with two African oars
  And rowed six weeks to the Cote d'Ivoire (coat dee-VWAR).
- It wasn't too easy to find the Zambezi (zam-BEE-zee)
  So I got on a plane, flew directly to Spain,
- Took fourteen buses plus too many trains
  And moonwalked all the way to Marseille (mar-SAY).

SEE IF YOU CAN LOCATE THESE PLACES ON A WORLD MAP. (YOU PROBABLY KNOW SOME OF THE CLUES, TOO.) IF YOU HAVE A BULLETIN BOARD MAP OF THE WORLD OR A PLACEMAT MAP, FINISH BY PUTTING IN A PIN OR STICKING ON A NOTE FOR EACH OF THE PLACES. THE PLAYERS WILL WANT TO KNOW WHERE ALL THESE WEIRD CLUES WERE LEADING. TO FIND ALL THE ANSWERS AND PLACES, LOOK ON PAGE 321.

PLAY WORLD-SIZED MARBLES
(AN OUTSIDE PARTY GAME)

Playing marbles is one of the oldest games in the world, with hundreds of different ring designs and sets of rules. It's such a popular game because you can use any kind of ring to play, and design any rules you want.

Maybe the around-the-world party could have its own versions for your friends to play outside. What about a giant, world-sized game that uses balls instead of marbles?

You'll need enough outside space for a playing circle about 80 feet (24 meters) in diameter. This game is good for 6 or more players.

Here's what you need:

A thick marker

4 strips of cardboard, each about 6 × 20 inches (15 × 50 centimeters)

A basketball

6 tennis balls

8 fairly big stones to mark off the big playing circle

Here's how to get ready for the game:

1. With a thick marker, mark each cardboard piece with one of these city names: Cairo, New York, Rio de Janeiro, and Tokyo. Take them and the basketballs and tennis balls out to the playing area.

2. Lay out the playing circle with the stones. The exact size is not important, but you do need to make it big.

3. Pretend that the circle is the Earth. To the left is North and South America. In the center is the Atlantic Ocean. To the right are Europe, Africa, and Asia. Lay down the cardboard cities roughly where they belong.

Then put the 2 basketballs side by side in the middle of the Atlantic Ocean.

4. Divide the players into 2 teams and decide which team gets the first turn. Then give that team the 6 tennis balls and tell them the rules.

Here are the rules for the game:

1. The first team tries to move the basketball by throwing 6 tennis balls at it from outside the circle. The goal of the first team is to make the basketball roll over Rio de Janeiro, then Tokyo, and then out of the circle. If the first team throws its 6 tennis balls without success, then the second team gets its turn. Put the basketball back into the center of the circle.

2. The goal for the second team is to make the ball roll over first New York, then Cairo, and then out of the circle. If the second team throws the 6 tennis balls without success, then the first team gets another turn.

· · · · · · · · · · ·

PLAY WORLD-SIZED MARBLES
(AN OUTSIDE PARTY GAME)

continued

3. The team that gets the ball through the cities and out of the circle first is the winner.

4. A player can throw from anywhere around the circle.

EVERYBODY WILL HAVE FUN WITH THIS. IT'S NOT EASY TO KNOCK A BASKETBALL IN AN EXACT DIRECTION, AND IT'S A LONG WAY TO TOKYO FROM RIO DE JANEIRO, AND A LONG WAY FROM CAIRO TO THE EDGE. YOU CAN PLAY THE GAME AGAIN AND USE DIFFERENT CITIES.

PLAY TAG AROUND THE WORLD (AN OUTSIDE PARTY GAME)

. . . .

This is an old Chinese version of tag, and a good one that you and your friends may want to try at the party.

Here's how to play:

1. Line everybody up, so that each person is holding the shoulders of the person in front.
2. Tell them that they've just turned into one big dragon that is good at twisting around.
3. The head of the dragon—the person at the front—is trying to chase and catch the tail.
4. But that isn't easy because the person at the back tries to keep away, with everybody in between helping.
5. Nobody in the whole dragon is allowed to let go of the shoulders of the person in front.

When you start the game, what happens almost right away is some amazing dragon-twisting. Everybody in the line has to dodge and twist around quickly to keep the head away from the tail and the tail away from the head.

When the tail does get caught, that player becomes the head, and the game keeps going. If different people want to try being the head, stop the game for a minute and rearrange the line.

> YOU CAN INVENT OTHER WAYS TO PLAY TAG. PEOPLE PLAY TAG ALL AROUND THE WORLD IN ONE FORM OR ANOTHER. THERE ARE PLENTY OF SPECIAL VERSIONS—AND NO REASON YOU CAN'T INVENT MORE.

· · · · · · · · · · ·
SOLUTIONS
· ·

Play the Weird Clues Game, page 317:

Weird Clues #1:

- D.C. is the District of Columbia, the location of the capital city of the United States. D.F. is the Distrito Federal, the location of the capital city of Mexico, Mexico City, and the surrounding area.
- Chihuahua is a state and a city in northern Mexico, as well as a breed of little dog, originally from Mexico.
- Tabasco is a state in southeastern Mexico, as well as a hot sauce.
- San Diego is a city in California, and El Paso is a city in Texas. Both are on the border between the United States and Mexico.

   The answer is Mexico.

Weird Clues #2:

- Rome is the capital city of Italy (42°N, 12°E).
- Quebec is both a city and a province in Canada (47°N, 72°W).
- Cancun is a city on the Yucatan Penisula in southeastern Mexico (21°N, 88°W).
- Caracas is the capital city of Venezuela (10°N, 67°W).
- Ougadougou is the capital city of Burkina Faso in west Africa (12°N, 2°W).
- Cote d'Ivoire (Ivory Coast) is a country in west central Africa (5°N, 5°W).
- The Zambezi is a river in Angola in central Africa (14°N, 24°W).
- Spain means you're getting close, but you're not at the right country just yet (40°N, 5°W).
- Marseille is a city in southern France (43°N, 5°E).

   The answer is France. You never quite made it to Rome.

GLOSSARY

Altitude	Height, especially the height of something, such as a hill, above sea level or above a spot on the Earth.
Aquifer	An underground layer of rock, sand, or gravel containing a large volume of fresh water.
Arctic Circle	The latitude 66° north of the Equator. The Antarctic Circle is at 66° south.
Asteroid	A small piece of rock that travels around the sun. Most of these thousands of small planets orbit between Mars and Jupiter. An asteroid can sometimes fall onto the Earth.
Atlas	A book of maps, charts, or tables describing the world, a part of the Earth, or the universe. Also a collection of maps or diagrams dealing with a subject such as anatomy. In Greek mythology, the giant, Atlas, supports the Earth on his mighty shoulder.
Attack point	A point on the map that a hiker chooses to walk toward because it is easy to find and to identify. A way of making sure directions are correct. It may be the top of the hill, road junction, railroad crossing. An attack point is the same as a *Checkpoint*.
Back bearing	The opposite direction from which a hiker or navigator came, the beginning point. A back bearing is also called a reciprocal bearing.
Bay	A wide inlet of water. Part of a sea or lake that forms a large indentation into the land. A bay is usually smaller than a gulf.
Bearing	One of the 360 degrees directions of a directional compass. Or a direction stated in degrees. Used in surveying, hiking, orienteering, and navigating.
Cape	A point of land extending or jutting out into a body of water.
Cardinal points	The four primary directions: north, south, east, and west.
Cartographer	A mapmaker.
Cartography	The science and art of mapmaking.
Cartouche	A decorated scroll or tablet on a map. The cartouche gives the title of the map and often other information, such as date of the map and the name of the mapmaker.
Cassava	A type of tropical plant with edible starchy roots used to make flour for bread and tapioca for pudding. Cassava is also called manioc.
Checkpoint	A known and obvious feature at some point along a trail or in navigation. Used to make sure directions are correct. A checkpoint is the same as an *Attack point*.
Circumference	The distance around the rim (or perimeter) of a circle.
Circumnavigate	To go completely around the world by water. To travel around a place, such as an island.

Climate	The pattern of weather that one region has over a long period of time.
Comet	A bright body that travels around the sun. Comets are made up of frozen gases, ice, and dust particles. They have bright heads and usually show a long, bright tail.
Compass	See *Directional compass* and *Drawing compass*.
Compass rose	A sign or card drawn to show directions on a map or for use along with a directional compass. A compass rose may show only the four primary directions (north, east, south, west). Or it may show 32 directions of a directional compass and the 360 degrees of a circle.
Continent	A major land mass, such as Africa, Antarctica, Asia, Europe, North America, or South America.
Continental shelf	The part of the ocean floor that starts at the shoreline of a continent, slopes outward to sea, and then ends in a steep drop-off. A continental shelf can vary in width from almost nothing to about 1,000 miles (1,600 kilometers).
Contour	The shape or outline of an object such as a hill, mountain, lake, or ocean. A contour map shows shapes of hills, mountains, lakes, oceans, and other physical features of the world.
Contour interval	The distance between contour lines on a map. Contour intervals help show how steep an area of land is. If the contour intervals are very close together, for example, that means a steep rise such as a cliffside or a sharp drop-off such as a canyon. If the contour intervals are far apart, that means nearly flat land.
Contour line	A line connecting the points on a map that have the same height or depth. Contour lines help show the shape of hills, mountains, and underwater terrain.
Cyclone	A powerful windstorm in which the winds blow in a circle. South of the Equator, the winds blow clockwise. North of the Equator, they blow counterclockwise. A cyclone is another name for a *Hurricane*.
Cylinder	A long, round shape. An empty soup can is a cylinder.
Desert	A very dry area of land, with a sandy or icy surface. A desert can be hot or cold.
Diameter	A straight line segment that passes through the center of a circle.
Directional compass	A device used to determine directions. A compass often works with a free swinging magnetic needle that always points to magnetic north.
Dividers	A map-reading device used to measure or mark off distances or to divide lines.
Doldrums	A very calm region near the Equator with little surface wind.
Drawing compass	A device used to draw circles or measure distances. A drawing compass has two arms joined at the top. One arm ends in a point, the other arm holds a pencil.
Drought	A long period of little or no rain that may lead to a dangerous shortage of water.
Earthquake	A shaking or trembling at the surface of the Earth, caused by movement in the crust below or by volcanic eruptions.

Eclipse — The shadow cast when the path of one heavenly body crosses between the source of light (such as the sun) and the path of another body. In an eclipse of the moon, the shadow of the Earth passes over the moon. In an eclipse of the sun, the moon passes between the sun and the Earth and blocks out the light from the sun.

Elevation — A height above sea level or some other chosen point above the surface of the Earth. Altitude. A rising or lifting up.

El Niño — An unstable ocean current in the Pacific Ocean that appears from time to time and may cause changes in climate and weather around the world. Because El Niño appears in South America around Christmas time, it is named for the birth of Jesus, the boy child.

Epicenter — The exact spot on the Earth's surface that is directly above the underground center of an earthquake.

Equator — The imaginary line circling the Earth at latitude 0°, and the starting point for measuring distances north and south on a map or globe. The Equator is halfway between the North and South Poles, and it divides the Northern and Southern Hemispheres.

Equatorial — The areas around the Equator or the conditions there. Weather on and near the Equator is usually tropical and hot.

Equinox — One of two each year—around March 21 and September 21—when day and night are exactly the same length all around the world. At these two times, the sun is exactly above the Equator.

Erosion — The slow wearing away of rock, land, or buildings by the weather or the sea.

Eurasia — The single, connected land mass that combines the European and Asian continents. Also can refer to the countries in the midsection of the combined land mass.

Export — A product made in one country and sold or traded to another country or the act of sending products to another country.

Fossil — Remains, traces, or impressions of an animal or plant that lived a long time ago. Usually found hardened in rock.

Geographic North Pole — The true North Pole of the Earth, located at latitude 90°N. The northern end of the Earth's axis that points toward Polaris, the North Star.

Geography — What this book is about—the science of location and place on the surface of the Earth, plus the patterns of natural and human activity. Also can mean the natural features of any part of the world.

Gerrymander — To change shape and size of voting districts so as to influence an election. The word combines "Gerry," from a governor of Massachusetts, Elbridge Gerry, who died in 1814, and "-mander," from salamander, the strangely lizard-like shape of one of Gerry's voting districts.

Glacier — Huge mass of ice that moves slowly downhill. Glaciers form high up in mountains where snow melts only partially.

Grade — The steepness of an elevation.

Grid	A network or pattern of equally spaced vertical and horizontal lines, all perpendicular to one another. The squares formed can be useful in locating or scaling objects. On a map, latitudes and longitudes form a grid that helps show location and direction.
Grid references	Grid numbers and letters that mark precise points on a map.
Gulf	A large, deep inlet of an ocean or sea that is partly enclosed by land. A gulf is usually larger and deeper than a bay.
Gyre	A whirlpool pattern, with water—or air—circling around a center.
Habitat	The specific natural surroundings in which animals and plants live. The icy waters and shores of the Arctic form the polar bear's habitat.
Hemisphere	Half of the total Earth. The Equator divides the planet into Northern and Southern Hemispheres. The Prime Meridian and the International Date Line divide the Earth into Eastern and Western Hemispheres.
Horizontal	Straight across. Parallel to the horizon or to a base line.
Horse latitudes	Two worldwide belts—near 30°N and 30°S—where weather tends to be clear and calm, with light winds. This region may have been named after horses that did not obey their masters, just as the winds did not do what sailors wanted.
Humidity	The amount of moisture carried in the air. High humidity means dampness. Low means dry.
Hurricane	A very tropical windstorm with winds blowing in a circle at least 75 miles per hour (120 kilometers per hour) and accompanied by heavy rains. A *Cyclone*. Hurricanes usually start in the area of the West Indies.
Import	A product that is brought into a country from another country or the act of bringing in products from another country.
International Date Line	An imaginary line located at longitude 180°. When you cross this line, you find that the date changes.
Landmark	An obvious feature on land that identifies a place or leads toward it.
Latitude	One of the imaginary lines that runs parallel north and south of the Equator. Latitudes are measured in degrees, from 0° to 90° south. Latitudes are also called *Parallels*.
Legend	A key for explaining symbols on a map. Also can mean a story passed down through many years.
Lodestone	A mineral with magnetic properties, able to attract iron.
Longitude	One of the imaginary lines that measure distance and time east and west from the Prime Meridian to the International Date Line. Longitudes are measured in degrees, minutes, and seconds. Longitudes are also called *Meridians*.
Magnetic North Pole	The direction point of the Earth's magnetic north toward which the north poles of all magnets are attracted. The location varies but is close enough to true north for most purposes.

Mercator projection map
A method of making maps developed by Flemish mapmaker Gerhardus Mercator (1512–1594) in which the surface of the Earth is shown as a flat rectangle. This sort of map accurately gives directions, but it distorts areas. The farther areas are from the Equator, the more they are enlarged compared to their actual sizes.

Meridian
A line of longitude running north and south on a globe. (See *Prime Meridian.*)

Meteor
A small lump of rock or metal that appears streaking across the sky and leaving a bright trail of light. Also called a shooting or falling star. Meteoroids or *Meteorites* are sometimes called meteors.

Meteorite
The remains of a fairly large meteoroid or meteor that has fallen to the Earth's surface without burning up.

Migration
The regular, patterned movement of animals, birds, or fish from one region or climate to another, usually to visit feeding and breeding grounds. Also can mean the act of moving from one place to another.

Millennium
A time period of 1,000 years or ten centuries.

Minute of latitude or longitude
One sixtieth of a degree of latitude or longitude. Each degree of latitude and longitude is divided into 60 minutes, as an aid to precise measurement.

Navigation
Plotting a course from one point to another, whether on the water, on land, or in the air.

Ocean currents
Large streams of ocean water flowing in the same direction.

Orbit
The path of a celestial body, such as that of a planet around the sun.

Pace
A step used for measuring distances.

Pangea
The theory that millions of years ago, the continents and islands of the world were one giant landmass, called Pangea. The idea is that the supercontinent slowly broke up and drifted apart. *Pan* means all, and *geo* is the root word for earth.

Parallel
Going in the same direction and always the same distance apart. Two parallel lines never meet or cross. The term is sometimes applied to the latitudes, which all run parallel to the Equator. For example, 50°N can also be known as the 50th parallel.

Peninsula
A finger of land surrounded on most sides by water or an area of land jutting out from the mainland and surrounded by the sea on three sides. Examples of peninsulas are Florida; Baja, California; and Cape Cod.

Planet
A Greek word meaning wanderer, and used to describe the large celestial bodies that move around the sun or another star. The nine planets of our solar system are Mercury, Venus, Earth, Mars, Jupiter, Saturn, Uranus, Neptune, and Pluto.

Plates
Large, separate areas of the Earth's crust, locked together and constantly pushing against one other. The boundaries between them receive tremendous pressures and frequently buckle, causing large and small earthquakes.

Population
The number of people living in an area such as a city. The number of animals or other organisms in a particular area or habitat.

Population density	The number of people living in a measured area such as a square mile.
Prime Meridian	The zero longitude that runs through Greenwich, England. It is the starting point for measuring longitudinal distances east and west on a map or globe.
Projection	A way of drawing curved surfaces of the global Earth onto flat maps. Each method results in its own view of how the Earth looks when drawn flat.
Proportion	The relationship of one part to another. The relationship may involve size, number, or amount. Four quantities, *a,b,c,* and *d,* are said to be in proportion if $a/b = c/d$.
Ratio	A comparison between two numbers or things. It is expressed as a quotient. Example: a/b or $a{:}b$.
Relief map	A map that uses raised figures to show the features of the Earth, such as hills, mountains, and depths of sea. A relief map is one type of *Topographical map.*
Richter Scale	A mathematical way to measure the strength of earthquakes. Each number on the scale represents a shock ten times greater, so that 5 is ten times stronger than a 4. Named for Charles Richter, who invented the scale in 1935.
Savanna	Large, grassy plain found in tropical or subtropical areas. A savanna has few or no trees.
Scale	The ratio of a distance or area on a map to the actual, real-world distance or area it represents. Also refers to the key on a map that uses a small measure to represent a larger area on Earth.
Schematic map	A map that shows a system, such as a train line or highway routes, without showing other features. A map that is a diagram, often without proportion or scale.
Sea	Usually a close-to-shore section of an ocean, fed by rivers and often named for the land area it touches. Sometimes used to refer to an ocean or a part of an ocean.
Second of latitude or longitude	One sixtieth of a minute of latitude or longitude. Each latitude or longitude is divided into 60 minutes. Each minute is divided into 60 seconds. A second of latitude or longitude indicates very precise measurement.
Seismograph	A machine that records the intensity of large and small vibrations within the Earth. A seismograph records the intensity, location, direction, and duration of earthquakes.
Solar system	The sun, along with the planets and other celestial bodies that revolve around it. Our Earth is part of the solar system.
Solstice	One of two times during the year when the sun is farthest from the Equator, either north or south. Solstice marks the beginning of a new season. In the Northern Hemisphere, the summer solstice occurs about June 22. Winter solstice occurs about December 22. In the Southern Hemisphere, the opposite seasons begin.
Sphere	An object shaped like a ball or globe.
Terrain	The surface features of a piece of land.

Time zone   A part of the world in which the people agree on one time. The Earth is constantly revolving so sunrise occurs at different places in the world. Because of this, an international system of 24 main time zones was established in the 1880s. Each zone differs from the next by one hour, and so on around the world. This means that people need to adust their watches when they travel.

Topographical map   A map that shows the features of the Earth, especially changing elevations such as hills, mountains, and depths of the sea. A topographical map may be flat and use symbols to show the Earth's features. Or it may use actual raised figures to show the Earth's features in proportion, in the same way that a *Relief map* does.

Topography   The science and art of making maps that show the Earth's features. The surface features of the Earth's land areas—hills, valleys, plains, mountains, lakes, rivers, forests, and deserts.

Tornado   A violent windstorm, with winds whirling at speeds high enough to uproot trees and destroy buildings. The storm looks like a funnel-shaped cloud dipping down to Earth. A tornado that moves over water is called a waterspout.

Torrid Zone   The areas just north and south of the Equator, where sunlight is intense and direct during parts of the year. Extremely hot compared to other latitudes.

Tropical depression   A windstorm that originates in tropical oceans and that has a wind speed of less than 39 miles per hour (62 kilometers per hour). As it gains strength, a tropical depression may become a tropical storm.

Tropical storm   A windstorm that originates in tropical oceans and that has a wind speed of 39 to 73 miles per hour (62 to 116 kilometers per hour). As it gains strength, a tropical storm may become a hurricane.

Tropic of Cancer   Latitude 23°27'N. The northern boundary of the Torrid Zone.

Tropic of Capricorn   Latitude 23°27'S. The southern boundary of the Torrid Zone.

Typhoon   A powerful tropical cyclone that happens in the area of the Philippines or the China Sea. A *Hurricane*.

Vertical   Straight up and down. Perpendicular or at a right angle to the horizon or to a base line.

INDEX